Patrick Barclay is one of the UK's most highly respected football writers. A former Sports Journalist of the Year, he began covering the game for the *Guardian* in 1976 and has since been a leading commentator for the *Independent*, the *Observer*, the *Sunday Telegraph* and *The Times*. Patrick is the author of *Football–Bloody Hell! The Biography of Alex Ferguson*, which was shortlisted for the British Sports Book Awards, and *Mourinho: Further Anatomy of a Winner*. *The Life and Times of Herbert Chapman* was shortlisted for the Football Book of the Year award at the Cross British Sports Book Awards. He has attended every European Championship since 1980 and every World Cup since 1982. He lives in London, where his day-to-day thoughts on the game appear in the *Evening Standard*. He remains a lifelong supporter of Dundee FC.

THE LIFE AND TIMES OF
HERBERT CHAPMAN

PATRICK BARCLAY

WEIDENFELD & NICOLSON

A W&N PAPERBACK

First published in Great Britain in 2014
by Weidenfeld & Nicolson
This paperback edition published in 2015
by Weidenfeld & Nicolson,
an imprint of Orion Books Ltd,
Carmelite House, 50 Victoria Embankment,
London EC4Y ODZ

An Hachette UK company

1 3 5 7 9 10 8 6 4 2

A CIP catalogue record for this book
is available from the British Library.

ISBN 978-1-4746-0079-8

Typeset by Input Data Services Ltd, Bridgwater, Somerset

Printed and bound by CPI Group (UK) Ltd, Croydon CR0 4YY

www.orionbooks.co.uk

To the Owl and the Pussycat

CONTENTS

ACKNOWLEDGEMENTS

The idea of a book about Herbert Chapman came from Alan Samson, whose support has been constant, and its realisation would not have been possible, let alone such fun, but for the assistance, friendship and relentless mockery of Ken Chapman. It was a pleasure to meet another family member, Peter Barwick, and Shirley and Trevor Burns.

At Arsenal, Samir Singh and colleagues could not do enough to help, while I'll never forget sitting opposite the incomparable Ken Friar as, eyes twinkling, he told me that the great carved-wood desk between us had been Herbert Chapman's. Thanks, too, to Mark Gonella, and to members of the wider Arsenal family: Lois Langton, for introducing me to Ron Jennings; Mark Andrews and Andy Kelly, of the Arsenal History Society, for their kind anxiety to guide me away from myths; and Darren Epstein, for priceless insight.

David Sykes at Huddersfield answered every call, while Helen Skilbeck provided perhaps the most memorable of all the little breakthroughs (the story of J. C. Whiteman). Friends rallied round. Lois Langton and Mark Gonella apart, they included Jonathan Wilson and Phil Shaw – the most generous of fellow football writers – David Luxton and Philippe Auclair. Thanks to all the characters in this book, my new heroes, among them Herbert's brother John, James Catton and Billy Sudell, Walter Tull, Jimmy Spiers, Evelyn Lintott, Vivian Woodward, Alex James, Herbie Roberts and Cliff Bastin. And finally to Herbert Chapman, the greatest of them all.

HERBERT WHO?

A visit to Kiveton Park is liable to give you a sense of life's mainstream passing by. This is not so much because Kiveton Park lacks the vibrancy of, say, downtown Shanghai or Times Square in New York (though naturally it does on a weekday mid-morning when many of the 6,500 inhabitants are working in Sheffield or attending to family chores) but because in order to reach the semi-detached home of Ken Chapman on the erstwhile coal-mining community's western fringes it is necessary to cross a bridge over the M1. Below, the endless grey ribbon whooshes and whines. The occupants of some vehicles might be preparing to turn off for Sheffield or Hull or continuing northward to Newcastle upon Tyne. Those travelling in the opposite direction might be contemplating Leicester or Nottingham or wondering if a steady foot on the pedal might get them to London in two and a half hours. Many might have done their journey a thousand times and been unaware of Kiveton Park's very existence, concealed as it is by the grassy crests of the motorway cutting. Yet Kiveton Park could claim (if it were that kind of place, which it is not) to have been a cradle of two revolutions, one industrial and the other sporting, and beyond question it is the birthplace of at least one great man, widely considered the father of football as we have come to know it.

Herbert Chapman was Ken Chapman's uncle. Herbert's parents had travelled the 28 miles north from Ripley in Derbyshire in 1869 because Kiveton Park, hitherto little more than a rural hamlet, had been present at the infancy of deep mining. The main seam had taken 18 months to sink but now Kiveton Park grew quickly with the fuel of heavy industry that was making Britain the economic engine of Europe. Rows of houses were built for the miners and the population went from dozens to thousands in a couple of decades. By 1929, long after Herbert Chapman had left the area and become nationally known for his work in football – he had built a triple-championship-winning team at Huddersfield Town and was about to do the same for Arsenal – employment at the colliery peaked at 2,244. Across the length and breadth of the United Kingdom the coal industry was providing jobs for nearly a million men. But the conditions in which they worked conspired in their politicisation.

The industry was nationalised by the Labour government led by Clement Attlee after the Second World War and yet, at what seemed the height of their powers following two successful national strikes in the 1970s, the miners under the leadership of Arthur Scargill encountered a deceptive foe in Margaret Thatcher at a time when they were relatively well paid and coal suffering unfavourable price comparison with the new oil and gas from the North Sea. The miners fought the Conservative government's plans to shrink their industry, but the most bitter dispute of the Thatcher era ended in 1985 with a victory for the Iron Lady. Now pits closed almost by the dozen. Kiveton Park met its fate in 1994 at the cost of a thousand jobs. Some buildings remain – the original administration offices, which have been recycled for the use of a vibrant community, and the evocatively utilitarian pit baths built in 1938 – but landscaping offers no hint of the industrial relics buried far, far below the feet of joggers and dog-walkers, and you could almost mistake for natural the nicely grassed slag-heaps on which James Toseland learned to tame motorcycles.

James Toseland is the most famous son of Kiveton Park. Certainly in Kiveton Park he is. In a wood-panelled room at the old pit offices one day in 2012 a group of local women were studying family history. Mention of Herbert Chapman produced mainly blank looks. But there was recognition of James Toseland, the local boy whom sport had made good. James was born in 1980, more than a century after Herbert Chapman, but had a harder start in life, at least emotionally. When he was three, his father walked out. He was raised by his mother but even the emergence of a father figure, when she began a long-term relationship with Ken Wright, contained the seeds of tragedy: James was 15 when Wright committed suicide. And yet Wright's legacy was priceless. It was he who had introduced James to motorbikes. The boy had become obsessed with motocross, using the slagheaps for endless hours of practice. While the miners resisted the hastening demise of their industry, he acquired skills that were to equip him for the succession to Barry Sheene and Carl Fogarty. Shortly after Kiveton Park lost its pit, James Toseland became World Superbike Champion for the first time. That was in 2004. He took the title again in 2007 and ascribed his success to emotional knocks: 'I never got angry ... probably because I had the motorcycle to jump on and wrestle the hell out of. I had my tantrums on the bike.' After retiring he married the singer Katie Melua. Their wedding at the Royal Botanic Gardens in Kew was attended by, among 200 others, Prince Pieter-Christiaan Michiel of The Netherlands. But Toseland was not one to lose touch with his roots, as those back in Kiveton Park would testify. One day a telephone rang in the old pit offices. It was Toseland, offering to contribute to the community newsletter. 'Oh, James,' he was told, 'I'm so sorry, love, but we're rushed off our feet today – could you ring back?'

If Herbert Chapman had been listening from on high, he would have smiled in recognition. For fame doesn't bowl Kiveton Park over quite as easily as it might Los Angeles, say, or parts of Essex. Chapman was celebrated more in London than Kiveton Park. He was feted farther afield, notably in the footballing coffee-houses of Europe, and even had influenced the game in Brazil, where his 'WM' formation took hold (put the first letter above the second and you can see how the third defender reshaped football). But how he was celebrated in London. The flower-bedecked cortège carrying his coffin to St Mary's church in Hendon in January

1934 was watched by crowds three or four deep and eight decades after his death the circular blue plaque erected by English Heritage on a wall of his final home at 6 Haslemere Avenue remained the only one relating purely to football.

A bronze bust of Chapman, commissioned by a group of his friends shortly before he died and crafted by Sir Jacob Epstein, was placed in the Marble Halls, the grand entrance to Arsenal's Highbury Stadium, so that no manager – no Bertie Mee, no George Graham, no Arsène Wenger – or player of Arsenal or their opponents could ever pass through to the dressing rooms unaware of his legacy, and in 2011 a statue of Chapman was unveiled outside the Emirates Stadium, which had replaced Highbury five years earlier, along with similar representations of the revered players Tony Adams and Thierry Henry. Even when, the following year, Arsenal unveiled a new home kit, it was noted by the manufacturers that both the shirt and shorts – fashioned from 'ground-breaking recycled polyester, making it Nike's most environmentally friendly kit ever' – featured details genuflecting to Chapman's WM.

In 1996, while Wenger was seeing out his obligations to Grampus 8 of Nagoya, the Japanese club for whom he had been working when Arsenal invited him to succeed Bruce Rioch as manager, a journalist rang. He wasn't trying to catch the Frenchman out, just interested in how versed he was in the history and tradition of his new employers, much of which had originated in the Chapman era. Wenger knew Herbert Chapman all right. 'That was the guy who put the numbers on the shirts,' he said, 'and had the Metro station renamed "Arsenal".' Wenger knew because of his long friendship with David Dein, the club's vice-chairman at the time, who was steeped in that history and tradition. He didn't know that Londoners called their underground railway the Tube. But he knew how Chapman had put the name of Arsenal on the map.

At Huddersfield's Galpharm Stadium there is no statue, but a replica of the Highbury bust was gratefully received from Arsenal on the club's centenary in 2008, when Wenger took a team to play for the Herbert Chapman Trophy. Arsenal won 2–1 and the cut-glass cup was presented to Johan Djourou, the captain of a young side featuring Theo Walcott and Jack Wilshere, by Ken Chapman from Kiveton Park. But Huddersfield Town have never cherished Herbert's memory in the Arsenal way. Is it because, having made Town the first club capable of completing a hat-trick of championships, he forsook them for the lure of greater potential, just as Bill Shankly was to do when Liverpool beckoned in 1959? Only death separated Chapman from Arsenal.

Huddersfield Town hardly disintegrated upon his departure. They won their third title, finished second in consecutive seasons and, after two years in mid-table, were restored to what would now be called Champions League contention, drawing their record attendance of 67,037 to an FA Cup tie against Chapman's Arsenal at the old Leeds Road ground in 1932. But in 1952 they were relegated for the first time and in 1975 they sank as far as the Football League permitted, to the Fourth Division. They have risen again but remain nowhere near as close to glory as Arsenal with their metropolitan advantages and moneyed structure. When Chapman joined Huddersfield in 1921, Burnley were about to become champions and only three London clubs were among the top division's 22. Today there are more likely to be six or seven from the capital out of 20. Perhaps it is understandable that some of the textile towns once familiar with footballing achievement are less inclined warmly to embrace the game's history than the modern aristocrats from north London.

Little Kiveton Park played more than its part in football's development. Being a mere 14 miles from Sheffield, whose outer limits can be espied today by those on bracing walks along Kiveton's higher lanes, helped because Sheffield could claim to have been the original hotbed. Sheffield FC, now of the Northern Premier League Division One South, is the world's oldest surviving club and the local cup final, played under Sheffield Rules, drew bigger crowds – 8,000 in 1876 – than the FA Cup final. The first recorded floodlit match in Britain took place at Bramall Lane in 1878 and pulled in (if you take the upper estimate) 20,000. Even Scotland v England at the original Hampden Park that year attracted only half as many. The first professional, inevitably a Scot, had been playing for The Wednesday (as Sheffield Wednesday were initially known) from 1876. And Kiveton had caught the mood. A team from the village had been taking part in Sheffield games for at least a dozen years before Kiveton Park FC was formed in 1892 as a founder member of the Sheffield League.

Among those showing early promise were Herbert Chapman and his brothers Harry and Tom. All went on to have professional careers, Harry a distinguished one, featuring a man-of-the-match performance in the FA Cup final of 1907 when The Wednesday beat Everton in front of 84,584 at the Crystal Palace in London. In all, some 30 footballers have either graduated from Kiveton to the League game or eked out their playing days there. Ian Mellor, a spindly attacker once of Manchester City and Sheffield Wednesday, where he scored one of four unanswered goals in the 'Boxing Day Massacre' of Sheffield United, and Ricky Holden, a winger during Oldham Athletic's happy times under Joe Royle, come into the latter category.

The club went out of existence for several years when the pit closed and its main source of financial support was lost but returned to the Central Midlands League in 2000. It spent the 2012–13 season in – to be precise – the Black Dragon Division North of the Windsor Foodservice Central Midlands Football League. That was the first team. There was also a reserve team, a youth team and teams for a variety of age groups beginning with Under 7s. So Kiveton Park FC was thriving. Matches were played at the Hard Lane ground with its capacity of 2,000, of whom 200 could be seated in its single grandstand. This was built for the club's move from its original ground around 1920, by which time Harry Chapman had died tragically early of tuberculosis and Herbert, having made a bit of a name in management at Northampton Town only to endure the taint of scandal when with Leeds City, was about to take his career to new levels at Huddersfield.

He would be delighted to note how football has adapted to the changes in his home village. The Kiveton of today, with its clean air and private housing where many of the old rows used to be, is no pit village but respects its heritage, as the enthusiasm of the local history group emphasises. Many residents commute to Sheffield or smaller towns by road or rail but there are a variety of factories providing employment. One makes steel items and wire, but surely the most durable, founded in 1927 by Edwin Talbot Sutherland, produces sandwich spreads of distinction. It is hardly an exaggeration to say that Sutherland's and Potted Beef – 'a right tasty Yorkshire recipe' – are synonymous and the notion of Herbert Chapman enjoying an early version of this treat on his evening return to Haslemere Avenue from a match at Highbury is as hard to resist as it is impossible to confirm.

Both the school Herbert attended until he was 13 and the pit offices where he subsequently queued with his father to receive wages are put to good use. The red-brick school is home to Kiveton Park Youth and Community Centre and the offices, also of red brick but more imposing with their Gothic clock tower facing in all four directions, house a miscellany of businesses and local societies, along with the studio of Redroad Radio, a community station awarded a five-year licence in 2010 and designed to appeal to the musical tastes of local young people.

Music is also the driving force behind Jade Kiveton. This looks like a shop but offers 'an alternative to the street culture of our area'. You can learn music production or deejaying. It is claimed that a sharp reduction in anti-social behaviour has been measured. The centre at the school concentrates on teenagers and includes a 'detached' programme reaching out to the shy or reluctant and offering 'fun, exciting, challenging opportunities to raise self-esteem, confidence and aspirations'.

Young Herbert got all that from football and cricket and his aspirations grew through adulthood until one day he declared an intention to make Arsenal the greatest football club in the world. He died too young – just short of his fifty-sixth birthday – and would not, in any case, have lasted long enough with the club to obtain the rough measure provided by European competition, which Real Madrid dominated from 1956 to 1960. But he did everything that football could ask of a mortal. Indeed, he did more.

Although not indisputably the greatest of all tacticians, he fostered the essential quality of teamwork as no coach had done before – and millions were to strive to do after. He established a balance between attack and defence as none had done before. He mapped new directions in training. Off the field, he pioneered 'football in the community'. And, yes, he lived to see numbers on shirts, if only in one League match and one in the Cup. On the first day of the 1928–9 season, Chapman and his friend David Calderhead, the long-serving manager of Chelsea, sent their teams out numbered – Arsenal away to The Wednesday in Sheffield and Chelsea at home to Swansea Town – as an aid to identification. The Football League promptly banned the innovation until 1939, when it was made compulsory throughout the four divisions by the then supreme Football Association, which had adopted it in the Cup final, starting with the Wembley event of 1933, the last before Chapman's death.

He wanted Arsenal's name on the Tube station at Gillespie Road and got that done. He advocated European club competition at a time when the British authorities would not contemplate leaving their island except to play, and usually win, international matches. He signed foreign players when it was very unusual (and proved just too far ahead of its time in the case of the Austrian goalkeeper Rudi Hiden, who had to be un-signed almost as soon as he had set foot on British soil). He picked a black player when that was even more unusual (and came to appreciate that Walter Tull's heroism went far beyond the boundaries of football metaphor). But Chapman didn't introduce floodlit football. How he tried: he had lights installed at Highbury and he argued strongly for their application to the competitive fixtures of the League and FA. But he argued with a lack of success that is astonishing given the essential role floodlights have come to assume in the drama of the modern game.

He was allowed to use them only for training at first and then for the occasional friendly. He had been dead for 16 years when they were sanctioned for official matches in 1951, starting with a reserve fixture between Southampton and Tottenham Hotspur, and more than 20 years before they were permitted to enhance League or Cup occasions. He would have been proud that Arsenal became the first club from the top division to play under lights, first in a friendly against Hapoel of Tel-Aviv in September 1951 and then, a month later, against Rangers in what had become an annual contest with the Glasgow club.

But floodlights were not Chapman's idea. When Britain's first floodlit match took place, it was true that the event was held not far from his home. But Herbert was less than nine months old at the time and, while you had to grow up fast in nineteenth-century England – his father started work aged seven and the practice of using children as chimney sweeps was not finally, unequivocally, banned until 1875 – you didn't have to grow up quite that fast. Others organised the Bramall Lane experiment and there were further floodlit matches involving, among others, Blackburn Rovers and Thames Ironworks (later to become West Ham United), whose opponents included the then Woolwich Arsenal.

When Chapman encountered the opposition of the League and FA, it seemed that the night game would be kept out of the competitive arena for ever. But a series of exciting friendlies involving Wolverhampton Wanderers and others against leading foreign clubs swept away all scepticism and football would never be the same again. It would reach the new planes of excitement now ascribed to the Champions League and prove Chapman to have been, once more, not years but decades ahead of his time. He argued for so much that would eventually come to pass, even artificial pitches and the idea of restricting transfers through a window; he felt it should be open in the summer only.

If the start of international football, the seed that grew into the World Cup, was Scotland v England in 1872, the involvement of British clubs in competition across borders could be said to have origins in the friendship between Rangers and Arsenal that Chapman made flourish in the early 1930s. It went back to Arsenal's financial troubles of 20 years earlier, when they nearly went out of business. Their team was looked after by George Morrell, a Glaswegian said to have been in charge of Rangers' reserves before making his name with Greenock Morton, and the bigger of his former clubs answered a general plea to buy Arsenal shares by taking two at £1 each. After Arsenal had won their first trophy, the FA Cup, in 1930, Chapman recalled those who had come to their aid in harder times and suggested that his board send some more shares to Ibrox by way of thanks: 14 were duly despatched.

Chapman and Bill Struth, his equivalent north of the border, the winner of five consecutive Scottish championships among 18 in all, got on well. In September 1933 they enjoyed a round of golf at Turnberry together before Arsenal met Rangers in the first leg of an unofficial British championship. The return at Highbury a week later saw the Scots emerge triumphant 5–1 on aggregate. From then the fixture between the clubs became annual, a single match alternating between London and Glasgow, and it lasted until 1968. The final Highbury occasion took place the previous year, with Alex Ferguson on the wrong end of a 3–0 defeat and George Graham among the victors.

But the most memorable was that of 1951. There is a wonderful photograph of a packed house watching the action under the lights' benign glare. This was the football of Chapman's dreams: sport and theatre fused. A few miles away, in the pitch black of a north London graveyard, was his tombstone and deep below Kiveton Park the miners' lights shone – for the latter half of Chapman's life had contained the rise of socialism in its various forms, from the Bolsheviks of post-revolutionary Russia to such kindly democrats of the British Labour Party as his elder brother John – on seams of nationalised coal.

In the Methodist chapel at Kiveton was one memento of Herbert Chapman: an ornamental altar chair of carved wood which he had donated to the chapel at Easter in 1931 in gratitude for happy days spent there in his youth. But even that was to follow the road south, for in the autumn of 1979 the chapel and its contents were put on sale and this came to the attention of

Cliff Crookes, a former Plymouth Argyle director, and his friend Harry Hutton, who had been born in Kiveton and attended the school and chapel and remembered the chair, which they bought and resolved to give an appropriate home. They took it to Highbury and presented it to the Arsenal chairman, Denis Hill-Wood, in a little ceremony after a 3–1 win over Coventry City. It may be seen today in the club's museum, where it shares a large glass case with a black bowler hat of Chapman's and other memorabilia. In Kiveton Park only a small plaque affixed to a wall of the village hall in 2008 commemorates Herbert Chapman and it is there only because Ken Chapman thought there should be something.

LUCKY ARSENAL

LEADING THE GREATS

Herbert Chapman lived through momentous times without ever leaving a clue as to how he viewed them. He confined his many public utterances to football and its immediate hinterland. Among the subjects for discussion by the wider populace were women's place in society – when he first came to London to play for Tottenham Hotspur, his wife Annie had to convince local politicians of her right to pursue her career as a school teacher – and the rise of Marxism, which many Britons saw as a greater threat to their way of life than fascism as practised by Adolf Hitler and Benito Mussolini and recommended by their own country's vain saviour, Sir Oswald Mosley. Before the Great Depression and the spread to Europe of seeds that were to grow into the Second World War had come that most futile example of man's inhumanity, the First World War, during which Chapman excelled in management at a munitions factory, boosting production of shells for the Western Front, where footballers familiar and, in some cases, close to him were dying or suffering injuries amid the hideous conflict.

As a 'great friend of the Jewish people' – to quote Chapman's obituary in the *Jewish Chronicle* – he would surely have recoiled, had he lived beyond 1934, from the Hitler of whom Winston Churchill strove to warn the appeasing establishment as represented by Neville Chamberlain and, at least initially, the Foreign Secretary, Lord Halifax, who went to see the Führer in 1937 and told him (to paraphrase) that, although Britain had a few minor issues here and there, he was doing a damn good job in suppressing those communists. But even the growing influence of trade unions, a cause dear to the heart of Chapman's brother John, was something on which Herbert remains silent, for a letter he dictated to the forerunner of the Professional Footballers' Association, officials of which had been anxious to discover why membership at Arsenal was negligible when the Huddersfield squad had been so solidly unionised, was never found. Of Chapman's politics and philosophy it can be said only that he was both an elitist, contending that players were highly strung performers requiring special treatment, and a collectivist who promised that no player in any of his teams would ever receive more money than another. Like many a football manager since, he often defied interpretation, or at least categorisation.

Where he can be safely filed away is among the great managers of all time. Of his time, he was certainly the greatest. Of his ilk, he was undoubtedly the first; he scythed the path along which all British managers have walked. But of all time? Was he the greatest that the game's homeland has ever produced? Anyone claiming that – anyone seeking to place him above Sir Matt Busby and Sir Alex Ferguson of Manchester United, above Bill Shankly and Bob Paisley of Liverpool, above Jock Stein of Celtic, Don Revie of Leeds United, Bill Nicholson of Tottenham Hotspur, Sir Alf Ramsey of Ipswich Town and England or Brian Clough of Derby County and Nottingham Forest – would have a case. A case and a bit. Not just in terms of those championship hat-tricks at Huddersfield and Arsenal, the first interrupted by his ambition and the second by his death; not just because no one other than Chapman and Clough, in his remarkable partnership with Peter Taylor, has ever managed two clubs to English championships; as if such sturdy evidence required support, it could be advanced through the fundamentally important criteria of what he inherited and what he left.

At both places he took a club that had won nothing from near the bottom of the First Division and, after introducing it to the glories of League and FA Cup triumph, left it so firmly geared for further success that over the ensuing five years Huddersfield, apart from their further title, reached two Cup finals – losing the latter only to Chapman's Arsenal – while Arsenal without him continued like the machine all his teams became, winning no fewer than three more titles and a Cup in a similar five-year span. Three-quarters of a century before the word 'legacy' became a sporting cliché, Chapman gave it substance.

At Huddersfield his influence continued to be felt for decades. At Arsenal it endures today. Some of the staff he put in place were still around Highbury when Bertie Mee arrived in 1960. Mee joined as a physiotherapist and, in 1966, followed in the tradition set by Chapman's protégé Tom Whittaker by being appointed manager. In the spring of 1970 he was interviewed by the *Sun*, which pictured him standing next to the Chapman bust in the Marble Halls under the headline: 'We've Stopped Living In The Past'. Within a few weeks Arsenal had won their first trophy in 17 years, the European Fairs Cup, and the following season they did the Double of League and Cup. Among those whom Mee had signed as he built that team was George Graham. After retiring, Graham went into management with Millwall and did well enough to prompt the Arsenal board to appoint him in 1986. Seldom can a predecessor's greatness have been embraced with such relish as Graham had for the example of Chapman. He impressed it on young players in order to build their allegiance to the club and was especially proud to win two League titles – plus the League Cup and European Cup-Winners' Cup, neither of which had been invented when Chapman was around – because of the footsteps in which he followed and whose imprint he so closely studied. Graham remained in the job until 1995 and the following year Arsène Wenger came with his own – initially more sketchy, but soon to improve – grasp of history.

It is still often said that Arsenal 'have a way of doing things'. This, too, lingered from the era when Chapman supervised every facet of the club. The Arsenal way was his way: polite, dignified, urbane, outgoing (and, below the surface, rigorously competitive).

Visitors were greeted warmly and employees, especially players and those who trained or tended to them, accorded respect by the man they all knew as 'The Boss'. Five years after his death his successor, George Allison, decided to reward some players for loyalty with gifts of £500 each, to be invested by the club on their behalf, a practice Chapman had instituted. It was not until the late 1970s that this pre-war gesture came to light, being casually mentioned by one of the former players, Alf Fields. The chairman, Denis Hill-Wood, a son of Sir Samuel Hill-Wood, under whose chairmanship Chapman had flourished, immediately ordered that the club's books be searched until each of the players involved had been identified. Interest was then calculated and the sums paid.

This was recalled towards the end of the 2012–13 season by Ken Friar, whose association with the club began in 1946. Friar was a 12-year-old Highbury schoolboy then, playing football outside the stadium with friends. The ball rolled under a car and Friar was endeavouring to retrieve it when a voice boomed out: 'Boy! What are you doing?' He looked up and there was Allison, who told him to report to the stadium the next morning. When the boy arrived, expecting a reprimand, he was found match-day work in the ticket office. He rose through the ranks to the post of company secretary in 1973, succeeding Bob Wall, whose first job had been to open and answer Chapman's mail. Friar became managing director in 1983 and, although replaced by Keith Edelman between 2000 and 2008, remained on the board, more than active. In his late seventies, diminutive but indefatigable, he sat behind a solid wooden desk with leather inlay on the fourth floor of the club offices between Highbury – its twin façades now incorporated into a housing development, the pitch a communal garden – and the Emirates Stadium.

It was a very big desk Friar sat behind: it was Chapman's last desk. Friar sat on a modern chair to ease his creaking back. But in the corner of the room was a fine leather chair: Chapman's last chair. Across a corridor was a reconstruction of the old Highbury boardroom where Chapman gave progress reports to Sir Samuel and the other directors. Complete with original panelling and, for Friar, memories. He served throughout the chairmanship of Denis Hill-Wood, where matters of general football policy to be decided at an imminent League meeting would always, at some stage, be addressed with the same question: 'But what about Doncaster?' These, said Friar, were the values handed down from the Chapman era: 'What Denis meant was that, although a policy might be right for Arsenal, it should not do undue harm to the game as a whole.' When Arsenal moved home, Edelman, anxious to do everything possible to balance the books, suggested that Chapman's desk might be sold. 'No,' said Friar. He added politely that he would defend it with his life and the subject was never raised again.

On the outer walls of the Emirates Stadium, eyed by Chapman's statue, are giant murals of star players from his time, arms linked with those of more recent counterparts. But Chapman would also have approved of Wenger's concern for young and unknown aspirants. Although he had a naturally keen interest in the wellbeing of senior performers such as Alex James, whom he sometimes indulged, it was significant that less than half a day before his death – indeed, conceivably a contributory factor to it – came an excursion to Surrey to keep an eye on the youth-infused third team, his 'lads'.

Shoddy behaviour or lapses of professionalism were not, however, tolerated and once at Arsenal, as at Huddersfield, he unceremoniously transferred a player for committing a rash foul. Tommy Black might have gone at the end of the 1932–3 season anyway, but his boots never touched an Arsenal sock again after he had conceded a penalty amid the seismic event at Walsall that remains almost synonymous with the expression 'cup shock'. Generally, Chapman showed players at all levels a paternal care to which they responded with filial affection. Few put it better than Alex Jackson, whom he put much effort into signing for Huddersfield just weeks before his switch to Arsenal: 'Chapman knew when to blow you up and when to blow you down, when to be the big boss and when to be the family friend. He was a genius and that's the fact of it.'

In dealing with the players' audience, Chapman was equally sure-footed and just as well received. Although he harboured a lifelong detestation of 'barracking' – the audible derision of footballers' shortcomings – he made his point reasonably. He was a great communicator and such a fount of ideas that just about everything introduced into the game since his death could be traced back to his column in the *Sunday Express*. A notable exception would be the ascribing of bad faith to opponents. If Chapman encountered ire, he absorbed its lessons privately. Most of the time; he did have the occasional loss of temper from which Arsenal employees suffered. Otherwise the Christian example as described in the chapels and churches he faithfully attended throughout his life – born into Primitive Methodism, he died a regular attender at his local Anglican church and must have heard a few ways of putting the message across – was given flesh.

For a man of such substance, he exuded an abundance of bygone style. Although not handsome, although a little ruddy and a little chubby – seeming shorter than his 5' 9½" because of the paunch that formed after his retirement as a player and certainly done no favours by a penchant for plus-fours – he commanded earnest attention. His eyes 'twinkled and searched at the same time', as Tom Whittaker put it. Chapman had presence, to the extent that his brilliant left-winger Cliff Bastin, when asked to describe the extraordinary charisma of Mussolini – the England squad had been invited to meet the dictator while in Rome to play Italy under Chapman's guidance – replied that it had contrived to exceed even that of 'The Boss'.

Not that every aspect of Chapman was universally popular. He was loved by Arsenal's supporters and respected elsewhere but not always regarded as a friend of the game his teams dominated. It was during his years at Highbury that the cry of 'Lucky Arsenal!' became prevalent. This was the forerunner to the 'Boring Arsenal' chant of George Graham's day, later to be adopted by Arsenal's own fans during the Wenger era and used ironically to celebrate the new beauty and attacking emphasis of their club's football under the tutelage of the man from Alsace. What Chapman instituted – and both Mee and Graham recreated – was an attritional quality. From today's perspective there was nothing untoward about either this or the high spending that brought Chapman's Arsenal another tag: they were the first to be dubbed the 'Bank of England club'. It was just that the game found itself unprepared for organisation on such a scale and, as ever, took various views of a novel approach.

A distant view shows Chapman to have been, apart from everything else, a highly successful businessman, an entrepreneur with the perpetual restlessness that tends to go with such territory. This was noticed even in his heyday by an especially perceptive observer, the journalist Donny Davies, who wrote for the *Manchester Guardian* as 'An Old International' up to his death in the Manchester United air crash of 1958. Davies had intended to publish memoirs and, when the part-written manuscript was found by his survivors, it included this passage: 'Herbert Chapman sat down to organise football much as a business magnate settles down to organise profits. In his view, every device used by the industrialist to speed up the production of goods could be used equally well to speed up the production of goals.

'Specialisation? The Arsenal team became a household word as a group of specialists whose tasks were outlined for them with a clarity never before envisaged. Functionalism? Was there ever a team where the players were more strikingly suited to the parts they had to play? Up-to-date machinery? Chapman left no stone unturned to get the best football machine brains could devise or money could buy. Salesmanship? None knew better than Chapman how to market his ideas, whether to his directors, who were cozened by his ready tongue, to his players, who had faith in his keen tactical insight, or to his competitors, who were only too willing to follow the lead of a manager who appeared able to harness success to his very chariot wheels. Publicity? There was never a manager before or since who could use publicity more skilfully, or guide it more surely for his own ends.'

In those 12 sentences, Davies provided an unbeatable summary of Chapman the football manager. But it was the second sentence – 'every device used by the industrialist to speed up the production of goods could be used equally well . . .' – that defined the philosophical battleground.

There had always been in football a tension between the functional and the artistic but the prevalence of the intricate short-passing style developed in Scotland maintained peace to a degree, even though by the mid–1920s goals had become so hard to come by that Chapman's first championship team at Huddersfield averaged little over 1.4 per match. By the end of the decade even relegated teams were doing better than that and the reason was a tweak in the laws of the game that the British-dominated international board of FIFA had made on the very day – 15 June 1925 – that Chapman joined Arsenal. But goals have always been an oversimplified measure of football and the change of formation that Chapman brought about led to much protest.

At length there came a scathing verdict from Willy Meisl – younger brother of Hugo Meisl, the manager of Austria's Wunderteam – whose book *Soccer Revolution* traced a link between WM and the humiliation of English football represented by a 6–3 defeat at home to Hungary in 1953 and subsequent 7–1 beating in Budapest. The Hungarians were advised, as the Austrians had been, by Jimmy Hogan, whom historians have recognised as an enormously influential proponent of the Scottish approach. More than two decades after Chapman's death, the battle lines had been redrawn.

Yet Chapman, Hogan and the elder Meisl had been friends who naturally pooled ideas – and opinions. Only months before Chapman's death Meisl called him the world's leading football man, while a year earlier Chapman had deemed Meisl's fine side unfortunate to lose 4–3 to England in London, extolling the virtues of their creative play. In the same newspaper column, he had enthusiastically forecast the start within two years of a West Europe Cup (presumably to run alongside the Mitropa Cup already involving Austrian and other Central European club teams) to be contested by the champions of England, Scotland, Germany, France, Belgium and Spain. Chapman was an ardent internationalist and had been since the outset of his managerial career, when he took Northampton Town to Nuremberg. In addition to the annual fixture with Rangers, he had begun a relationship between Arsenal and Racing Club of Paris. Each year the clubs met, usually in Paris, to raise money for war veterans and these matches were to last until 1962.

Nor was his vista restricted to football. His obituary in the *Manchester Guardian* mentioned that, on the very day of his death, he had been intending to play host to the Australian rugby league tourists at Highbury, where they duly watched Arsenal's 1–1 draw with Sheffield Wednesday amid the general gloom. The Kangaroos had been in England since August, when Chapman had greeted them. No one in football had been doing more than he, the *Guardian* added, to encourage matches against European teams. 'More often than not when a foreign country sent a side to play international or club matches . . . Chapman would be at the station to welcome the party.'

He also threw Highbury open to other sports, letting England's cricketers receive treatment before their 1932–3 expedition to the Antipodes – since that was the Bodyline tour, the medical attention might have been better reserved for the battered Australians afterwards – and being especially proud that Tom Whittaker's healing hands had taken less than a fortnight to get Bernard Gadney, the England rugby union scrum-half, fit for a match against Ireland at Twickenham in 1933 when there had been fears that an ankle injury might end his career. Fred Perry, soon to claim the first of his three consecutive Wimbledon singles titles, was a regular visitor to the Highbury treatment room.

Chapman loved to read, so it was no burden to him to carry textbooks on his travels as a young player. 'I'd made up my mind to be a mining engineer,' he once recalled. 'To achieve this had always been the ambition of my life. Study had always been a fascination to me.' And clearly remained so. 'My leisure time always finds me with a good book in hand from which I might learn something.' Sad to say, the odd quote from Kipling is the sole evidence of his literary taste. For Chapman, information seems always to have been a more powerful lure to the page than entertainment.

He was certainly no philistine in terms of football philosophy. Portrayal of him as such, interested only in results at the expense of entertainment, is contradicted by both his own word – Austrian one-touch football was 'a delight to watch . . . designed to please and none the worse for that' – and accounts of his teams' performances. The trouble, according to Hogan, was poor imitation of Arsenal after his development of the WM formation there: 'Other clubs tried to copy Chapman but they had not the men and the result was, in my opinion, the ruination of British football.' Through the 'big kicking game', Hogan added, the players had lost their 'touch and feeling for the ball'.

Willy Meisl certainly agreed with that. He regretted the 1925 law change, which provided that an attacker was free of the offside trap if two opponents remained between him and the goal, instead of three; defences attempted to tighten by moving the centre-half, hitherto in the second line of outfield players, to a new 'stopper' role between the full-backs. Hence the WM shape, with three at the back, two lines of two in midfield and three – two wingers and a centre-forward – up front. But Chapman had already been moving in the direction of a third back at Huddersfield, using the splendid Tom Wilson there on no less an occasion than the FA Cup final of 1922, and he was not alone; Charlie Roberts, a player of unusual tactical awareness, had performed a version of the role for Manchester United. The process of evolution would surely have occurred without Chapman; it was just that he hastened it with such skill and efficacy.

Nor was he such a systems man at this substantially advanced stage of his career – Chapman had won two League championships and an FA Cup when he arrived at Highbury – that he made his new club adopt the third back straight away. He had to be persuaded by his first signing, Charlie Buchan, whose persistent advocacy at team meetings and in conversation with the manager turned into angry scorn after a 7–0 defeat at Newcastle in the ninth match of the season; Buchan had just come south from Sunderland so it would have stung like 17–0. Chapman didn't discipline him. He listened to Buchan's argument that Newcastle had used a third back, Charlie Spencer, to good effect and soon the team shape was adjusted. It was three more years before Chapman's near-perfect stopper, Herbie Roberts, was integrated into the side and another year before the machine was fully functional. Then it became a destroyer of attacks, a punisher of defences and a breaker of hearts.

The method was to retreat and set up a seven-man barrier, letting opponents have the ball and drawing them forward confident in the knowledge that someone, sooner or later, would leave space for quality raiders such as the wingers Joe Hulme or Cliff Bastin to exploit. Hence the appearance of luck in surviving pressure. But in their first two title seasons they scored 127 and then 118 goals and it is difficult to understand how such figures could be recorded by an austere team. Especially one featuring Alex James, who, although under orders not to bother scoring the goals he had been in the habit of contributing to previous clubs – he had rattled one in every three matches for Preston North End – fully merited his place at the very top of the bill.

James is said to have been what Dennis Bergkamp would have been if fate had cast him as a little Scotsman in baggy shorts and directed him into the midfield. James, like Herbie Roberts, made a position in the Chapman plan seem his own. This was why so many imitations went wrong. They lacked a master in the art of turning defence into attack. James, for Arsenal, was the missing link. He was a great footballer by any standard: always at least a couple of moves ahead of the play, with perfect control and the ability, unusual in the days of the old-fashioned leather ball, not just to pass it over long distances but to curve its trajectory if necessary. And a great entertainer whose changes of direction, by wrong-footing opponents, often had audiences in fits of laughter.

When James died of cancer, Davies recalled in tribute: 'The Arsenal defenders all played to the same rule, namely, pass the ball to James whenever possible, and leave it to the baggy-trousered Napoleon to direct offensive moves as he saw fit. How well he did so is part of the Arsenal saga.'

MAN OF VISION

Ron Jennings saw the football of that time. He was taken to his first match by his mother in 1930, two days after Arsenal had won their first trophy. It was a Monday and the FA Cup was paraded around the pitch before Chapman's heroes lost 1–0 to Sunderland. 'They're all bloody drunk!' Those were his mother's words, remembered 82 years on. 'That's exactly what she said. And I think perhaps they were.' Jennings experienced the 'absolute perfection' of James's passing and, while acknowledging its fundamental importance, felt that teamwork was the key to Arsenal's success. 'During the same era,' he said, 'Aston Villa went out and bought five or six extremely talented individuals and still got relegated because the players could not work together. Chapman made his players into a team. You'd see one hit a ball and say "What's that?" And suddenly another Arsenal player would be moving on to it. Because he'd have known what was coming. Joey Hulme liked the ball in front of him, for instance, and that's where Alex James would always put it. The players must have trained so hard together.'

To Highbury, with their devastating efficiency, they drew crowds that blurred society's class divisions. 'For He's a Jolly Good Fellow' rang out when the Prince of Wales opened the West Stand in 1932 and the ground was made even more alluring with invitations to celebrities such as Anna Neagle, who had become Britain's most popular screen actress through her role as Vicki in the romantic musical *Goodnight, Vienna* and was to make many more films under the direction of Herbert Wilcox, her future husband. Wilcox accompanied her to Highbury with relish, for he had been a keen football fan since his schooldays in Brighton, where once Derby County visited and he was enthralled by Steve

Bloomer, who had not only scored a hat-trick but, upon knocking an opponent flat, stopped to tend to him until the trainer arrived, scorning an opportunity to continue a run on goal. Wilcox later mentioned the episode in his autobiography: 'A handshake and the incident was closed. No fuss, no ill-feeling – those were the days!' He was writing in 1967 and was to live through most of the turbulent Seventies.

Amid the throng on the Highbury terraces was a teenage Ron Jennings and his pals from a factory in Holloway. 'We worked until about one o'clock on a Saturday and, because it was quite a distance to Highbury, often had to run all the way because in winter, with no floodlights – well, not that Mr Chapman was allowed to use anyway – they often had to kick off at two or two fifteen. There was no time to stop for a bit of dinner and no food stalls in our part of the stadium in those days. What we used to have was chocolate. A guy used to walk round the pitch with a tray and we'd all chip in and throw the money down to him and he'd throw the chocolate back. Then we'd share it.'

Chapman made sure the club got a share, too. Among the countless tasks he set himself was that of weeding out pirate chocolate pedlars. The lads, happily munching, would have approved because it was all for the greater glory of their place of worship. Ron Jennings kept watching Arsenal as the decades passed and, while deeply grateful for the pinch-yourself times Chapman brought, rated the peak of the Wenger era as even more entertaining. 'It's hard to say this but, for me, Wenger brought football of greater excitement because it was done at a higher speed. In the Thirties the game was conducted at a slower pace, probably because the pitches were so heavy.'

Chapman's Arsenal still became too quick and clever for their contemporaries. Donny Davies wrote of them – again finding the *mots justes* – as 'a team with a personality of its own' and Chapman, who had formed that personality, argued that it played to the rhythm of the times. 'I doubt very much,' he reflected in his *Express* column, 'whether the public would today be satisfied with the old football, with all its precision and deliberate accuracy. It does not fit modern tendencies. It would be out of tune with the bustle and excitement of everyday life.'

This exciting bustle was probably more evident in London, where his legacy included a stadium exuding Art Deco confidence, than the unemployment-ravaged cities Arsenal visited. But times were changing and Chapman never looked back with debilitating nostalgia. He did wonder if the authorities, had they known the consequence of the change in the offside law, would have proceeded – but then took advantage of it more forcefully than anyone else. He saw that the football of the Golden Age, the football that had packed St James' Park, Newcastle – firing him with an ambition to build such a citadel in the metropolis – and Villa Park, was obsolescent.

Part of him yearned for football as fun. He even expressed a wish that something could be done to encourage the aesthetic impulse by diluting the importance of League points (and came up with the radical idea that the top-half clubs in the Second Division could swap places with the bottom half of the First at the end of each season) yet conceded shortly before his death: 'Thirty years ago, men went out with the fullest licence to display their arts and crafts. Today they have to make their contribution to a system.' The elitist-cum-collectivist could also find room for ideals amid his triumphant pragmatism. He was also a most collegiate autocrat, instituting early in his career, and never departing from, the habit of the weekly team meeting at which players would be encouraged to and, if necessary – for not all shared the mental fecundity or assertiveness of Buchan – cajoled into making suggestions. For much of his career he even had a miniature pitch painted on his desk on which toy players could be moved around to illustrate moves and patterns. Individuals were welcome to air their ideas, too. The door to his office was, at least figuratively, always open.

Another paradox was that he ruled by both fear and kindness. Few – the occasionally abrasive James apart – would dare to upset 'The Boss' and yet tact was among Chapman's great virtues. As early as 1914, when he was at Leeds City, a local journalist put it thus: 'I am certain he could discuss the value of eyesight with a cross-eyed man without giving his auditor the slightest feeling of annoyance.' The Arsenal defender George Male noted: 'He had a soft voice.' And yet it was Male who, in 1932, went into Chapman's office a fringe-of-the-side left-half and emerged convinced he was a right-back. Not only that: 'I knew I was the best right-back in the country!' And, filled with the courage of Chapman's conviction, Male made his career there, going on to succeed his clubmate and fellow full-back Eddie Hapgood as England captain.

Chapman was an autocrat who knew when to delegate. Early in his career he said: 'The manager's right-hand man is his trainer or his representative in the dressing-room. A good trainer is a blessing. He has the confidence of those under him and above him, knows how to keep the boys happy and good-tempered, and heals minor injuries before some trainers would know about them. Personally I have been very fortunate in this aspect, able to make the fewest changes.' He was presumed to be paying tribute to Dick Murrell, who had followed him from Northampton Town to Leeds City, but it could just as easily apply to Whittaker, who was to be his key assistant and eventual successor at Arsenal – or it could have been Bill Shankly talking about Bob Paisley between 1959 and 1974 at Liverpool.

Tactically, Chapman would have moved with any change in the time allowed him. He responded to criticism with a rhetorical question: 'Why change a winning system?' But he was also said to have told his friend Meisl: 'Look, Hugo, it works. When everyone has copied it [adapted to WM with the expertise of Arsenal, presumably], we'll think of something else.' Whatever this was would not have countenanced waste, to which he was opposed on and off the field; he once bemoaned 'the holes in a football club through which money may escape unless someone with a hawk eye is constantly around' and that was to become more deplorably true by the decade.

He made no attempt to hide his contempt for the careful and delicate working of the ball to the wings, from where a cross would be floated to 'just in front of the goalmouth, where the odds are nine to one on the defenders'. He thought – to borrow a phrase that became fashionable amid later English debates – that teams thus 'overplayed' and it is hard, when envisaging his Arsenal and those they eclipsed, not to agree. From his very first days in management at Northampton, he knew what he wanted from wingers. He always liked them to cut inside and go for the jugular, as great ones have done, from Cliff Jones at Tottenham Hotspur in Nicholson's Double side to the early Lionel Messi at Barcelona, before he was moved inside to become a 'false' centre-forward. Chapman's basic instruction was to head towards the near post and look for a pass.

The great Matt Busby was with Hogan in regretting inferior interpretations of WM, which might just as accurately be described as 3–4–3, or even 3–2–1–1–3 given that the link man – James during the machine's most productive years – would play in a free role but well behind his fellow inside forward – David Jack, say – who would be more like a creative second striker in the style of Kenny Dalglish, or a goalscoring midfielder of the Frank Lampard type. The key to Arsenal, as Busby pointed out, was less the shape than the number of goals created from defensive beginnings. And this art of counter-attack, or 'transition', as it has come to be called, is still being assiduously practised at the highest level of the game more than a century after Chapman first preached it at Northampton.

Much is made of his immortal advice along these lines: 'You start the match with one point – make sure that at least you keep it.' But this, too – this emphasis on the importance of not conceding a goal – was hardly against the spirit of the game as we have come to recognise it. Anyway, Chapman was less defensive than perfectionist, a trait memorably impressed on his team after a 7–1 victory over Wolverhampton Wanderers at Molineux in November 1932. They reported back for training on the Monday bubbling with confidence and yet, as one player recalled: 'The only goal he talked about was the one we gave away.'

Chapman's perfectionism intensified with his age and capacity to make improvements through the transfer market. Mere months before his death, with Arsenal atop the English game, he was confiding in journalists that his attack needed pepping up, chasing the signature of the potent young Ted Drake, designing the new team George Allison was to supervise, preparing the stage on which, with a fourth title in five years, the hat-trick would be performed.

That it would be done a second time emphasises that Chapman's is not simply a story of Arsenal. It is not even a story of Huddersfield and Arsenal, even though he brought off a remarkable feat by breaking his first Arsenal record when still with Huddersfield, supervising Highbury's joint heaviest defeat – 5–0 – four months before he journeyed south on a permanent basis in the summer of 1925. His managerial debut at Northampton had been significant enough, for there he had developed the cat-and-mouse tactics that were to win so much. His first title, that of Southern League champions, was won on the counter. 'A team can attack for too long,' he had observed the previous season, after losing a match his men had dominated territorially. But when Northampton learned to counter-attack they struck lethally enough to score 90 goals, a League record, and that was Chapman's basic method laid down. The rest was a question of refinement.

What he did at Huddersfield becomes even more remarkable when it is taken into account that crowds there were below the First Division average, even as the club rose to uncharted heights. Huddersfield when he came had had less with which to build than Derby County or Nottingham Forest when Clough and Taylor arrived. And Huddersfield made history at a time when a trio of titles was unprecedented. Competition was closer than now. The championship changed hands much more frequently. In the sixteen years between Chapman's death and Manchester United's first title under Matt Busby, it was shared among no fewer than 11 clubs; in the first 16 years after the Premier League's formation in 1992, only four clubs won it. Resources were spread more evenly then and the maximum wage and transfer regulations were further instruments of financial fair play, as continued to be the case well into the 1950s, helping Preston North End, for example, to hold on to the great Tom Finney for his entire career.

So up to 1934 only one man had been able to build teams capable of staying on top for three years. And he had done it twice. And no one else was able to do it for half a century. Bob Paisley's Liverpool completed their hat-trick in 1984, by which time conditions had changed radically, conspiring in the concentration of power that enabled Manchester United to complete two hat-tricks in little over a decade culminating in 2009. Were a Chapman around today, and at a club as mighty as he made Arsenal, even Sir Alex Ferguson's achievements might be surpassed.

It was Manchester United, by coincidence, who appointed, in Busby, the manager most comparable with Chapman in terms of his effect on a club. United succeeded Arsenal as English football's most internationally renowned institution in the decade between the Munich crash and Busby's producing the first English team to win the European Champions' Cup. But Chapman had set the standard. It was Chapman who had changed everything, redrawn a background of widespread assumption that clubs were best run by directors who would pick or at least influence the selection of the team and leave the manager and/or players to work out such tactics as were deemed useful, if any. All the great managers, beginning with Busby, must be considered in Chapman's debt.

'What was significant,' argued Jonathan Wilson during an account of Chapman's Huddersfield years in his history of tactics, *Inverting the Pyramid*, 'was not merely that he had a clear conception of how football should be played, but that he was in a position to implement that vision. He was – at least in Britain – the first modern manager, the first man to have complete control over the running of the club, from signings to selection to tactics to arranging for gramophone records to be played over the public-address system to keep the crowd entertained before the game and at half-time.'

Only a chairman had taken such responsibility to such effect before: the remarkable William Sudell, who built Preston's 'Invincibles' in the 1880s, guiding them to the Double in the first season of the League. Sudell's pioneering of professionalism is properly recognised – but not the organisational ground he broke while Chapman was still in short trousers. Sudell was a football manager in all but title. His work was, however, to be largely overlooked for many years, no doubt partly as a result of the embezzlement from textile mills at which he was employed that came to fund the club's subsequent exploits. After its discovery, Billy Sudell was sent to prison and ended his days, rehabilitated by a second career in sports journalism, in South Africa.

Chapman's methods were applied more sustainably as he changed football for ever. The advantage – not least to directors – of giving managers their head began to dawn, however gradually, and after the Second World War the advance guard of the tracksuit brigade appeared, led by Busby.

It had been more than 20 years earlier, while Chapman's Huddersfield were on the way to their second title, that the *Sporting Chronicle* asked: 'Do clubs realise . . . the importance of the man who is . . . in control? They are ready to pay anything up to £4,000 and £5,000 for the services of a player. Do they attach as much importance to the official who will be in charge of the player? The man behind the scenes who finds players, trains talent, gets the best out of the men at his command and is the most important man in the game from the club's point of view?'

One club chairman who realised that was Sir Henry Norris of Arsenal. He still behaved, in the relatively short time he and Chapman had together at Highbury, as if he were the most important man at the club. But Norris deserved more credit than, in his lifetime, he received for having brought Chapman south with the highest salary in the game, one that dwarfed, because of the maximum wage, those paid to Alex James and the other players.

After Norris had gone, disgraced and cursing his own vision – he blamed Chapman for his demise – Chapman appeared liberated, pushing for stadium refurbishments and airing his brainwaves.

More than half a century before Ferguson arrived at Manchester United, Chapman had established the concept of a manager's total control of a football club. Indeed, he had felt obliged to do it twice. The pivotal incident at Arsenal occurred when a long-established club servant, George Hardy, made the mistake of rising from his seat alongside Chapman during a match and, unbidden, calling instructions to the players. It was his last contact with the first team. His job went to Tom Whittaker, whom Chapman had earmarked for it anyway. Whether the change could have been made more elegantly is debatable, for Norris was still chairman at the time and valued Hardy; had he not been away from the club that day, there would surely have been crossfire between two strong personalities. But what could not be disputed is that Chapman, faced with the option of the nasty way, went ahead and took it. Although not confrontational in the sense of many managers of the past two or three decades, he did have that ruthless streak.

Perhaps he learned from his experience at Leeds City, where scandal saw him suspended indefinitely from the game along with board members. When the investigators moved in at Arsenal, it was Norris alone who found himself exposed and friendless. What Norris had done was hardly evil. He had siphoned money from the club to make illicit payments to players – not unusually in the game at that time, and almost certainly with the knowledge and approval of Chapman – and used Arsenal money for the wages of his chauffeur. Having invested considerably in the club, he felt entitled to the odd dip into the petty cash. But there was no mercy from the authorities and he was cast out of football. Chapman proceeded to take the club beyond the heights Norris had envisaged. Norris was left with his fine house, his Rolls-Royce and the glories of the Côte d'Azur. And plenty of time in which to ponder.

Chapman never had that. Yet what had flashed by him. He had been born to the clack and creak of horse and cart and died to the sound of an occasional aeroplane propeller overhead (with Frank Whittle working on the jet engine) while at ground level more than an occasional ambulance would chime in, for there were more than a million cars on the roads in 1934 and so recklessly were they driven that nearly 7,500 people a year died – three times as many as today. He was born to word of mouth and long before his death he could make telephone calls, listen to radio (with television just around the corner) and pose for photographs or introduce his team to the public through the medium of newsreels. He was born vulnerable to the cruelties of nature and he died only just short of the application of antibiotics, which might have saved him. If only. Fifty-five years, 11 months and 18 days of Herbert Chapman added up – even though the perpetual fidget with what Whittaker called 'that restless, electric, planning brain' had crammed so much into his time – to nowhere near enough.

VICTORIAN VALUES

DISTRESS IN SHEFFIELD

Herbert was the eighth child of John and Emma Chapman, but Isaiah and Lilly had perished in infancy and Anna Louisa, the first-born, was to die at the age of 15 within months of Herbert's arrival. This left him with three brothers – Thomas, John and Matthew – and a sister, Martha. There followed Henry, Ernest and Percy, although Percy died aged five. Life was anything but a right; it was almost a privilege.

Not that it seemed so for the disadvantaged (how hollow today's euphemisms ring) of Sheffield, the great smoke-belching conurbation served by the railway that passed through Kiveton Park on its way from Grimsby, bearing fish in that direction and steel and coal for distribution from the East Coast docks in the other. 'Distress in Sheffield' was the title of a national newspaper account published on the day Herbert Chapman was born: Saturday, 19 January 1878. It told of many cases of 'extreme hardship' among families. There was no social safety net for the unemployed, sick or injured in 1878.

One report read: 'Hunger has become a normal state of things. The whole of the furniture in the place would not fetch five shillings [this would have been about a day's wages for luckier ones] under the hammer. There are three children at present, one of which is sickly and afflicted with a disease of the spine. Perhaps before this is in the press a fourth may be added to their number.

There is nothing, can be nothing, in preparation for the little stranger.'

The writers continued: 'In Kenninghall Street we saw a family of five, where everything disposable had been disposed of [possibly to one of the many pawnbrokers who traded money for goods that might fetch a higher price if not reclaimed]. They sleep in the little clothing they possess, and all lie close to keep each other warm. The wife is so hoarse from a cold she can scarcely speak.

'Next comes a family of five children, one an idiot and a cripple. The father ill in bed of bronchitis and consumption. No bedding except the clothes they wear.'

And so it goes on: 'Neighbour to these was another family where even worse destitution prevailed. Furniture, beds and bedding, and clothing gone.'

And: 'The poor wan face of the mother, with a four-month child at her breast. A single covering only serves, and barely, to hide their nakedness. They are simply starving.'

This was in the *Illustrated Police News*, a paper with no aversion to melodrama, but, lest its exposé be discounted, *The Times* confirmed the extent of Sheffield's distress the following winter, when Christmas Day arrived bearing the generous gift of a severe snowstorm. The situation, it was reported, was 'now far more serious and more extensive than was the case last year'. Soup kitchens were to be opened and food taken to children. The Mayor pleaded for a bolstering of his relief fund, contributions to which had included one from 'a gentleman signing himself "C.D.J." and stating that, although he had no sympathy with the men, believing that the distress was in great measure owing to their own suicidal policy in unreasonably raising the cost of production in every branch of trade by high wages and shorter hours, he could not help feeling for the suffering of the helpless children and wives'.

By shorter hours he meant only eight a day rather than 10 or 11, and only five and a half days a week instead of six. It was hardly a luxurious life for the foot soldiers of industrialisation, those drawn to the swelling urban centres – Sheffield already held more than 300,000 people and Birmingham, Manchester and Liverpool more than 400,000, while 2.5 million made London the most populous city in the western world – by work in the factories and mills. Protection from the hazards of machinery was often scant. A decline in British agriculture was conspiring in this migration. It coincided with massive consumption of alcohol – today's figures almost pale by comparison – by those who turned a deaf ear to organised religion's warnings. The working class was split in this sense: drink and God fought a constant battle for the right to offer refuge.

Herbert Chapman was directed towards the latter. His parents made sure of it. John Chapman had been two months old when his own father, a quarry labourer, was killed in a rock fall at work in Crich in Derbyshire. His mother remarried and, with William Booth, had a further six children. John kept the surname Chapman, except when seeking to evade possible arrest; he was supplementing his income as a coal miner by fighting bare-knuckle in pubs, an illicit but popular entertainment which often paid a sovereign (£1) per bout to the winner (purses were said to go as high as 50 sovereigns, but 'Battling Jack Booth' was not quite in that class). At the age of 20 he met Emma Haynes, who was 16 and worked in a cotton factory, and they were married in the stone Methodist chapel at Holloway, near the Derbyshire house where Florence Nightingale and her family spent their summers, in 1862.

John and Emma lived in the Haynes family home in Ripley, into which another miner, Samuel Fletcher, moved in 1865 when he married Emma's sister Louisa. Four years later, the pit where John and Samuel worked having neared exhaustion, they all embarked on a train journey to Yorkshire. In Kiveton Park the coal company had built houses for the miners. Here the families could rent one each. There was more space in which John and Emma could build their family – and a pit that would never be exhausted.

Kiveton Park had yielded shallow coal for centuries, being a useful source of income for the Dukes of Leeds in their edifice of brick and the local limestone with extensive manicured grounds and handsome parkland through which the hunt could howl and thunder. The first Duke built Kiveton Hall in 1698 and the sixth demolished it in 1812 when, citing whiffs of smoke from the proliferating chimneys of Sheffield, he moved to Bedale in the fragrant north of the county. Stone from the quarry had been in demand, most notably when a large quantity was ferried by canal to London for the reconstruction of the Houses of Parliament that began in 1840. Now, however, was the moment for the Osborne family to make serious money from their mining rights: an appreciation that the Manchester, Sheffield and Lincolnshire Railway ran almost straight over a deep but extremely rich seam of coal left little to do but licence the newly formed Kiveton Park Coal Company to call in the sinkers, who took 18 months to complete their operation. They reached the Barnsley seam in December 1867 (a second, the High Hazel, was to follow in the 1880s). Sidings were laid so the coal could be ferried from the pithead to waiting railway wagons.

Meanwhile the erstwhile agricultural hamlet was drawn into the extended boundaries of the adjacent village of Wales, with its church bearing Norman features and name testifying to the continuing presence of a Celtic community when the Anglo-Saxons arrived in the late fifth century. Wales is a variation of a Germanic word for foreigners or outsiders; the country of Wales probably got its name in much the same way as the Yorkshire parish that now included Kiveton Park.

Some of the miners came, like John Chapman, from Derbyshire, others from Nottinghamshire or farther afield. Barnet Kenyon had been born and brought up in South Anston, two miles away, but at the age of 13 had walked 20 miles for work upon hearing from a cousin that the Denaby Main mine was opening. 'It was just as big an adventure to me as the celebrated journey of Dick Whittington,' he later wrote in a memoir, after he had served as Liberal MP for Chesterfield. 'I had heard that there was always more money to be made at a new pit than at an old one.' In his first week he made 27 shillings – 'it seemed a fortune, I began to fear I had robbed somebody' – and sent some home to his family.

Kenyon had been born in 1850 – 'just after the Hungry Forties' – and begun work aged seven in a quarry not far from Kiveton Park. His parents were reluctant but had little choice: his father earned the equivalent of 75p for a six-day week and the 15p (sixpence a day) that the boy could bring in made a difference. He was one of five children. 'My dear mother was an excellent manager and, poor thing, she used to say she could make a two-pennyworth of liver go as far as some people could make a joint of meat.

'My job at the quarries was to fill a wheelbarrow with the stones that the men had broken. Limestone is cold to handle at any time, but on a frosty morning it is no joke. One particular morning, when I had been on the job about four years, my little hands were absolutely numbed. So I put one hand in my pocket to warm it while I put stone in the barrow with the other. Hardly had I done so when I heard a voice from the top of the quarry. I looked up and saw the ganger – I remember he was a member of the village choir. He shouted down in a voice of thunder "You young devil – do I pay you sixpence a day to stick your hands in your pockets? Get home to your mother." I went home filled with remorse and shame because I knew what that sixpence a day meant to us all. But my mother was not angry. She comforted me and told me not to worry as something would turn up.

'I remember those times distinctly. I used to go to work without a proper breakfast – tea without sugar, bread without butter. We never had such a thing as a coal fire. The fire was made of sticks we collected. The Dukes of Leeds had a steward who lived close to Kiveton Park station and he let us pick bits of wood from the estates.

'There was one very hard winter, five months of solid frost. My father could not work and there was no unemployment benefit. One night there was a knock on the door and, as we lived on the turnpike road between York and London, I felt sure it was Dick Turpin or one of his successors who had come. We were sleeping three in a bed to keep warm and I made my way downstairs in fear and trembling. To my pleasant surprise I found that the visitor was not a burglar but someone from the village butcher's who had sent some meat and bones. I always think gratefully of that butcher.'

The trek to Denaby was young Kenyon's first excursion. 'South Anston at that time was a remote country village which, in winter, was cut off from civilisation.' It was no different at Kiveton before the pit, and, even after, people could spend their entire lives within a mile or two of their place of birth. Kenyon had the spirit of adventure that Herbert Chapman was to exhibit a generation or two on. But, because the search for a living left Kenyon little choice but to hew coal, it entailed a surfeit of injury and trauma; he arrived at Barnsley in the aftermath of an explosion that caused the death of 388 miners and rescuers and helped to retrieve some of the bodies. He returned to Kiveton for the opening of the pit there.

At Denaby, whose notoriety exemplified the perception among polite society that underground mining was one vast den of vice – until the 1840s women and girls worked often scantily clad among naked men in the sweltering tunnels – he learned to sup and scrap and follow the frowned upon sport with which John Chapman supplemented his income. 'I could drink a pint with the rest,' he confessed, 'and the boxing ring found in me an enthusiastic supporter.'

Kiveton, however, offered Kenyon a different influence. Unlike Denaby, it had no colliery pub and he worked alongside men from Leicestershire, earnest Christians who would neither start their shift without a prayer nor break for 'snap' (lunch usually of sandwiches carried in a metal tin) without first singing a hymn. 'Other men were also devout,' he recalled, 'and no one dreamed of mocking them.' John Chapman was one. He may even have kept a bible in his tool box; it was not unusual according to Kenyon, who became literate as well as religious and, through trade unionism, went into politics. He was firm in asserting the virtue of Primitive Methodism (a movement second only to the Wesleyan before the Methodist Union of 1932): 'It was undoubtedly the salvation of the miners about the 1880s and before . . .'

John Chapman practised it while taking the proceeds of illicit pugilism, which competed with such other spectator sports as bull-baiting, badger-baiting and cock-fighting (the imminent spread of football was to prove an extremely good news story for the wild and domestic animals hitherto regarded as sports equipment). Considerable scepticism over the influx into Kiveton Park and Wales had been harboured at the parish church, where in 1868 the curate, James Catchpole, had submitted a report to the new Archbishop of York about young miners coming in 'with the vicious habits all too common of that class' – drinking and fornication, no doubt – and tempting locals to overcrowd their houses with paying tenants. Such fears can only have been assuaged by the likes of John and Emma Chapman, who worshipped at Catchpole's church before a chapel was built at Kiveton Park in 1876.

THE BEST OF PARENTS

The coal seam that lured John Chapman to Kiveton was 1,200 feet below the surface and the men hurtled towards it in cages. Some found the experience exciting, others less so. There was no element of choice in this or many other matters of safety and explosions or other mishaps took the lives of 1,000 miners a year nationally. One had died at Kiveton in 1876 and both John Chapman and his first son, Tom – aged 15 and already in his third year at work – survived the loss of four men in a gas blast in 1880.

As for pay, it was liable to be cut; there was a strike against this at Kiveton in 1878. Men and boys, the 300 protesters were members of the South Yorkshire and North Derbyshire Miners' Association. Trade unionism had nowhere near the muscle that was to be flexed in a national strike to establish the principle of basic pay in 1912, or by the NUM in the 1970s.

Sheffield had been a true battleground. Its success at steel production had entailed long working hours in conditions evolving with painful slowness from those depicted by Charles Dickens in his great novel *Hard Times*. Dickens, through his journalism, had campaigned on behalf of those neglected amid Great Britain's drive to remain the supreme economic and political power. In *Hard Times* he helped to change middle-class opinion by showing how industrialists treated workers as little more than parts of machinery. In the cause of Sheffield steel, they certainly wore out or broke: there were such graphically titled ailments as 'grinder's asthma' as well as horrific injury. Agitation by workers became accordingly bitter and was opposed by a great editor of the *Sheffield Telegraph*, William Leng, who denounced 'howling mobs' and alleged their organisations' complicity in violence against both employers and workers who declined to join. The formation of a Liberal government under William Ewart Gladstone led to more sympathy for organised labour and a year after Dickens had succumbed to a stroke the Trade Union Act of 1871 made unions legal.

The previous year had seen the Elementary Education Act and this was greatly to influence the life of Herbert Chapman. Kiveton embraced the obligation to provide schooling for all from the ages five to 12 and not just the minority who attended church schools. Gladstone and his ministers were endeavouring to satisfy a variety of requirements: for a better qualified workforce, to keep the wheels of growth turning, but also for a more educated electorate of the urban males who had been given the vote in 1867. Young Herbert and his brothers would prove only too anxious to oblige.

Growing numbers of children prompted the coal company to provide the purpose-built school in 1872. It was a 'British School'. The system of education used in these establishments had been designed more than half a century earlier by Joseph Lancaster, a Quaker from the East End of London. He wanted it to be affordable for all but the very poorest families and so only a couple of teachers could be engaged, their work being supplemented by monitoring: older and more able pupils, once they had mastered a lesson, would be rewarded for passing it down to juniors. Lancaster took his idea to the United States, where its reputation suffered amid reports of low standards and occasionally humiliating methods of discipline. Eventually he was removed from his own foundation, which was renamed the British and Foreign School Society and continued to offer charitable aid to education projects in the United Kingdom and overseas into the twenty-first century.

The British School in Kiveton Park was run by James Royds and his wife Mary when Herbert first attended at the age of five. His brothers Tom and John had left and were working at the colliery but Matt, two years Herbert's senior, was there. Herbert learned with the aid of slate and chalk and lesson sheets, prepared by Mr and Mrs Royds, which the monitors would take down from the walls before gathering a group of up to 10 younger pupils.

Herbert left at 13 to become an apprentice at the colliery, where he did clerical jobs such as checking the weight of loads of coal. He worked alongside his brother John and never had to go underground. Except as part of his further studies; he was always determined to pursue his education, as suddenly the son of an il-literate miner could do. His impulse to manage was felt. He spent days at the recently constructed Sheffield Technical College – a robust and ornate edifice, in keeping with the civic style of the time – attending lectures and reading for a diploma in mining engineering. The trams were still horse-drawn; electric ones did not start to replace them until the end of the century. Street light-ing was by gas and perhaps the most significant progress was subterranean, for sewage, since 1886, was no longer just pumped into Sheffield's rivers. There was a public library in case Herbert needed to supplement his textbooks.

He was taking steps on the road to prosperity. His eldest brother had already got as far as Grimsby, where, having escaped the pit, Tom was making a career in the railways (he had also played as an amateur for Grimsby Town). John was to become a pillar of the Labour Party, chairman of the Rother Valley divi-sion, parish, district and county councillor, leader of the Kiveton Park miners' union, member of too many committees and boards to list, keen amateur footballer and cricketer and pioneer of provision for other recreations such as tennis and bowls, school governor, progenitor of the local war memorial and, somehow, father of six. Matt followed Tom to Grimsby, where he rose to become the town's chief sanitary inspector. Harry (christened Henry) became an outstanding professional footballer for The Wednesday in Sheffield. Ernest – father of Ken Chapman – briefly tried the licensed trade before returning to the pit and becoming a deputy, or safety supervisor. There should also be mention of Herbert. He did quite well too.

The parents lived to see some but not all of it. Emma Chapman died in 1908, the year after Harry starred in the FA Cup final, and her husband John in 1909, during which Herbert hinted at things to come by guiding Northampton Town to the championship of the Southern League. But they would have gone assured that the boys and their sister were on the Christian path to fulfilment. Martha had married William Rodgers, a supervisory worker at the pit, and, although five of their first six children did not survive to a first birthday, the exception, Emma Haynes Rodgers (named after her grandmother), became a singer and music teacher whose gifts took her beyond the Kiveton Park Operatic Society to the orchestral halls of Sheffield and Manchester.

The love and respect that flowed back to John and Emma Chapman from their children was evident on the joint gravestone that remains in the churchyard of St John's, Wales. The inscription reads: 'The best of parents'. They didn't have an easy or always kind existence but, despite the inauspicious deaths of two babies and a teenage daughter in their first few years at Kiveton Park, John and Emma had found there a better and richer family life than could ever have been envisaged on the day they were wed in the Derbyshire hills.

CHRISTIANITY AND THE HOOLIGANS

In America around the time of Herbert Chapman's birth, Thomas Edison had patented the phonograph, which eventually permitted the playing of recorded music. Edison's company had plenty of other projects: electric lighting, for instance, and the telephone.

They all took a while to get to Kiveton Park, where gas dimly lit the muddy main street. Even in Herbert's first summer of 1878 the wheels of carts and hooves of horses would churn the thoroughfare, for it was an unusually wet summer, with farmers lamenting the disease afflicting the feet of their sheep and disruption to a harvest in which miners lent a hand, earning useful extra income.

No photographs tell the tale. Photography was an infant, albeit one that grew quickly enough for the first Kodak box camera to come on the market a decade later. Regular radio broadcasting was nearly half a century away and television didn't even start until after Herbert Chapman had died. Yet change kept a brisk pace. By the time Herbert went to school in 1883, there had been electric light on a street in Godalming, Surrey – a historic event that failed to attract the attention commanded by Edison's flip of a switch in Manhattan, theatrically illuminating a square mile of New York's most fashionable borough, a year later – and a race to develop the telephone involving, among others, Edison and Alexander Graham Bell.

Gladstone's Liberals had beaten the Conservatives under Disraeli in the general election of 1880, which took place during the first Boer War, a successful rebellion by farmers against British rule in the Transvaal. Three weeks after it ended, Disraeli died. Others who left the world in the five years leading to Herbert Chapman's first walk to school included Ned Kelly, hanged in Australia, and Billy the Kid and Jesse James, shot along with other outlaws in America, where troops accepted the surrender of the Sioux leader Sitting Bull.

Chapman's life was to span enormous shifts in the power of nations, notably his own and its cousin across the Atlantic. It also saw the opening of a wealth of opportunity for managers. Chapman was naturally equipped, with his organisational skills, to manage in many a sphere; his oversight of a munitions factory during the First World War was to be a considerable undertaking. But football was in his heart.

He grew up happily and not only played for the school football team but captained and managed it. The game had been with him all his short life. In every corner of the land, clubs were being formed. The year of Herbert's birth also saw the inception, a couple of miles from Manchester city centre, of Newton Heath LYR (Lancashire and Yorkshire Railway) Football Club. The men who built the rolling stock played for and, through the works canteen committee, ran the club, which initially took part in local competitions before joining the Football League in 1892–3, by which time its attendances had risen to an average of 10,000. They are now even healthier, and the club is called Manchester United.

Another club that formed in 1878 was St Domingo. Or, as it soon became known, Everton. The original title reflected the contribution of churches to the game's development. Quite a few clubs can trace their roots to them, including Manchester City, created as St Mark's (West Gorton) in 1880 by members of the church cricket team. This was for an especially admirable purpose. The church warden thought it might offer an alternative to gang warfare, or 'scuttling', as it was known in Manchester. Other afflicted cities had their own terms: Birmingham had its 'sloggers', while London's 'hooligans' were to leave a semantic legacy.

Gorton, whose image problem has proved equally durable – Ian Brady and Myra Hindley lived there while committing the first three Moors Murders and *Shameless*, the tragi-comic televisual depiction of life on a contemporary Manchester estate, was largely set in the area – was among the theatres of scuttling. The conflicts were territorial and involved male teenagers in a sort of uniform: clogs with brass tips, bell-bottom trousers, heavily buckled belts which would be removed for use as weapons (along with the obligatory knives) and distinctive haircuts with long fringes sometimes plastered over an eye with drying soap. Each side might number only a couple of dozen or, for special fixtures between areas such as Gorton and Openshaw, as many as three hundred. There was much stone-hurling and knifing – reports told of the assailants' proud sneers as wounds were horrifically detailed in court – but mercifully little fatality.

Scuttling was blamed – by the *Manchester Guardian*, which was not alone – on the parents. Credit for its recession towards the end of the century was to be shared among the city fathers who cleared the worst slums, the pioneers of the youth club movement and the increasing popularity of street football.

There was the concept of 'muscular Christianity' and what sport, football included, might do for the young men about whom society and the clergy fretted, not just those who might fall victim to the perceived vices of masturbation and homosexuality but the unruly who formed the gangs. The phrase 'muscular Christianity' was first used in the 1850s, in a review of a novel by Charles Kingsley, who later wrote: 'In the playing field, boys can acquire gifts no books can give them . . . self-restraint, fairness, honour . . .' A similarly hopeful view on the other side of the Atlantic led to the invention, for the Young Men's Christian Association, of basketball. And, in fathering the modern Olympics that began in 1896, the Baron de Coubertin alluded to the imperative not to win but play the game well. How much football, with its incendiary effect on the passions, brought to the movement for nobility in sport is hard to judge, even now. But it did help to get the scuttlers, sloggers and hooligans off the Victorian city streets. And it certainly seemed to dovetail with the Christianity of the Chapmans of Kiveton Park.

In Kiveton it was a life of generally wholesome leisure, when it came, this era in which the new expression 'weekend' came to be used for the period of now one and a half or even two days between the end of work and its bleak Monday resumption. There were local orchestras, chapel choirs and dances. But no cinema yet and none of the earthy glamour that blew in with the popularity, spreading from London, of the music hall. This could be enjoyed in Sheffield. Marie Lloyd was music hall's brightest star. When still in her teens, she was said to earn £600 a week, which would not have been greatly exceeded by the income of the population of Kiveton Park put together. Not if you set aside the Duke of Leeds and the pit owners.

Lloyd, born in the slums of London's East End, sang perkily

of the grim everyday – 'My Old Man (Said Follow the Van)' was about eviction – but tended to go down better in the capital than Yorkshire. Not that she shied from the notion of a north–south divide. Far from it. Coolly received in Sheffield once, she yelled at the audience: 'You don't like me? Well, I don't like you. And you know what you can do with your stainless-steel knives and your scissors, you can shove 'em up your arse.'

She was to take an interest in football – or at least a footballer – attending Sunderland matches in London while having an affair with Dick Roose, the charismatic 'prince of goalkeepers'. Later she formed a relationship with the Irish jockey Bernard Dillon and married him after her second husband died. But Dillon was a heavy drinker with violent tendencies and Lloyd herself developed an alcohol problem that eroded her health and her performance. One night in 1922 she collapsed on a London stage – the audience laughed, thinking it part of the act – and three days later she died, aged 52, so loved for the gay mischief of her prime that 100,000 attended the funeral.

MURDERER ON THE KIVETON EXPRESS

Herbert Chapman, growing up with his brother Harry, two years his junior and destined for greater fame in the short term, was 10 when the Football League began. Newspaper coverage of the now-professional game was considerable and the better players became celebrities, if not quite to compare with Marie Lloyd or the great sporting hero of willow and leather W. G. Grace, who had marked the first Test match ever played in England by scoring a century against the Australians in 1880 and went on to dominate cricket to within a few years of his final match for the Gentlemen of England against Surrey in 1908. Herbert could read all about it. The rise of Grace was news and Herbert, like millions of other children of his generation, could consume it. Schooling opened their eyes to a world that was to have more and more time for sport in general and football in particular.

There were descriptions of more lurid matters for the literate youngster to peruse and these included the hangings of murderers. Around 20 of these poignant ceremonies took place, on average, during the first 10 years of Herbert's life. Two women were among those executed in 1879, one for killing an illegitimate child and the other for the murder of her husband. Prominent among the men hanged that year was Charles Peace, whose notoriety proved so durable as to gain mention decades hence in short stories by Mark Twain (1907) and the Sherlock Holmes author Arthur Conan Doyle (1924). Peace was another celebrity, albeit posthumous, of the era in which Herbert grew up.

Peace came from interesting stock, being the son of a miner who, after losing a leg in an accident, made use of a gift for lion-taming in an animal park before seeing out his days as a shoemaker. Charles was born in Sheffield. At the age of 14, he was lamed by a leg injury in a steel-mill accident and by his late teens he had turned to crime. He served substantial sentences for burglary, the latter aggravated by the wounding of a police officer who had trapped him when collecting buried loot, and, while trying his luck in Manchester, committed his first murder, through another shooting of a policeman. Another man was tried for this and Peace watched from the public gallery as he was found guilty and condemned to death. Two days before the date of execution, the sentence was commuted to life imprisonment.

By now Peace had befriended a couple, the Dysons, in the Sheffield suburb of Darnall, and was said to be having an affair with Mrs Dyson. The couple moved to another suburb, Banner Cross, after threats from Peace, but he found them and shot the husband dead. He fled to London and, despite a £100 offer for information leading to his arrest, was able to resume burgling for a couple of years, until in November 1878 he was caught in the act and used his revolver for what proved the last time in injuring one of the officers involved in his capture.

Even then he was defiantly set on escape. Accompanied by two prison officers on the journey back to Sheffield to face a preliminary hearing, he asked to be allowed to use the lavatory every time the train stopped at a station. The officers instead gave Peace bags to fill and throw out of the window. As the train slowed near Kiveton Park, the window was opened and he took the opportunity to leap through it. Although grabbed by a foot, he kept kicking until released. He was later discovered with a severe head wound. A fortnight later, he was deemed fit enough to be tried and, despite the arguments of his solicitor, William Clegg, who suggested that Mr Dyson, jealous, had started a fight during which the gun went off, committed to the higher court at Leeds.

Clegg – later Sir William – was a keen footballer. Along with his brother Charles, also a lawyer and also to be knighted, he played for both The Wednesday and England, although his duties with Peace did cause him to miss the first 15 minutes of an international against Wales at Kennington Oval. Having worked late in Sheffield on a Friday with the doomed killer and the futile version of events they were rehearsing, he was obliged to take the morning train to London and snow delayed it. England won 2–1. There was little left to do for Clegg's client. Peace was found guilty at Leeds, the jury taking 10 minutes to reach their verdict, and sentenced to death. At least, while awaiting his demise in Armley prison, he confessed to the Manchester murder, allowing the man falsely convicted to be released and compensated from public funds.

Peace's execution was vividly featured in the *Illustrated Police News*. Photographs did not appear in newspapers until the 1890s, but drawings of notable events would be commissioned and this one showed the executioner preparing to slip a blindfold over the stone face of Peace, to whom a robed chaplain was reading from the Bible, with the outline of a trapdoor below the prisoner's feet and several guards in alert attendance. Such was the interest of even the more serious newspapers in murderers and other outlaws that a satirical journalist devised a scornful term for it: 'criminal-worship'. There must have been a severe outbreak of artist's cramp when, in 1888, just as the Football League was getting under way in the north and Midlands, the nation fell agog at the series of murders of prostitutes in the East End of London who had their throats cut by Jack the Ripper.

Not that young Herbert needed to read newspapers to be acquainted with horror. Word of mouth would have conveyed the all too real and tragic tale of the single mother (a state of shame) Alice Middleton, the body of whose baby was fished from the canal at Kiveton Park. In her defence it was stated that she had been 'the victim of some man's lust' while in a workhouse but had walked several miles to Kiveton, where a brother lived, in the hope of finding some employment, only to be beaten and rejected. It was added that she had not eaten for several days before the baby's death and had pleaded with at least two local women to take the girl in. She was nonetheless found guilty of murder, but in May 1888 the death sentence was set aside.

Among the cases that came before Sheffield's busy coroner, Dossey Wightman, was one concerning the death at Kiveton Park of a 14-year-old pit-pony driver, Isaiah Pinches, from a skull fracture sustained when a metal box was thrown at him underground. A workmate was later tried for manslaughter. Misfortune abounded. Wightman's court also heard that a sinker helping to repair a ventilation shaft had gone to fetch a spanner and forgotten that some planks had been removed; witnesses heard him hit first some scaffolding and then the pit bottom, 400 yards below. Away from the pit, a 69-year-old labourer had been sent to collect a load of stone in a wagon with three horses. He was returning, walking alongside, when the whistle of a railway engine passing through Kiveton Park station frightened the horses, which bolted. A wheel passed over one of Pinches's legs and he died on a train taking him to hospital in Sheffield.

Although it is not known whether young Herbert took note of momentous events (the rise of football aside) beyond his community, inquiring minds among his elders would have digested the fatal stabbing in Phoenix Park, Dublin, of Lord Frederick Cavendish, the newly appointed Chief Secretary for Ireland, and his principal assistant; the death of General Gordon in Khartoum; the construction of the Forth Bridge and, even closer to home, the conversion of sections of the rivers Mersey and Irwell into the Manchester Ship Canal. But neither seasoned observers nor wide-eyed boys could have ignored the exploits of a great football team that in 1889, when Herbert had turned 11, became the first to win the Double of Football League and FA Cup in the same season.

It was the inaugural season of the Football League and Preston North End went through it unbeaten. They never so much as conceded a goal in the five Cup matches that culminated in a 3–0 victory over Wolverhampton Wanderers in front of 27,000 at the Kennington Oval. How they merited the resonance of their sobriquet: they were the Invincibles.

THE GREAT SUDELL

Preston had a manager with more than a claim to have defined the role in advance of Herbert Chapman. William Sudell was also, like Chapman, a game-changer, in that he was instrumental in guiding football towards overt professionalism. Sudell was officially Preston's chairman but in truth did everything but play. He guided the club to either first or second place in each of the first five League championships and, although Preston were to have some notable times long after he had gone, winning a second FA Cup in 1938 and being runners-up with the great Tom Finney twice in the 1950s, Sudell's feats remained untouchable. What Real Madrid were to European football in the teenage years of Alex Ferguson, you might say, Sudell's Preston were to the English game in the formative years of Herbert Chapman.

Lean and darkly charismatic, Billy Sudell was of the Prestonian middle class, a privately educated cotton-mill manager and officer in the local Volunteer Force (a precursor of the Territorial Army) with a fondness for sport, rugby especially, that led him to join the North End club when in his teens and become chairman in his twenties.

He played rugby and cricket and, when the club started football in 1878, tried that. Briefly; he wasn't very good. So he stopped and took responsibility for management. The club resolved to play football only but competition in Lancashire was fierce and once the mighty Blackburn Rovers, boasting Fergie Suter and other professionals from Scotland, came to Deepdale and won 16–0. Sudell learned his lesson and began recruiting north of the border. In 1883 he persuaded Nick Ross, the captain of Heart of Midlothian, to forsake Edinburgh for a job as a slater in Preston and the odd underhand payment; professionalism remained illicit.

Ross was no glamour boy but, despite discoloured teeth through which he hissed as he played, switched from attack to become a 'demon' defender in England, the best of his day according to the football writer James Catton, who wrote in a memoir published in 1926: 'This was the beginning of modern football, because, after The Wednesday of Sheffield and the Rovers of Blackburn had their Scottish allies who were called amateurs, the North End did not rely on half measures.' Sudell used jobs at his mill among other lures. He signed so many Scots that the Scottish FA, whose opposition to professionalism was harder than their English counterparts', at one stage outlawed no fewer than 11 of his players among a total of 68 blacklisted for moving south.

In 1883 Preston qualified for the fourth round of the FA Cup by winning 9–1 at Eagley and then drew 1–1 with Upton Park, who protested to the FA that Sudell's team had been loaded with professionals. Sudell and an Upton Park representative were called to face the FA committee at Kennington Oval, where Upton Park provided statements from Glasgow and Edinburgh that might have been more damning but for Sudell's open confession. Yes, his inquisitors were told, he paid players; he had to, because it was common practice and Preston would otherwise be at a crushing disadvantage. He defiantly added: 'Gentlemen, Preston are all professionals, but if you refuse to legalise them they will be amateurs. We shall all be amateurs, and you cannot prove us otherwise.' Preston were disqualified from the Cup, but Sudell's candour had left an impression on FA notables such as Charles Alcock, whose initiative had led to the Cup's foundation, Lord Kinnaird, who had won three finals with Wanderers and two with Old Etonians, and Major Francis Marindin, a veteran of the Crimean War and Cup runner-up with Royal Engineers whose reputation as a referee was now so high that he handled every final, missing not one between 1884 and 1890.

The opposition to professionalism was fierce among representatives from Sheffield – including William Clegg's brother Charles – and Birmingham. Among their arguments was that it might entrench the malign influence of betting. Alcock and colleagues were more pragmatic; they felt it best to legitimise professionalism but control it with conditions such as residential qualifications. Sudell, who would not have liked the sound of that but realised the value of oiling the lock on the door, continued the campaign and in October 1884 a meeting of 19 mainly Lancastrian clubs in Blackburn resolved that, if professionalism were not recognised, they would break from the FA and form a rival 'British Football Association'. This was reinforced by a second gathering, of 31 clubs, in Manchester.

The prospect of a split prompted the FA to form a subcommittee including Sudell and others from Lancashire. Alcock emerged from it with a fresh proposal that was carried by the FA at a meeting at Anderton's Hotel in Fleet Street, London, in July 1885. Professionalism had been accepted. Sudell was now almost an establishment figure. Not enough of one, however, to prevent the FA from again disqualifying Preston in 1885–6, after they had won 3–2 away to Bolton Wanderers, who were themselves put out of the Cup two rounds later. The residential rule had been Preston's downfall, for Bolton had argued that Geordie Drummond had been working in Edinburgh at the time of the match. The temptation to make a tit-for-tat complaint (they were not unusual amid the hypocrisy Sudell deplored) was irresistible to Sudell, who had Bolton eliminated before they could take on Old Westminsters.

In 1886–7, North End reached the semi-finals only to lose to West Bromwich Albion. 'The Major', as Marindin was known, was refereeing and, although his fairness in applying the laws went unquestioned on that and most other occasions, a distaste for the obligation to allow imports from Scotland became evident afterwards as he strode into the Albion dressing room and asked: 'Are you all Englishmen?' The reply was a unanimous affirmative. 'Then I have very much pleasure,' he continued, 'in presenting you with the ball. You have played a very good game and I hope that you will win the Cup.'

They lost to Aston Villa. The following season Albion reached the final again and who should be waiting for them but Preston? By now North End had become fearsome. They had begun their campaign by beating Hyde 26–0, then Bolton Wanderers 9–1, and went on to overcome Halliwell 4–0 before taking on the holders, Villa, who were beaten 3–1 on their own ground, as were The Wednesday in Sheffield. Crewe Alexandra lost 4–0 to Sudell's men in the semi-final and so at last it was off to the Oval. Such was the team's progress over the past year that few gave Albion a chance. Least of all Sudell and his Preston players, who asked Marindin if they could be photographed with the trophy beforehand so their kit would be clean. 'You'd better win it first,' growled Marindin. And when he blew the final whistle North End had fallen again. Reports of the refereeing included an observation that on one occasion Marindin had awarded Albion an inexplicable free-kick – no appeal, as prescribed by the law of the time, had come from them – as Preston were about to score. But there was no lapse of sporting dignity from the mercenaries from Deepdale, who blamed their preparation – it had included a morning visit to the chilly banks of the Thames to watch the Boat Race – for a below-par performance. Nor did Albion lack grace. 'I do not pretend for a moment,' said their captain, Billy Bassett, 'that we deserved to beat them.'

The clubs met again a year later and this time Preston won 1–0 in a semi-final at Bramall Lane. By now they were carrying all before them, including Wolverhampton Wanderers in a final that had lasted only 15 minutes before Marindin was supervising its restart, Preston having taken the lead through their captain, Fred Dewhurst, who was one of four Englishmen in the side. There was a Welsh goalkeeper, Robert Mills-Roberts, and six Scots, including Jimmy Ross, the younger brother of hissing Nick (who was absent, having made an ill-timed decision to move to Everton for more money). Jimmy Ross scored Preston's second before half-time and Sam Thomson rounded off the comfortable win with which history was made.

Preston had finished their League programme as runaway champions six weeks earlier. They were the first Double winners at the first time of asking. And their achievement stands the tests of both time and rudimentary analysis. Adding their League and Cup results produced figures of 85 goals for and 15 against. In other words, they outscored the opposition by an average of 5.67 goals to one. Such a ratio has only been approached since by the relentless machines that were Bob Paisley's Liverpool (85 to 16 in the First Division in 1978–9) and José Mourinho's Chelsea (72 to 15 in the Premier League in 2004–5). Aston Villa, when they became the second Double team in 1896–7, scored 90 and let in 44. There was something very special about Sudell's Preston. He was the very first Special One.

Sudell had vision and a gift for organisation that truly would merit his mention in the same breath as Chapman. As his team grew and peaked, its glories were chronicled by James Catton, who became to sports journalism what Herbert Chapman became to football management and was to exert a major influence over Chapman's career in helping to connect him with Arsenal. Catton wrote in 1926 that Sudell had been 'responsible for the finest football team I ever saw'. This opinion was ventured in the year in which the Huddersfield built by Chapman completed a hat-trick of titles.

It is not known if Catton, who died in 1936, revised his opinion of Sudell's work in the light of Chapman's efforts in London, but the assumption that he stayed loyal to Preston would be reasonable, especially as he continued to describe Sudell as 'a great gentleman' long after the latter's fall from grace.

Catton was also born in Preston. In 1875, at the age of 15, he had become an apprentice journalist on the local *Herald* and specialised in sport, covering rugby, cricket and, to his great good fortune, North End in the time of Sudell. He had started writing under a pseudonym for the Manchester-based weekly *Athletic News* and proceeded to its editorship when the Football League began; in recognition of the need to salute its first champions, he postponed publication of that issue from Saturday to Monday. Preston were champions again the next season (with Nick Ross happily restored to the fold) and runners-up in each of the succeeding three. The circulation of Catton's magazine kept soaring: it doubled to 100,000 between 1891 and 1893 and was to keep increasing until the years between the world wars, when newspapers got the message that football sold and the quest for mass circulation embraced the game firmly, almost as Rupert Murdoch was to do in the age of satellite television.

But 1893 was the year in which Sudell lost control of Preston North End. An annual general meeting – the first in four years – was called to discuss the club's financial difficulties and, although Sudell, oddly irascible in answering questions, survived a vote of confidence, it was against his wish that the club became a limited company. Two years later, having gone to live by the coast at Morecambe, he was arrested and charged with a long-running fraud. In 1886 he had been promoted, put in charge of all of his employers' mills, and since 1890 he had been siphoning money from them to the club: some £5,326 in all, a massive sum in relation to, say, the British transfer record, which did not reach £100 until Aston Villa bought Willie Groves from West Bromwich Albion in 1893. The club had paid too much for its success. More than it could legitimately afford.

Although the average attendance of paying customers at Deepdale in the Double season, 6,725, had been exceeded only by Everton's 7,400, the Preston figure remained more or less consistent over the succeeding years as other clubs' gates rose steadily. Meanwhile Sudell entertained generously on the club's behalf and enjoyed being nationally known as well as a local celebrity. He had been treated as a manager: the first to have his work personalised by the press as with Chapman and Brian Clough and now just about everyone. And as a proprietor he had rubbed shoulders with the Prince of Wales. In 1887, Queen Victoria's Golden Jubilee year, he had sat next to the future King Edward VII at the celebration match between North End and the Corinthians at Kennington Oval.

Eight years later, the Prince, whose favourite sport was horse-racing, was getting excited about the promise of his thoroughbred Persimmon, which was to win the Derby, the St Leger and the Ascot Gold Cup over the next two years. Sudell, meanwhile, was being found guilty of embezzlement. He was sent to prison for three years and thereafter went with his family to live in Cape Town, where, having earned respect for the fairness of his reports on rugby, his first sporting love, and become sports editor of the *South African News*, he died of pneumonia in 1911.

Catton remained loyal to Sudell, possibly to a fault – he hinted that his friend had taken the rap for unspecified others – while working on, latterly updating the cricket records for *Wisden's Almanack*, a task that occupied the concluding four years of his life.

A very short and rotund man, Catton seems to have been relentlessly gregarious. He wrote of an encounter with the Aston Villa team that did the Double eight years after Preston: 'I went to their headquarters at the Tavistock Hotel, London, the day after they had received the Cup. While I congratulated them I rashly remarked that I could not help feeling sorry that they had deprived Preston North End of their unique record . . . The Villa players naturally objected . . . The discussion became heated and even reached the stage of a threat to drop me out of the window into the courtyard . . . Presumably they remembered that they were twelve or thirteen to one – and such a very little one, so small indeed that even "Fanny" Walden smiled when he first met me and said with his soft voice and winning way that it was not often he had the pleasure of gripping the hand of a man on whom he could look down!' One of the players did, however, deliver an unkind verbal cut: 'Preston? Ha! Football was in its infancy then. They had no one to beat.'

But Catton and his pseudonyms, first 'Ubique' and then 'Tityrus', were universally respected: he was as much part of the game as its diarist. He was the father of football journalism, to the extent that some of the phrases, rhythms and characteristics that sprinkle his 1926 legacy, *The Story of Football Journalism*, could be detected in the work of the modern master, the great Brian Glanville, who was born in 1931.

Might Sudell have likewise influenced, however indirectly, the style and approach to management of Herbert Chapman? Any aspirant could certainly have done worse than adopt the principles of teamwork as set out by John Goodall, leading scorer in the first League-winning season, in conversation with Catton: 'Every man in the team was a master of his craft. What is more, every man was a partner. That made our success. We never bothered about who got the goals. They belonged to the team – not to the man.' Catton added that they fitted 'like fingers in a glove' and Sudell can only have been responsible for that. Chapman was to earn uncannily similar praise.

At a time when teams tended to be picked by committee, Sudell had complete control. Except over his players' drinking. Bear in mind that the booze culture had been rampant as they grew up and now they had money in their pockets. A lot of players liked a drink and Preston were as keen as most. There were unsavoury reports: of damage to a hotel on a tour of Scotland and, more serious, an incident at Wigan railway station involving a barmaid, much broken glass and a train guard badly beaten. Sudell kept pleading with his players, stressing that a cleaner diet would make them even more effective on the pitch, but to little avail.

In every other context, he had their ear. He encouraged versatility and initiative; the players even had a private system for signalling to each other during matches. He taught tactics by using a blackboard – the first recorded instance – or chess pieces set out on a billiard table. His teams were distinctively systematic because he believed that 'less roughness and dash' was the game's future. His men liked to keep the ball on the ground and pass in the Scottish manner: naturally enough, although skipper Dewhurst, the side's only amateur and a master at Preston's Catholic Grammar School, represented Englishness with appropriate vigour. More than once Sudell took them to watch the opposition in advance and he also had the idea of having a cobbler accompany the players to away matches in case their footwear needed adjustment to cope with unfamiliar ground conditions. Of all his brainwaves, that was perhaps the most Chapmanesque.

He preceded Chapman, who was to sign the heroic Walter Tull for Northampton Town in 1911, in engaging a non-white player. Arthur Wharton was the goalkeeper of the Preston team that reached the Cup semi-finals in 1887 but left to become a professional sprinter. It was strange that he played in goal, for Wharton was so quick that in 1886, when only 20, he had won the 100 yards at the Amateur Athletics Association meeting at Stamford Bridge in a time of 10 seconds flat, equalling the world record.

Born in Jamestown, Gold Coast (now Accra, Ghana), to a Ghanaian mother and father who was half Scottish and half Grenadian, he had been brought to England to be educated and given encouragement to follow in his father's footsteps as a Methodist minister, which initially he accepted. He was training to be a missionary when sport began to obsess him; as well as excelling at sprinting, Wharton did well at cycling, rugby and cricket and in football his goalkeeping prowess took him to Darlington, where the crowds loved him. Having been persuaded by Sudell to move to Preston, he established himself as a terrace favourite there, too, with his courage and eccentricity; accounts of his style conjure up a familiar image in the minds of those who experienced Bruce Grobbelaar at Liverpool. Not that every critic appreciated Wharton's improvisations. 'Is the darkie's pate so thick,' asked the man from the *Athletic Journal* on one occasion, 'for it to dawn upon him that between the posts is no place for a skylark? By some it's called coolness – bosh!'

Even admirers knew Arthur as 'Darkie' Wharton, for it was the best part of a century before semantic sensitivity began to dawn on the white majority. He wasn't the first non-white player in Britain – the Guyana-born Andrew Watson had won the Scottish FA Cup with Queen's Park and represented Scotland three times – but Wharton was the first to earn a living from the game in England and before his career ended he had tried his hand as a coach, assuming charge of Stalybridge Rovers, where he took on a teenage Herbert Chapman. Wharton did make it into management, but of pubs, which proved his downfall because he developed a drink problem and died penniless.

He must surely have come to regret not settling at Preston because, as North End marched on to claim their glittering prizes, he found no fulfilment on the professional sprinting circuit. He returned to football, sometimes combining his career with the running of a pub, as at Rotherham, where he married a local girl, Emma Lister, and then Sheffield United, where his place in goal was taken by the formidable Bill 'Fatty' Foulke. There were two spells at Stalybridge and one at nearby Ashton North End before he finished up with Stockport County in 1902. He was 37 and, despite his drinking tendency, found work as a haulage hand at the Edlington Main colliery near Doncaster. He took part in the General Strike of 1926 and died four years later.

Wharton's grave at Edlington Cemetery remained unmarked for 71 years but then a memorial stone was erected and in 2003 he was recognised by induction into the English Football Hall of Fame at the National Football Museum. Among those similarly honoured that year were Gary Lineker and Wharton's fellow goalkeepers Pat Jennings and Peter Schmeichel.

That this ceremony should take place in Preston was in itself a tribute to William Sudell. The town was chosen as the original site for the museum in 2001 partly because it had produced the original League champions. Chapman might have campaigned for the renaming of a Tube station; Sudell's legacy was the siting of a national institution next to Deepdale. Alas for Preston, the museum was to remain there only until 2012, when it relocated to Manchester in order to attract more visitors. Among the first thing people saw when they entered the new building's airy foyer was a huge portrait of Arthur Wharton. At last he could be said to have achieved full acknowledgement of his place in football's history. William Sudell's time is still awaited.

THE GAME THAT WAS

UP FOR THE CUP

The football of Herbert Chapman's schooldays bore little relation to the football he was to bequeath. The football he left in 1934 was international and going from strength to strength in its birthplace, with the most popular clubs embarking on an era, to span the Second World War, in which attendance records of 60,000, 70,000 or even 80,000 would be set. The vast terraces of their stadiums were often complemented by two-tier grandstands, in Arsenal's case a towering edifice of recent construction, to be augmented a couple of years after Chapman's death with another so distinguished in its architecture that, by government order, the façade could never be demolished. There were solid crossbars and nets and trim, usually clean-shaven, players in crisp shorts. They were supervised by a referee who wore black and carried a whistle and was assisted by two similarly attired linesmen with flags. Only the goalkeeper could handle the ball, and he could do so only in his penalty area. The pitch markings were much as today. And a Football League championship augmented the FA Challenge Cup, whose final invariably drew a full house of 92,000 (to rise gradually to 100,000 in time for the 1953 match that took its unofficial title from the great Stanley Matthews) at the national showcase known as Wembley.

The professional football of Herbert's first schooldays was illicit – he was seven when the FA let players be openly paid – and the record attendance for a Cup final at the Kennington Oval had just been set at 8,000. Although grounds were being improved, a single modest grandstand represented the state of the art; ambitious Preston had just opened a 600-seater. Crossbars were optional; a tape stretched between the tops of posts was all the laws demanded. The pitch was defined by flags but the lines between them were undrawn, a matter of judgement. As for nets, even the leading clubs had yet to use them. There were frequent disputes about whether the ball had passed inside or outside the post and these were to continue for several years, presided over by the umpire for the relevant half of the field. The umpires dressed as for the street in coat and hat. One was nominated by each side and only if they could not agree was a decision handed over to the referee, who otherwise stayed off the field. Gradually the idea of a net was to dawn and, following a particularly drawn-out controversy at Goodison Park, a regular attender at Everton's matches, John Brodie, had the wisdom to take out a patent on the 'net pocket', which became familiar in football and other sports from 1891 after he had been interviewed by the FA and an experiment conducted during the annual North v South match in the January of that year. This was not Brodie's only achievement; he went on to design the Mersey Tunnel.

The game as Herbert first heard of its heroes, as he learned of the local conflicts beyond the hills in Sheffield and, farther afield, of the national struggle between old school and new in the FA Cup – the League existed only in a few creative minds wondering how best to raise money to pay the new professionals – featured no penalty area. Offside existed, but with the requirement to have three opponents between the attacker and the goal-line rather than two. The goalkeeper could use his hands anywhere on the field – so long as it was 'for the protection of his goal' – and wore the same colours as the rest of the team, being distinguished only by a cap if he chose to don one. Boots more than covered the ankles. Shin-pads were buckled over socks and their upper edges almost met the lower hems of the shorts, which usually had pockets.

The players almost invariably sported moustaches. There was even the occasional bearded one, a classic example being Kinnaird, whose handstand celebration after Old Etonians had won the Cup in 1882 was to prove a last hurrah for the amateurs, mainly former public school boys, whose clubs – the Etonians, Wanderers, Royal Engineers and others – had dominated the competition since it began.

In 1883, when Herbert went to school, the Cup was brought north for the first time. What was more, Blackburn Olympic, who did it by beating the Etonians, showed that record-breaking 8,000 crowd at the Oval, including many top-hatted toffs and the humbler opinion-formers of the press, the shape of football to come. Olympic mixed their dribbling with passes that switched the focus of play from side to side. It was not exactly an unknown style, for the Royal Engineers had adopted passing through the influence of two Scottish lieutenants, Henry Renny-Tailyour and John Blackburn, and reached four of the first seven Cup finals. But Olympic demonstrated conclusively that the Scottish 'combination' game could prevail over superior physique, vindicating the long-held view of Charles Alcock, the FA secretary and former England captain, whose feel for the soul of a still-infant game is so impressive in distant retrospect.

The evidence of the early internationals, which Alcock also did much to bring about, was already strong. The annual fixture between England and Scotland had officially begun in 1872. The first, at the West of Scotland Cricket Club's ground in Glasgow, was scoreless and England then won 4–2 at the Oval but, of the ensuing 14, the Scots won 11 and drew 3, losing only 1. In the year of Herbert's birth they beat England 7–2 (and Wales 9–0) and further victories over the English by 6–1 and 5–1 followed before Herbert took that first walk to the school in Kiveton Park. Almost as soon as the English had devised the game, the Scots had all but reinvented it for the enhanced enjoyment of a wider public and the spread of the passing element that made the difference can be traced back to the formation of the Queen's Park club, whose desire to find something subtler than the forms of sporting combat that had emerged from public schools south of the border was to benefit the English game as much as their own. More, in fact, because the English were first to lure Scottish players south and then to acquire the right to buy them openly for as long as they were good value for money, which turned out to be the best part of a century, beginning with the likes of Fergus Suter and Jimmy Love and ending, more or less, with Kenny Dalglish and Gary McAllister. There was the further and continuing benefit of managers, among them Matt Busby, who made a tradition for Alex Ferguson to uphold at Manchester United, Bill Shankly, the architect of the mighty Liverpool, and George Graham, among the finest to have shouldered the burden of Chapman's Arsenal legacy.

Before the Cup came to be seized by Blackburn Olympic and, more durably, their better-off neighbours the Rovers, another club from the area had made its mark. In the 1878–9 midwinter, Darwen had engaged Fergie Suter and James Love, who were initially paid by whip-rounds of members and later with the proceeds of benefit matches. It could be argued that a previously used method of circumventing the rules outlawing payment of players had rendered Jimmy Lang the first professional when he came south to Sheffield to join The Wednesday. He was given a job by a director whose firm made knives, but there is no evidence of his ever carrying out whatever the duties of his employment might have entailed, unless they were to pop in now and again and leaf through the newspapers.

Such a charade was avoided in Darwen's engagement of Suter. A confident 20-year-old with a precocious gift for reading play, he had arrived from Glasgow with the 31-year-old Love. Their impact was all but instant as they led a famously valiant attempt at giant-killing.

Having knocked out the Remnants, a Berkshire club for the well-heeled, Darwen, with mainly mill workers supporting the Scots pair, had gone farther than any northern team in the Cup's brief existence by reaching the quarter-finals. They were not only drawn against the formidable Etonians – Lord Kinnaird, Major

Marindin and all – but trailed 5–2 with 15 minutes left at the Oval. Somehow they got to 5–4 with the aid of what would now be called a 'big' decision. The ball was forced over the line after a scrimmage but Kinnaird protested that he had handled and so play should be brought back for a free-kick. Darwen replied that they had not appealed to the umpire and Charles Alcock, now refereeing, took their side against the wily Etonian with the thick beard and thin argument. The goal stood. Then Love struck to force a replay. This also had to be in London because FA regulations stipulated that all matches in the final three rounds had to take place there. Another draw ensued and the second replay saw Darwen lose at last, by 6–2, conceivably due to a combination of weariness after an overnight train journey and the challenge of a taller, heavier side who made no apology for using their advantages. To the Etonians' credit, they joined the FA in making a contribution to Darwen's expenses. But far greater sums were raised by public subscription in the town and a fund-raising concert; their joint proceeds of nearly £154 dwarfed the club's share of gate receipts and left historians in no doubt that FA Cup fever was established as a feature of the English winter.

THE GREAT DEBATE

The game that Chapman discovered, however, increasingly the opiate of the industrial north and Midlands, owed much to those among the amateurs whose instincts had been to civilise football. Even the original Sheffield club had been formed by Old Harrovians who opposed the holding, pushing and kicking of opponents and handling of the ball. At Cambridge University there had been similarly refined forces at work. But elsewhere the game known as football was excessively violent and individualistic. Until in 1863, as the autumn leaves drifted down from the trees by the Thames that overlook the Boat Race's final stretch, Ebenezer Morley resolved to start the process by which football arrived at a single code of conduct.

Morley was a solicitor and keen sportsman. He had come south from Hull to practise and made his home by the river at Barnes because of his fondness for rowing and on the village green nearby he found football. Actually, what he found was more like rugby. Indeed, it was hard to tell the difference because the games were developing side by side. A sense of obligation infused Morley. He was that sort of chap – he later became a member of Surrey County Council and Justice of the Peace – and what he did was form the Barnes club. It attracted public school old boys and naturally they disagreed on rules. So Morley wrote to *Bell's Life*, the sporting newspaper, suggesting that football should, like cricket, have one set of them. A meeting was called at the Freemason's Tavern in Lincoln's Inn Fields and, although most of the clubs that sent representatives were from the London area, Sheffield sent observers.

Morley, who had drafted laws in longhand at home, presented them and the debate began. At the first meeting the Football Association was formed and Morley elected secretary. A further five meetings were to take place, all at the Freemason's, before a set of official laws emerged from the smoky old inn on 8 December. The crucial disagreements were with Morley's draft Rule IX, allowing a player to run with the ball in his hands if he made a 'fair catch' – in others words, caught a ball last played by the opposition – and Rule X, letting him be charged, held, tripped or hacked (kicked on the shins) or have the ball wrested from his grasp. The only concession to mercy was that he could not be 'held and hacked at the same time'. The Cambridge representatives protested and there was help for them on the way in terms of an unflattering critique of Morley's ideas from Sheffield, who declared them 'against the spirit of football and more suggestive of wrestling'.

As a rowing man, Morley would have needed to know how the currents ran. He looked around the delegates, with their beards and pipes and top hats resting on sticks, and said: 'I don't mind it [running and hacking] myself, personally, but . . . I feel that, if we carry those two rules, it will be seriously detrimental to the great majority of the football clubs.' So now he agreed with Charles Alcock and his brother John, who had said hacking would drive from the game everyone who had 'reached the age of discretion', leaving it to schoolboys. There remained only the death throes of hacking, as enacted by F. W. Campbell, of Blackheath. 'If you do away with it,' he warned the gathering, 'you will do away with all the courage and pluck of the game and I will be bound to bring over a lot of Frenchmen who will beat you with a week's practice.' While he was almost certainly making his point with an element of self-parody, few reviewing it a century and a half later in the light of Zinedine Zidane and Thierry Henry would laugh as the gentlemen did while drawing on their coats and preparing to hail horse-drawn cabs on the clacking cobbles of Great Queen Street.

Campbell quit the FA on Blackheath's behalf at the sixth meeting and the split between 'association' football and rugby was now just a matter of time. It would have happened anyway because of professionalism, but at least the playing philosophies could now develop separately and in comfort. Blackheath members went on to perform for rugby the service Morley had done football and call the meeting at which the Rugby Football Union was formed in 1871.

The FA was strengthened when Charles Alcock joined Morley on the committee and began his advocacy of the innovations – the Cup and international football – that are the organisation's main sources of income to this day. But neither could have happened without agreement on law. Sheffield integrated in 1877 and the Scots, along with the Welsh and Northern Irish, joined the fold on the formation of the International Board (to become FIFA's law-setting body as well) in 1882.

This was all happily timed for the boy from Kiveton Park because there was one simple game when Herbert Chapman started to play it, one game civilised by the Scottish influence and the discernment of the Cambridge and Sheffield men, one game about to spread through the working class whence Herbert came like a forest fire in a drought, one game about to provide a living and almost boundless opportunity, one game ready to extend across

Europe so that eventually Herbert, having established himself as one of its giants, could meet and exchange ideas with the likes of Hugo Meisl. They spoke of formations, among much else, for fashions in team arrangement had changed rapidly since the founding fathers with their concentration on attack, two wingers on each flank and three more forwards inside them, all facing lonely, harassed defenders.

The number of all-out attackers dropped to five as Blackburn Olympic opted for a third half-back. In a decade the prevalent English game had changed from 1–2–7 to 2–3–5. The evolution of a midfield in the modern sense still had a long way to go – and Chapman was to take a massive hand in that – but the debt to Queen's Park was established. How to measure it against the refinements later made in Europe and South America is another matter. But there is certainly a point in looking at football as England might have settled upon it had the conservatives got their way.

Then the children of Herbert and Harry Chapman's generation would have been presented with something less fertile and inclusive than they were to receive when the League arose in response to professionalism, offering an increasingly tidy purse, if not a crock of gold, at the end of the rainbow that was the Chapman boys' football for fun.

THE FOOTBALL LEAGUE

The League arose from the thoughts of William McGregor, who took from cricket's county championship the concept of ranking clubs. Cricket had been unhappily wrestling with a system of assessment but football decided to award two points for a win and one for a draw and the principle, with no more than a bit of constructive tinkering from Jimmy Hill when he had the win upgraded to three points, was to stand the test of time. McGregor deserves to be ranked among the great men of football, for he helped the game to boom when it threatened to go bust.

Unlike Alcock, he wasn't much of a player but, having journeyed from his native Perthshire to Birmingham, he attached himself to Aston Villa because they had Scots, above all the inspirational George Ramsay.

If McGregor was to devise the League, Ramsay was to make Villa its most formidable force. He had arrived in Birmingham in 1871 to work as a clerk in a brass foundry. A couple of years later he saw the players, members of a Wesleyan Chapel bible class, practising on the public park next to the stately Aston Hall and, having asked if he might make up the numbers in their game, caught everyone's breath with Scottish skills so pronounced that he was appointed club captain the same evening. He gently suggested some amendments to their rudimentary style – 'a dash at the man and a big kick at the ball', as he later described it – and, once they had got used to passing, Villa became good enough to win the Birmingham Senior Cup in 1880.

Ramsay, obliged by injury to stop playing, left his job to become Villa secretary and no one doubted who was responsible for the success that followed. An FA Cup triumph in 1886–7, with Archie Hunter, Ramsay's key signing, becoming the first player to score in every round, was just the start. But McGregor, by now on the board, saw that the newly professional game had reached a crossroads. Clubs were struggling to attract enough spectators because, the Cup apart, there was no structure or meaning to the fixtures. To a meeting of clubs on the eve of the 1888 Final he suggested a competition, with each playing the others home and away, to be called the 'Association Football Union'. Billy Sudell of Preston didn't like the 'Union'; he thought it would cause confusion with rugby. When Sudell proposed 'Football League', McGregor countered that 'League' was too closely associated with politics. A few months earlier, the Irish National League had helped to organise the home-rule demonstration in London on what became known as Bloody Sunday because three died and hundreds were injured, while at the opposite end of the spectrum lay the Primrose League, named after Disraeli's favourite flower and recently formed in order 'to support and sustain God, Queen and country and the Conservative cause'. McGregor lost that argument: the

League it was. The FA, as if in response, announced that from the next season 22 clubs would be exempt from the early rounds of the Cup. The competitions became integrated, the knockout affair adding spice to the season as the year turned.

Although Sunderland were the immediate successors to Preston as the game's leading club, Villa soon took over, winning five championships in seven seasons, plus two more Cups. They did the Double in 1896–7 and Herbert Chapman, now 19, would have read plenty about the climax because not only was the Cup final a classic, Everton losing because they scored only two of the five goals that came in the space of 26 first-half minutes, but Villa clinched the League on the same day when Derby, the only team who could have caught them in the remaining three fixtures, failed to win. In the summer a trio of Villa players joined Celtic, yet Ramsay simply rebuilt and Villa were champions the next season but one, and the season after that. They won the title again as late as 1910, by which time Chapman had set out on his own managerial career with Northampton Town.

Ramsay was to remain in what had always amounted to the manager's job until 1926. Villa reached the fifth round of the FA Cup that year; they were knocked out, after a replay, by Chapman's Arsenal. Villa also finished a respectable sixth in the League; Chapman's Arsenal came second, below only the Huddersfield Town that Chapman had left behind. As one great manager took a well-earned rest at the age of 71, Ramsay slipping into a vice-presidential role, another was about to reach his peak and for Chapman the sense of achievement must already have been considerable, given that Ramsay's Villa had surpassed Sudell's Preston and the Sunderland of Tom Watson, to which Chapman's friend Catton also doffed his cap, as the model of sustained success.

If Ramsay inspired Chapman, so, too, must the growth in Villa's scale fostered by Fred Rinder, a local authority surveyor who became financial secretary; among his means of boosting income was the installation of turnstiles.

The ground to which Villa had moved, in Perry Barr, was not

of the required size and standard for trophy contenders, however, and in 1893 the overcrowding caused by the admission of some 27,000 to a Cup tie against Preston brought near-disaster, with cavalry called to help mounted police to restore order. Two years later the club returned to Aston, to convert the failing Lower Grounds amusement park into the finest home in football. It opened a week after the Double and naturally the ground was packed to its 40,000 capacity for the visit of Blackburn Rovers. House-full notices were to be posted frequently as Villa built a tradition so strong that in 1970, when the club suffered relegation to the League's Third Division, crowds still averaged nearly 27,000, which was more than any side in the Second Division and nine in the First. McGregor would have been proud of that; it was the commitment of great-grandchildren, their children and their children's children. On the field and around it, Villa had pointed football towards the future Chapman was to seize.

HEROES

Herbert had been 10 when the League kicked off on a September Saturday in 1888. Everton drew an estimated 10,000, the Wanderers of Wolverhampton and Bolton 3,000. Preston's 6,000 was about average and their 5–2 win over Burnley a warning of things to come. Yet for Herbert and his schoolmates, when the first League table was published in November it must have seemed a little distant. Of the initial League participants, the nearest to Kiveton Park were Derby and Notts County, each a little over 35 miles to the south. But The Wednesday's performances in the Cup – they were finalists in 1890 – helped to emphasise the wisdom of expanding the League and in the spring of 1892 it was agreed to create two 'Divisions', a First of 16 clubs and a Second of 12. The Wednesday were put in the First and Sheffield United the Second. The League had come almost to the Chapmans' doorstep. It had come to the city at whose technical college Herbert was about to study. And there was to be great excitement for the family as Harry fulfilled his abundant potential with The Wednesday, helping to win two League championships as well as the Cup and even briefly engaging in fierce rivalry with his elder brother, who was to spend the 1902–3 season with United, by now also in the First Division.

This was the stuff of the Kiveton boys' adolescent daydreams: the fortunes of the League clubs were covered by the Sheffield papers available in Kiveton and, while of no use to Herbert's father and mother, avidly read by the new generation. The papers stimulated word of mouth and the game became embedded in working-class consciousness, just as its earlier versions had appealed to the public school pioneers, with the north of England now setting the pace. The real north in the case of Sunderland, who, after Everton had been the first to deprive Preston of their title, took over as the country's top side, finishing top two years in succession and obliging Sudell's North End to accept the consolation of a hat-trick as runners-up.

Sunderland, guided by Tom Watson, were dubbed by William McGregor a 'team of all the talents' and the procession of expertise began in goal, where Ned Doig, a Scot so sensitive about his baldness that he always wore a cap, was not only an ever-present during those five years of League pre-eminence but still giving unbroken service when Sunderland collected yet another championship in 1902.

Doig was among the game's leading personalities as Herbert Chapman left school. Archie Hunter had been one – until the Villa star was suddenly lost to the game. Having collapsed with a heart attack during a League match against Everton in 1890, he never played again and died aged 35. The story that, on his deathbed, he asked to be raised in order to watch once more the crowds trudging to Villa's ground did nothing to diminish his near-legendary status.

They were so admired, these 'Scotch professors', engendering in English audiences the affection that those of the late twentieth and early twenty-first centuries were to accord the wave of civilising influences from Europe: the likes of Dennis Bergkamp and

Gianfranco Zola. Stars of English and Welsh as well as Scottish origin began to proliferate in the 1890s and Chapman, while pursuing his studies in Sheffield, could almost reach out and touch a few of them, because the city was beginning to punch its footballing weight.

The Wednesday, from 1891, had Fred Spiksley, a left-winger from Lincolnshire who, James Catton wrote, 'could do almost anything he wanted with either foot and was a sure marksman'. By 1893 Spiksley was scoring for England: hat-tricks in each of his first two matches against Wales and, even more impressively, Scotland, according to the memoirs of Sir Frederick Wall, the former Royal Engineers player who began a long stint as FA secretary in 1885. 'Conjurers have sleight of hand,' wrote Wall. 'Let me vary the phrase and say that Spiksley had sleight of foot.' United, meanwhile, had a player who might be considered the club's best ever and became Herbert's hero: Ernest Needham, known as 'Nudger', was from the nearby Chesterfield area, an outstanding left-half, short but quick and unflagging, an all-purpose midfield player in what might be imagined as the Bryan Robson manner. Chapman, who played up front, was never in Needham's class as a performer – though they were briefly to share a dressing room towards the end of Needham's career – and yet those qualities of zest and unselfishness were always evident in his game.

Needham got into United's team at 18 and went on to captain his country as well as the club where he spent his entire career of nearly 20 years, the most successful period United have known. Needham also played county cricket for Derbyshire with his great friend Bill 'Fatty' Foulke, the United goalkeeper. Derby, meanwhile, had one of the brightest of football's stars in young Steve Bloomer, already scoring impressively for County and breaking into the England side. Billy Meredith, after first working as a pitpony driver in North Wales at the age of 12, had been brought to Manchester by City and was already drawing crowds with his attacking skills and apparent insouciance, emphasised by the lodging throughout the 90 minutes of a toothpick in his mouth.

HERBERT'S TRAVELS

MIXED BLESSINGS AT GRIMSBY

Herbert had no ambition to join the ranks of the full-time professionals, let alone become an outstanding one – he wasn't good enough to hit the heights for which his younger brother was destined and knew it – but he was also aware, from his initial displays for Kiveton Park in the local competitions, that his talent had some value. He had played for the club while an apprentice at the pit and continued to offer his energetic attacking during the time when he also went to Sheffield 'Tech'. He saw a future in the game as a part-timer and duly topped up his earnings from a variety of jobs as he hopped hither and thither on a tour of the Pennine foothills close to Manchester. The itinerary took in Ashton-under-Lyne (later immortalised as the birthplace of Geoff Hurst and, more surprisingly, Simone Perrotta, the Italian midfield player who emulated Sir Geoff by obtaining a World Cup winner's medal in 2006), nearby Stalybridge and then Rochdale. Herbert was also to sample Grimsby in the Chapman tradition and to have that season in the First Division with Needham at Sheffield United. But in 1896, when Spiksley was scoring two goals for The Wednesday as they won the Cup final against Wolves, delighting nearly 49,000 at the Crystal Palace with back-heels into the bargain, the 18-year-old Chapman was on his more obscure travels.

He had left Kiveton the previous year to take an office job with a ticket-printing firm in Ashton-under-Lyne. It paid 10s. a week, which was less than the cost of lodgings, so his mother topped up his earnings, as did football in a modest way. Having been introduced to the secretary of Ashton North End, George Johnson, Herbert was signed by the newly elected Lancashire League club. He joined as an amateur but was promised expenses of 5s. a week. Ashton was no mean football town in those days. Hurst, the club now known as Ashton United, had staged the first FA Cup tie in the Manchester area in 1883 and set a ground attendance record of 9,001 two years later for a Lancashire Cup tie against the FA Cup holders, Blackburn Rovers. Their list of distinguished former players was to feature not only Alan Ball – as a schoolboy when his father, also Alan, was the manager – but Dixie Dean. North End, had they survived, could have responded with only Herbert Chapman and Arthur Wharton. But North End didn't survive. The club went bankrupt in 1899, failing to complete a decade of existence.

By then, Herbert had long gone. He had left the ticket firm to work in the shipping department of John Hill and Sons and, after just a season at North End, joined Stalybridge Rovers on enhanced 'expenses' of 10s. Rovers were to last only until 1908, after which the town was represented by Stalybridge Celtic, briefly in the Football League. Rovers, though, provided an enjoyable environment for Chapman. At the time of his arrival, Wharton was with the club. He had left Sheffield United, defeated by Fatty Foulke's excellence in goal, and combined the step down with a bit of coaching, which would explain his link with the recruitment of Chapman. Soon, though, Wharton and the club committee fell out and he went to North End until their demise. Chapman, meanwhile, caught the eye of Rochdale, then also of the Lancashire League, and fitted in well. At inside-right in the five-man forward line that was now *de rigueur*, he contributed much effort and a few goals, and appears to have been better paid there to judge from a quote: 'Fancy all these folk paying to see me play, and paying me to play. Why, I would play for nothing.'

Maybe they paid him too much. The Rochdale club had been

founded only in 1896 and was to last just four years (the current club formed in 1907). But again Chapman was not around. Grimsby Town, unaware that he was becoming a bit of a jinx, signed him in the summer of 1898, several months before his twentieth birthday, thus bringing him into the Football League. Into some rarefied company as well, for, although this was the Second Division, its clubs included a Manchester City graced by Meredith and they provided the opposition in Chapman's first home match at Grimsby. City won 7–2 but for Chapman there was the consolation of having scored both goals against a side to be promoted as champions. If he saw this as a harbinger of kindly fortune, it proved cruelly false. Grimsby's great achievement was to finish in mid-table after a dismal first half of the season in which 17 matches yielded just 14 points (a total admittedly envied by declining Darwen, who were to pick up nine over the entire campaign) and the opposite of relief was provided by the FA Cup's first round proper, in which Grimsby were beaten 7–0 by Preston. This was beneath the expectations of the support, for Grimsby had challenged strongly for promotion twice under the direction of Frank Hazelgrove. The requirement of his successor, Harry Hickson, had been to rebuild – hence Chapman and others – and the bricks were all over the place. Indiscipline and low morale affected performances and, although Chapman and Wilson Greenwood, his partner on the right side of the attack, tried to rise above it by working on their joint game, devising ploys as few others even attempted to do, it did not save Chapman from the crowd's scorn. He felt it less often than some team-mates, for it was recognised that he spared no effort in the team cause. Stocky and persistent, he was recognised as a trier. But the aural backcloth to failure at Grimsby caused him pain he never forgot.

It must have been the worse for the presence of his elder brothers Tom and now Matt, who, with their wives, lived next door to each other in the town. Tom had become a regular attender at the Abbey Park ground after moving to Grimsby and playing for the club as an amateur in relatively obscure times. He gave it just a season before quitting, though he continued to play cricket. Tom married his first wife in 1890 but four years later she died of tuberculosis, leaving their two-year-old daughter. He married again in 1896 and Tom and Jane were to be together some 54 years, until her death. Tom dominated his household with self-mocking good humour, regaling visitors and family with tales of his supposed travels – 'When I was in [for example] Patagonia . . .' became the signal for a ritual chorus of 'Where you've never been!' – and showing off his gift for mental arithmetic. As the decision to stop playing football emphasised, Tom's priority was his work for the railway company.

Matt, though he had played football and cricket at Kiveton, by now had forsaken team games, preferring bowls, for which he was to give Tom a taste; they became doubles partners. Matt had married a Kiveton girl in 1895 and at first they lived with his parents and Harry, now 15, in a house that had just lost poor Percy, the last of the 11 children born to John and Emma Chapman. Herbert was in Ashton-under-Lyne at the time. In 1897 Matt went with his wife Mary to Grimsby to begin his career with the council and the following summer Herbert arrived, unaware at first of the troubled environment into which he had carried his pale yellow football boots.

In truth it is difficult to place the stage of his journey at which Herbert started wearing boots of yellow – some accounts say 'canary' – leather. It was a most unusual habit and infinitely more likely, in the case of this enterprising but restrained young man, to be a practical rather than a narcissistic ploy. But if he wore yellow at Grimsby it didn't bring the club much luck and it was fortunate that Harry, who came over for a trial in the midwinter depths of the 1898–9 season, stayed a while longer at Worksop Town, nearer to home, awaiting the call to Sheffield. Herbert, if a good Methodist boy could do so, would have hated the treatment his team received for their undoubted shortcomings and he never quite found the appropriate retort on the field, despite the rally that saw Town finish with 35 points. At the end of the season, he was saying goodbye to his brothers and packing his bags once more. The next destination would be Swindon.

ELGAR AND THE WOLVES

In the midsummer of 1899, as Herbert Chapman wondered how life would treat him in Swindon, it smiled on Edward Elgar, the story of whose interest in football contradicts any notion that the game had been entirely taken over by the working classes. The *Enigma Variations* was premiered at St James's Hall in London and such was the acclaim that Elgar must have known his struggles were over; he would no longer despair over his gift's faint fulfilment. And soon he was to be established as the leading British composer of his generation. Whether he greedily seized celebrity as compensation for Wolves' drop from third place to mid-table in the League season just finished is open to question, but Elgar was among the many who had been drawn to football and Molineux housed the club closest to his heart. Tales of him cycling to the ground from his home in Worcestershire are probably a little less fanciful than the notion, still aired from time to time in the Black Country, that he had a Wolves season ticket – but only a little. He had other reasons for going to Wolverhampton.

Elgar, though a self-taught musician, had been born to highly cultured parents. His father played the violin and tuned the pianos of the county's fine houses when not at work in his shop, which sold instruments and sheet music. Edward left school at 15 and, after briefly working in the offices of a solicitor, gave piano and violin lessons for a living. At 22 he was appointed director of music at a mental hospital, or 'lunatic asylum', and conducting the band made up of staff and patients broadened his understanding of music and its instruments. He was increasingly drawn to composition. When visiting Leipzig in 1882 to hear the work of, among others, his favourite Schumann, he spent time with Helen Weaver, a student at the Conservatoire, and the following summer they announced their engagement. Why it was cancelled is unclear, but Helen went to live in New Zealand and Edward was heartbroken. From then on, although in 1887 he began a long and happy marriage to Alice, a former pupil who became his aid and inspiration, he was to develop close friendships with several young women, prominent among whom was Dora Penny, daughter of the rector of St Peter's in central Wolverhampton.

They met through Alice's friendship with Dora's stepmother. The Revd Alfred Penny and his wife Mary moved into the rectory in 1895. Wolves had taken possession of the nearby Molineux Grounds – like Aston Villa, they benefited from a leisure complex's decline – six years earlier and by 1896, according to a note in Alice Elgar's diary, her husband was attending matches. And not just picking glamorous ones. 'E. saw football match' was an entry in October that year. On the afternoon specified, the Elgars were indeed in Wolverhampton and the Wanderers' reserves beat Singers, the cycle-factory club soon to become Coventry City, by 4–0 in the Birmingham and District League. Afterwards, Edward and Alice travelled from the nearby railway station to Stoke-upon-Trent for a rehearsal at Hanley of his work *King Olaf*, returning to the rectory at 10.45 p.m.

With Dora he must have tasted first-team action, for her memoirs state: 'When they were with us for a long weekend . . . we were able to go to a football match. It all delighted him. The dense crowd flowing down the road like a river; the roar of welcome as the rival teams came on to the ground; the shouts of men calling to their player-friends by their Christian names – usually considerably shortened; the staccato "Aw!" at a mishap (a most remarkable sound from a crowd of sixty thousand); and the deafening roar that greeted a goal. He was much taken with the names of the players – particularly Malpass, a famous member of the "Wolves" at that time. I have known him say when we met "There you are. How's Malpass?" – a question I was not always able to answer.' Billy Malpass was something of a local hero. He had been in the team that brought Wolves their first trophy, the FA Cup in 1893, and also the side that had lost the Spiksley final in 1896, just a few months before Elgar and Dora made that short journey with the crowds down Waterloo Road to Molineux.

Dora's estimate of 60,000 was quite an exaggeration, because League records put the highest First Division attendance that season at 40,000 for the Merseyside derby and the all-club average at under 8,000. An explanation may be that her book was published in 1937, only two years before Wolves' record attendance of 61,315. But the atmosphere created by passionate congregations was already part of football's allure and Elgar had known where to find his, even before he visited the rectory for the first time in December 1895. 'He wanted to know if I ever saw the Wolverhampton Wanderers play,' Dora said, 'and, when he heard that our house was only a stone's throw from the ground, he was quite excited.'

Molineux didn't let him down and a highlight of his times there was a match against relegation-bound Stoke in February 1898. It must have been quite a display, for afterwards Elgar beseeched Dora to send him the local newspaper's account. Malpass had been outstanding and the report spoke of how, at the end of a fine move, he had 'banged the leather for goal', the phrase amusing Elgar so much that he set it to music, amending the lyric slightly to 'we bang'd the leather for goal' (with a sforzando, or accent, calling for sudden force, on 'goal'), and posted the three-bar score to Dora.

Was it ever heard in public, this short work, before 2010, when it was performed at a concert in aid of the St Peter's organ restoration fund? Legend insists that it was swiftly taken up as the first terrace chant and to let such a delicious thought perish would be churlish. More demonstrable, however, is Elgar's posthumous contribution to terrace culture, heard even today: the infinite adaptation by raucous choirs of *Land of Hope and Glory*, which he composed three years later. The most familiar introductory words – 'we hate Nottingham Forest . . .' – have a late 1970s feel. Elgar, though, always knew he was on to something popular with that first *Pomp and Circumstance* march, especially the slower middle section, about which he told Dora: 'I've got a tune that will knock 'em – will knock 'em flat.' After Henry Wood had conducted its debut performance at the Proms, the audience rose and roared and from that moment the Last Night became music's equivalent of the Cup final.

Elgar in middle age, with his elegantly receding temples,

Roman nose and immaculate walrus moustache, was a hand-some as well as gifted man and yet he had often suffered from insecurity. He was still fretting about his music and his finances when he met Dora. But in the *Enigma Variations* she featured as 'Dorabella'; the opening woodwind phrase is thought to poke fun at her stutter or, as some Elgar students contend, her laugh. Elgar was knighted in 1904 and, although he retained an allegiance to Wolves, had less time for football now. He and Alice even lost touch with Dora after her marriage to Richard Powell, the son of a Sussex rectory, around the beginning of the First World War.

SHEPPEY'S LEADING SCORER

It was at the height of Elgar's playful passion for Wolves that Chapman's favourites, the Sheffield United of Nudger Needham, basked in some of their greatest glories. They were champions in 1897–8 and, though the following season saw United suffer a temporary plummet down the First Division as the great Villa resumed supremacy, its culmination saw Needham and company overcome the Derby of Steve Bloomer in a Cup final watched by a record crowd of nearly 74,000 at the Crystal Palace. And Herbert Chapman was on his way into the Southern League.

Not that the Southern League represented utter obscurity, for since its foundation in 1894 some notables had found it a haven from the wage restrictions caused by the Football League's way of controlling players, the FA-facilitated registration system. Although a big offer by Tottenham Hotspur failed to tempt Billy Meredith, those who had gone to north London included Harry Bradshaw, the first man to represent his country while in the service of Liverpool. Southampton, meanwhile, had secured Brad-shaw's fellow England international Harry Wood from Wolves.

The League, seeking to achieve a spread of competition among clubs, had curbed the players' freedom of movement in order to prevent gravitation to the most moneyed and successful. An alternative would have been for clubs to pool gate receipts, the well supported helping the less so, as William McGregor had suggested, but this seemed to be taking the communal principle too far. Instead it was agreed that no player could change employment without the permission of his club. The consequence was the transfer system, with the fee acting as a sweetener. Or not as the case might be. The player was certainly at a disadvantage in seeking to improve his wages without a move – and a move was at his employers' discretion.

Talk of a union became reality and by February 1898 the 'Association Footballers' Union' (later to become Professional Footballers' Association) was helping members to negotiate. Its credibility was temporarily challenged by the departures of Bradshaw and Wood, both leading lights, in response to Southern League promises of riches beyond the reach of even household names in the Football League: lump sums of up to £100, wages of up to £5 a week with none of the reduction in the summer months that was to remain the Football League norm until the 1950s.

Even a top international like Needham would have struggled to match that kind of deal. Needham received from Sheffield United a basic £3 a week (averaged over the year) plus bonuses of 10s. for an away win and 5s. for a home win or away draw. On top of that would be as much as £5 for success in an especially important match. So in a successful season Needham might have averaged £4 a week. No wonder many players retained outside jobs. They were about 120 years behind times in which their successors' earnings, at the top level, might be confused with those of leading entertainers; Needham might have taken half a career to make what Marie Lloyd could collect for a short tour of the halls.

Yet the leading professional footballer was much more handsomely paid than the ordinary working man, who, depending on whether or not he was skilled, would collect between £1 and £2.50 a week (women tended to receive considerably less for humble duties). Herbert Chapman was an ordinary working man: still an amateur footballer, albeit on suspiciously rounded expenses for his football exertions. The deal that took him to

Grimsby had included a job in the office of a local solicitor and club enthusiast, John Barker. But he couldn't find employment at Swindon, despite the presence of the massive Great Western Railway engineering works where nearly 14,000 – a third of the town's population – worked, and had to rely on such expenses as the club provided.

Swindon Town had been amateur until 1894 and, upon entry to the Southern League's inaugural First Division, finished bottom, escaping relegation only when it was agreed to expand the division to 11 clubs. There followed five largely mid-table years, but Chapman lent quite a stimulus, scoring goals and laying them on and even earning praise for his defensive contribution; his wholehearted approach helped the club into third place behind Tottenham and Portsmouth. But Chapman clung to his amateur status and, having given up hope of finding a job in the area, resigned himself to another change of club.

It took him to Kent, to the Isle of Sheppey, farther than ever from home and the game's established strongholds, to within 40 miles of Dover's white cliffs and the waterway to France, with which Britain had reached accord only months before, finally averting the threat of a war between the contenders to become the principal colonists of Africa.

Almost as soon as that 1899–1900 season had ended, the amateur club Upton Park – not to be confused with the former Thames Ironworks, now West Ham United – had happily crossed the Channel to represent Great Britain at the Olympic Games, winning 4–0 in their only match against a team from the Union des Sociétés Françaises de Sports Athlétiques in front of 500 spectators at the Vélodrome de Vincennes in Paris. Only in 1906 would the French capital play host to an England amateur XI in the first international involving England and an overseas country (France lost 15–0). But as Chapman joined Sheppey United the leaders of the nations were grateful to have avoided a bloody conflict after a French expedition had journeyed from Brazzaville to Fashoda in the southern Sudan with the intention of gaining control of the Nile. A British flotilla sailed up the river and, as the sides exchanged courteous arguments, blitzes of rhetoric were launched from Paris and London. At length an appreciation that, although the French had larger land forces, Britain's naval power was crucially superior prevailed. It was one of the subtler examples of gunboat diplomacy.

The news from south of the Zambezi was not so good as Herbert Chapman journeyed to Sheppey, not far from Chatham and the vast Royal Dockyard at which the servicing of the Empire's seaborne armoury continued. The second Boer War was about to turn into Britain's most prolonged and lethal conflict since the Battle of Waterloo in 1815. The sieges of Makefing, Ladysmith and Kimberley had begun and Lord Salisbury's worried government increased the British commitment to 180,000 men. There was further setback when forces attempted to take a hill near Ladysmith. It was the highest for many miles around and the troops were ordered to scale it under cover of darkness thickened by mist. They encountered only a small Boer contingent and, after a skirmish, assumed possession.

When dawn broke it became apparent that they held only the lower part of the hill and were overlooked by Boers on three sides. The British lost some 250 men and had a further 1,250 injured or captured. Among the reporters who chronicled the terrible scenes was Winston Churchill. The stretcher-bearers included Mohandas K. Gandhi – a young lawyer later to be known as Mahatma Gandhi. The hill was called Spion Kop and six years later, when Liverpool Football Club built a massive bank of terracing behind a goal, the local *Daily Post* forecast that its nickname, already acquired, would stick. Among the other clubs that had Spion Kops were Sheffield United and The Wednesday, whose originally natural hillside is the second most famous.

Time, as always, eased the memory of the Boer War but, as its early stages took their toll, the people's appetite for football was accordingly dulled. And Chapman hardly found himself in an island of relish, for Sheppey United were the poorest team in the Southern League's First Division. By some way; they were relegated having won just three of 28 matches. But Herbert was not dragged into the morass as at Grimsby. He was Sheppey's leading scorer, excelling himself with a dazzler of a goal against lofty Tottenham, and did not suffer disappointment on a personal level until towards the end of the season when a fixture against Swindon brought no old pals' act but a good old-fashioned clogging match in which he may well have been targeted; at any rate he was crocked and, despite a valiant effort to return to the field after treatment, realised that both his match and his season were over. His time at Sheppey, too. Whatever job Chapman had done while playing there was not enough to detain him.

He headed back to Kiveton for the first summer of the twentieth century, to find a club for the next season almost on the doorstep, to get serious about his studies while enjoying his cricket – and to find time for a suddenly significant love life.

THE SUMMER OF ANNIE

Kiveton Park in the summer of 1900 was a community preparing for rapid expansion. The second coal seam, the High Hazel, had been sunk and overcrowding in the coal-company houses near the pit was rife. There being no pithead bath, men had to get clean at home and sometimes there were several mineworkers, from their teens to sixties, in a house with no running water. Hard-pressed wives faced extra difficulties in summers when supplies were short at wells and standpipes and carts had to bring water to the village – and this was one such summer.

Emma Chapman always coped. Her children had grown up and gone now anyway. As the family's driving force, she had always encouraged them to seek their fortunes away from Kiveton and now Herbert, who had been the most mobile, returned home to consider his priorities. Education first; he was 22 and, in career terms, mining engineering looked a lot more promising than football. And it would take care of the long term, which even the most distinguished of professional footballers could not secure in those days. Chapman had done his best to continue his studies, often poring over textbooks and writing up notes by the light of an oil lamp in his lodgings in Ashton-under-Lyne or Sheppey or wherever it might be, but the time had come to get earnest about the qualifications he would need when those pumping legs gave out and the yellow boots were hung up for the last time. So he enrolled at Firth College in Sheffield.

This institution, later to become part of the university, had been founded by Mark Firth, a steel manufacturer, shortly before his death in 1880. Firth had joined his father in employment at a steel works but left to set up his own business with his brother Thomas. As the company grew, so did the size of the products. Once the Firths exported the metal for Colt revolvers to the United States, but by the 1870s they were themselves making guns on an altogether different scale, massive naval cannon of up to 80 tons, to be mounted on battleships or shore emplacements. But that men of steel could have hearts was about to be vividly demonstrated in America by the Scots-born Andrew Carnegie, whose company had spread from Pittsburgh and fetched such a price that he was able to give away some $350 million in the remaining 20 years of his life and a further $30 million, the last of his fortune, to charity in his will. All this was during times when an American could have a family home built for $1,000. Mark Firth was not quite in Carnegie's league as a philanthropist, but he did give Sheffield, among other things, a public park and Firth College, which took advantage of the Cambridge University Extension Movement in bringing high-class further education to the burgeoning industrial cities. Chapman was lucky enough to receive this.

Something had to suffer in his determination finally to obtain the mining qualification and it was football. He got a club that summer, accepting an offer from nearby Worksop Town to play in the club's first season in the Midland League, but was to appear mainly for the reserves. What he contributed to the local cricket season is unknown, for the detailed records of the Kiveton Park Colliery Cricket Club date from 1904 when it joined the Bassetlaw and District Cricket League. Newspaper reports speak, however, of entertainment derived from watching Herbert and

Harry Chapman batting together, audaciously stealing runs, and Harry appears to have gone on to be a useful bowler in his summers off from The Wednesday, taking wickets at an overall average of 24.78 runs. Herbert picked up the odd wicket too and, in at least one season, also acted as club secretary.

Whatever else Herbert did in his twenty-third summer, his interest in girls flourished, for he spent time with two. The first was a local, Thirza Hart, but then he turned his attention to a newcomer to the village. Annie Poxon, the daughter of a Nottinghamshire colliery manager and sister of John Poxon, whom Chapman had known while attending Sheffield Technical College in his teens, had come to Kiveton as a teacher of younger children at the school. It was initially a temporary post. But to Herbert she proved permanent. In Annie he had found his partner for life; it appears to have been as simple as that. Annie was no adjunct, any more than Emma had ever been to his father, and was to prove a perfect companion on the upward journey. He must have known how lucky he was and gone to his lectures with a renewed sense of purpose.

If he read the newspapers or discussed current events on the Sheffield train, there would have been much pensive head shaking. Mafeking and the other settlements besieged by the Boers had been relieved but the war was still agonisingly tough going and it had become less popular among the British people, let alone those of mainland Europe whose sentiments had caused Queen Victoria to forgo her annual visit to France. Parliament was dissolved and the first 'khaki election' took place. Khaki had not been used for soldiers' uniforms before the conflict in South Africa, where it served as camouflage, and the term was to stick, being used to describe the British general elections after both world wars. On this occasion Salisbury's Conservatives held power with a large majority due to the high number of uncontested seats. The election of 1900 was also notable for the success of two candidates representing the newly founded Labour Party – Keir Hardie in Merthyr Tydfil and Richard Bell in Derby – but the miners of Kiveton Park were not diverted from the general working-class

Chapman in his kit at Northampton Town, c.1907 *(Popperfoto/Getty Images)*

The crossed arms of Herbert and Harry Chapman instantly reveal that they are the footballers in the family *(Kenneth Chapman)*

Northampton Town in 1904 *(top)* with Chapman second from right of the
standing row, and 1908 *(bottom)*, where he is a bowler-hatted manager *(both
Popperfoto/Getty Images)*

Leeds City, 1914 *(Colorsport/Corbis)*

Huddersfield Town, 1922 *(Popperfoto/Getty Images)*

The clock being fitted at Highbury, 1930 *(Personal collections of Lucas Pink, Andy Kelly and Mark Andrews)*

Highbury in 1927 *(Colorsport/Corbis)*

The 1927 FA Cup final players featured in *The Daily News (Personal collections of Lucas Pink, Andy Kelly and Mark Andrews)*

THE PIONEER MAGAZINE PAGE—SATURDAY'S Daily News.

The | ARSENAL

Col Sir Henry Norris, D.L.
Chairman of Directors

Mr Herbert Chapman
Secretary - Manager

T. Parker

D. Lewis

H. Cope

A. Baker

J. Butler

R. John

J. Hulme

C. Buchan

J. Brain

W. Blyth

S. Hoar

The Daily News FOR GOLF NEWS.

The 1927 line-up, with Chapman's key signing Charlie Buchan sitting third from left *(Getty Images)*

The wing wonders Joe Hulme and Cliff Bastin, 1930 *(Personal collections of Lucas Pink, Andy Kelly and Mark Andrews)*

Two of the stars of Chapman's Arsenal: *(below)* Bastin *(Popperfoto/Getty Images)* and *(right)* Alex James *(Personal collections of Lucas Pink, Andy Kelly and Mark Andrews)*

(left to right) Alex James, Frank Hill, Herbie Roberts and Cliff Bastin training at Highbury, January 1933 *(Getty Images)*

allegiance to the Liberals, who narrowly lost the Doncaster seat to the Conservative incumbent, Sir Frederick Fison.

As the shadows lengthened on Kiveton's surrounding fields, most citizens qualified to vote exercised their right. Suffrage had yet to be granted to women – that was not to happen until after the First World War – but in 1900 a majority of men at last had the vote and Chapman was one of those newly enfranchised, being over 21 and the owner or renter of property. He continued to live his life of unusual mobility, making journeys not only to Sheffield for education but Worksop for his football. He gave his all for the reserves and scored a few goals. On his odd appearance in the first team he played alongside Harry, at least until his gifted brother made the short trip to The Wednesday and fame. That was in the February of the season, when the FA Cup proper arrived to find the nation in mourning.

Queen Victoria had, as usual, spent Christmas at Osborne House on the Isle of Wight but became unwell soon afterwards and died at the age of 81, ending a reign of 63 years and seven months. Her successor was by her bedside and the Prince of Wales duly became Edward VII.

Herbert's club were already out of the FA Cup, having made their customary exit during the preliminary rounds, and when the game resumed any ambitions Harry might have entertained on behalf of his new colleagues were removed when The Wednesday lost at home to Bury. As winter turned to spring, however, Herbert's fortunes looked up with another spell in Worksop's first team, which turned out to be highly significant because one appearance was against Northampton Town, where fate was next to take him. Northampton were in only their fourth year of existence but doing well enough to earn an invitation to join the Southern League. They decided not to bother with half-measures, joining the trend among professional clubs to become limited-liability companies with a board taking over the duties of the committee and spending big on players – and one they chose was Herbert Chapman.

The secretary, Arthur Jones, ran the team but the decisions

were taken by the chairman, A. J. 'Pat' Darnell, and he had seen and heard enough of Chapman to offer a more than useful £3 a week. It must have been quite a fillip – almost like being asked to join Blackburn Rovers after Uncle Jack Walker decided to unfold his millions in the early years of the Premier League. The Southern League was on a high: Southampton had reached the FA Cup final the previous year and Tottenham gone one better, holding Sheffield United to a 2–2 draw in front of a world record football crowd of 114,815 (plus hundreds clinging to the branches of trees overlooking the Crystal Palace) before winning the replay at Bolton 3–1.

Scotsmen were continuing to make a difference. The native strength of the Sheffield side can be gauged by newsreels of Needham leading United out, his arms rocking the ball like a baby, with Fatty Foulke, demeanour as formidable as his bulk, close behind. Yet Spurs' Scottish contingent included John Cameron, their player/manager; he got the crucial equaliser at Burnden Park and Sandy Brown made history by scoring in every round. The annual international, a 2–2 draw at Crystal Palace, reflected that Scots dominance of the fixture had given way to a rough equality which was to persist until the English took the lead in terms of overall wins as late as 1983, six years before the series was abandoned.

The conveyor belt of talent from north of the border continued to roll as southern England began fully to engage in a professional game hitherto concentrated on the north and Midlands. At the turn of the century, the Football League map showed only Woolwich Arsenal, of the Second Division, below Birmingham. But Bristol City were to join them within a couple of years and both to be in the First Division by 1906–7, when Chelsea earned promotion. Further down the lower order were Clapton Orient, but the following season Fulham entered the League in robust health and in 1908–9 came the belated arrival of Tottenham, who were immediately promoted. The game was establishing itself ever more firmly in the capital, where Chapman's business was to be eternally unfinished.

NORTHAMPTON: FROM PLAYER TO MANAGER

THE COUNTY GROUND

First there was Northampton. Chapman became a full-time professional there for the first time. He still saw the future in engineering, but that could be deferred. He could live quite well on £3 a week, which was about average for a white-collar worker, and Northampton seemed as good a place as any to see where his talent could take him. The shoemaking town's population had grown to nearly 90,000 and must have seemed congenial with its new electric street lighting and absence of slums: a good place to start the century. He was to make friends and enjoy life in Northampton, and to return not once but twice.

There was a vigour of youth about the club and when, in October, he scored twice against Spurs, his progress as a full-timer was obvious. Not only that: Northampton were advancing through the preliminary rounds of the FA Cup. Having emerged triumphant from a derby at Kettering, they reached the first round proper for the first time ever and the town's excitement was hardly dimmed by a draw that brought the famous Sheffield United to the County Ground. For Chapman it could hardly have been a more piquant occasion: here he was on the crest of his career, about to face his idol Needham. And Fatty Foulke. And Alf Common, already showing the class to be recognised later in a £1,000 transfer, the first in football.

Northampton has always been associated with rugby union

but those who said football would never command the town's passion were contradicted now; all talk was of Sheffield United's visit. Not just among men. So great was the interest among women that a debate raged about whether they should pay the full admission price of sixpence (2½p); in a contest between avarice and chivalry, there could, even then, be only one winner. Purses were duly opened. As kick-off time approached, some may have been surreptitiously closed again, for there was a rush for the gates and as many as a quarter of the estimated crowd of 15,000 may have got in free. On this occasion it seemed all part of the fun, but that the consequences of football's rapid expansion were not always so trivial was to be emphasised in Glasgow later that year, when some 80,000 packed into Ibrox to see the Scotland v England match (it always meant a little more to the Scots) and a newly built section of wooden terracing collapsed, killing 26 and injuring 547. The match was completed for fear of further panic – many spectators did not appreciate the extent of the tragedy until the next day – but the 1–1 draw does not appear in the records of either country. It was replaced by the 2–2 draw that subsequently took place at Villa Park, the proceeds going to the victims' families.

At Northampton, happily, the fans all returned home to tell their FA Cup tales. They had seen Northampton lose 2–0 but acquit themselves well, notably Chapman, who must have been thrilled by not only Needham's private congratulations on his performance at the final whistle but the United captain's public declaration that he had played against 'one of the best inside-forwards I have seen this season'. Nor were the words offered lightly, for United were to engage Chapman at the end of the season and put him in the same team as Needham: the zenith, surely, of his playing career. Chapman's, that is.

The nadir of his first spell at Northampton had arrived in mid-winter, when Town journeyed to Southampton via London just after Christmas, their train from Waterloo stopping too often and too long for the comfort of Chapman and colleagues, who reached the Dell just in time for the kick-off only to discover that their boots were soled for frost and the pitch muddy. The ensuing 11–0 defeat remains the club's heaviest. Yet Chapman learned from it the value of meticulous preparation, just as he had learned from the chaos at Grimsby the necessity for a good team spirit; so much of what he was about to achieve could be ascribed to the lessons of unfortunate experience. And yet the season was hardly spoiled for Northampton or Chapman, who, though he missed some games due to injury, finished top scorer with 14 goals from 22 matches in the League.

There was the further reflection that it had taken quite a side to remove the Town from the FA Cup, for Sheffield United won the trophy for the second time in four years after beating Southampton in a replay. And Chapman had an offer to join them, one of the most renowned clubs in the land, and as near as any to Kiveton Park. How he must have enjoyed the end-of-season journey back to the village and Annie Poxon. They had quite a future to discuss.

If there was any doubt that Herbert and Annie made a level-headed couple, the decision that was to follow removed it. Far from being dazzled by his success on Southern League fields, persuaded that his offer to join the FA Cup holders in the First Division would let him live the dream he worked things out with a cold, hard realism. What mattered was not fame or rubbing shoulders with Nudger Needham but qualification from the Institute of Mining Engineers, and it mattered so much that he would forgo a professional contract at Bramall Lane in favour of a reversion to amateur status there. In other words, he would go back to the conditions in which his playing career almost foundered at Worksop. The risk seemed great but, to him, acceptable. The priority was to obtain practical experience in mining.

Whether he would otherwise have enjoyed a long and fruitful career with United is impossible to say. But the 1902–3 season proved his only one with the club of his youthful heart. It began with an unforgettable occasion for him and his family – a home derby against a Wednesday side featuring brother Harry, which United lost 3–2. They did win the return fixture 1–0 in October, however, and finished fourth, an improvement of six places, but even this was put in the shade by Wednesday's securing of a first League title at the end of a highly competitive season that saw only 10 points (or five wins in the currency of the time) separate the champions from Newcastle in fourteenth place, just clear of the relegation zone. Whatever Herbert did, such as earn praise for a late-autumn display against Liverpool, Harry tended to outshine, although they did replicate their cricketing gift for combination in the annual football match between Sheffield and Glasgow on The Wednesday's ground, where the visitors won 2–0. As ever, the elder brother hustled and bustled and threatened defenders with his spurts for goal, but a return of two goals from 22 matches at United hardened the view that more was required at this level.

Notts County begged to differ. They liked Chapman's direct approach to the game and towards the end of the season made an offer for his transfer that United, clearing the decks for a new wave of talent, accepted. Chapman took the opportunity to go professional again. He had received his mining diploma at last; it had come through during the summer of 1903, a Second Class Certificate of Competency as an Under-Manager of Mines.

The fee of £300 from Notts County, the first any club had paid for Chapman, hardly suggested he had failed at United. To put it in perspective: a year later it took only £200 more to shift Common, a current international, from Bramall Lane back to Sunderland, who sold him to Middlesbrough for the historic £1,000 a year after. Even some of the better players made frequent switches in those days (as now), though in Chapman's case his regular summer moves had more to do with a combination of relative journeyman status and the peripatetic, forever inquiring way of life he often pursued before marriage and fatherhood.

At any rate he was staying in the First Division, albeit with a club on the way down, one whose idea of team selection seemed to consist of perpetual reshuffles by the County directors. Chapman kept finding himself at the bottom of the pack despite frequent support from the local press and when, in March, the club visited Northampton for a friendly he enjoyed being among old friends so much that he pursued the notion of playing there again. County, while retaining his registration, let him return to the Southern League. They also lost their long-serving captain, Walter Bull, to Tottenham.

Before the forthcoming season, 1904–5, was out, Bull and Chapman would become reacquainted, to the latter's ultimate advantage. Those whom they had left behind at Notts County were at the bottom of the First Division and would escape relegation only because it was being expanded from 18 to 20 clubs. They had been swiftly removed from the Cup by Bury. Chapman's Northampton had observed tradition by falling in the preliminaries. Although they finished in the lower half of the table, Chapman did enough to suggest that, if Sheffield United had been slightly above his natural level, this was still below. He displayed his customary relish at centre-forward, where his bulky build helped to unsettle goalkeepers (the difference between centre-forward and attacking inside-right was not otherwise too radical is those times of 2–3–5), and once again pleased the Northampton fans. He had also caught the eye of Tottenham, who had finished fifth but harboured loftier ambitions, and a fee of £70 – paid to Notts County – took him to London. His pay was £4 a week.

WHITE HART LANE

There were men of quality at Tottenham: not just John Cameron, the mastermind of the 1901 Cup triumph, but the remarkable Vivian Woodward, something of an old-fashioned gentleman footballer in that he practised as an architect – following in the footsteps of his father, John Woodward, a Freeman of the City of London – and remained strictly amateur, never claiming travel or other expenses except when pressed by the FA after tours overseas. He captained Great Britain to gold-medal success in both the 1908 and 1912 Olympic Games – and then designed the main grandstand at the stadium built for the 1920 event in Antwerp.

As a goalscorer he was especially prolific for England, finding the net 29 times in 23 full internationals and 44 times in 30 amateur matches. Although these figures were achieved against sometimes hopelessly outclassed continentals, Woodward is not to be undervalued. He scored a goal every other match for Spurs and quite a few for Chelsea and yet always put his slight build at the disposal of the team, looking to serve those around him with helpfully deft passes.

Woodward was both popular hero and one for the connoisseur; James Catton described his game as 'all art and no violence', fearing for his safety in the face of desperate inferiors. Another observer called him 'the footballer with magic in his boots' and, as far as his head was concerned, many regarded it as the most effective in the land, despite his moderate height. A gazelle-like spring sent him soaring above helpless defenders. There are photographs to prove it; he truly was a remarkable exponent of the game, the originator of a Tottenham tradition that was to reach its apotheosis with Bill Nicholson's Double team in 1960–61. But when Chapman arrived Woodward was at a club under whose ambitious façade lay something between stagnation and decline.

While there were grand designs for the stadium, these served mainly to divert financial commitment from the playing staff. The Cup winners gradually dispersed to other clubs or, in Cameron's case, concentrated on management, at which he became gradually less successful. But Chapman looked a signing of promise. At least in the first half of the 1905–6 season: he scored in the opening match against Brighton and Hove Albion and was in double figures by midwinter. But the title always seemed destined for Fulham and the Tottenham crowd needed someone to blame in the latter half of the season. The fickle finger pointed at Chapman. He didn't like anyone being barracked and must, on some match days, have wished he were back at Northampton. The consolation was that every day now he went home to Annie.

In September they had been married in her home village of Annersley. They found a house in Edmonton, a favoured suburb for Tottenham employees, and Annie got a job as a supply teacher at Silver Street School. Even this, however, contrived to brew a local controversy, after a proposal at the November meeting of the Edmonton education committee that someone else be sought for the post because Herbert Chapman, on a footballer's wage, 'ought to be in a position to keep her at home'.

An argument that would be regarded as preposterously sexist today made sense to many then: a married woman should run the household (as Chapman's own mother had done) if the family could afford it, not go out to teach. Equally rational, however, was the contention that Chapman's £4 a week was a comfortable living only while he earned it and that, at 27, he might be only a couple of years from retirement. By a single vote, the committee decided to keep Annie in a job. The headmistress had testified that she was 'an efficient and up-to-date teacher and disciplinarian' who had already improved the performance of her pupils in a matter of a few months. But that was not yet considered the crux of the matter. Women's rights as they came to be understood were still a long way off. Emmeline Pankhurst had, however, just formed the Women's Social and Political Union, the term 'suffragette' was about to be minted and the long discussion was about to rage. An indication of the profundity of the still-prevailing attitude was that the right to vote in elections, when graciously handed to women in 1918, was for those over 30; equality with men of 21 or over had to wait a further 10 years.

The White Hart Lane electorate had yet to turn against Chapman as they ushered in 1906 and wondered what the Cup might have in store. His enthusiasm and courage – at Plymouth he suffered a mouth injury and had to play with sponge held to stem the bleeding – had impressed people and his goals suggested that Spurs might have found a worthy successor to the unfortunate Jack Jones, an inside-forward with a scoring knack who had contracted typhoid fever shortly before the start of the previous season and died within a couple of weeks. Jones had outscored Woodward, who was sometimes missing due to business or other sporting commitments such as his late-summer tennis and cricket, and Chapman was doing likewise – until form gradually deserted him. The press and public noticed and the scorn from the terraces, where expectations were so much higher than at Northampton, added to the challenge. His character was up to it – he kept fighting – but his skills had taken him as far as they ever would.

He completed two years at Tottenham, which by Chapman's standards was almost gold-watch territory, but left in the spring of 1907, around the time that Cameron abruptly resigned as manager, the Scot's terse explanation of 'differences with the directorate' alluding to the board's decision not just to invite Woodward to join their number but to put him in charge of team selection. Today it might have been a case of constructive dismissal. Cameron went to Germany to coach and, although Spurs did appoint a supposed successor in Fred Kirkham, a referee from Lancashire who was thought to be well connected at the Football League, which Tottenham now yearned to join, no one took him seriously in the manager's role and soon the directors were picking the team themselves, with or without Woodward's input.

Was Chapman a little sadder for his experience in north London? In a footballing sense, perhaps; he liked to please the people all of the time. But he had done his best and that was another principle of a lifetime. As far as life away from the game was concerned, he had been more than happy. Rather than head back to Kiveton for the summer of 1906, indeed, he and Annie had stayed in their new home; Chapman played his cricket for Spurs' team instead of with Harry in the Bassetlaw and District League. So sadder, no. But wiser, yes. He had clarified his view of how team management was best conducted – through yet another close-up of how it should not be done, courtesy of the Spurs board as they undermined Cameron. And for Chapman it was to prove a timely reminder, because he was about to enter management himself.

It had not been all bad experience at Tottenham either, for Chapman had seen more of the FA Cup than was his custom. Their appetites sharpened by annual midwinter trips to the Essex coast, with hot salt-water baths at Southend's recently completed

Kursaal amusement park, the team had twice reached the last 16. But the Southern League title eluded them and, in any case, Spurs' main intention was to go national, to follow Woolwich Arsenal and the rest into the increasingly prestigious Football League. Spurs achieved their ambition by a single vote in 1908 despite a modest seventh-place finish in the Southern League. Their first goal in the Second Division was scored by Woodward – and their second, as Wolves were beaten 3–0 on a rainswept but joyous occasion celebrated by a crowd of over 20,000 – and they went on to obtain promotion at the first attempt, spending the rest of the years leading to the First World War amid the lower ranks of the elite.

But the Southern League was where Chapman's immediate destiny lay. He stayed in it while changing club. It was one of the best moves he ever made: his third move to Northampton and his first step on the road to greatness. According to Shakespeare, some men are born great, some achieve greatness and some have greatness thrust upon them; Chapman had at least that first step thrust upon him.

It was towards the end of the 1906–7 season and, by his own recollection, the thought came to him in the bath. Not in the sense that a revelation made him cry 'Eureka!'. All Chapman thought was that he had 'had a thoroughly good innings' and it might be time, at nearly 30, to forsake football for that long-planned career in engineering. He was washing off the mud and dried sweat of what he expected to be his final appearance. 'I had no regrets,' he later wrote. 'It was goodbye to football and the start of a new life. But how curiously is one's life shaped. Before I left the Tottenham dressing-room that day I had made fresh plans.'

Another who had anticipated leaving Spurs at the end of that season was Walter Bull. The centre-half had been appointed player/manager at Northampton, with a remit to raise them from the depths of the Southern League. As Chapman dressed, Bull disclosed that he had changed his mind and preferred to stay another season at White Hart Lane. He then told Chapman: 'You will have to take my place at Northampton.'

Whether Bull was endeavouring to ease his conscience or not, he spoke of Chapman's greater suitability for the role with an authority that struck a chord. Such an idea must have at least fleetingly occurred to Chapman before, because he had helped his old chairman Pat Darnell by 'tapping up' Bull – privately checking his interest in the job – as the powers of Arthur Jones waned. Chapman strode from the dressing room on the Saturday evening and went home to talk to Annie. By Monday his letter of application to the Northampton board was in the post.

His reasoning was that mining management could wait a year while he tried football management. Darnell agreed to those terms and could hardly have argued with Chapman's salary request, which was that the board pay what they thought he was worth. He trusted Darnell to reflect any increase in gate receipts, which duly rose for his first match – there was much residual affection for Chapman in Northampton – but only to £67, the proceeds from a gathering of 2,000. During Chapman's two seasons away, the club had finished eighteenth of 18 and then, after the Southern League First Division had been extended to accommodate Leyton and Crystal Palace, twentieth of 20, with only five wins all season. Small wonder that attendances had dwindled.

TAKING CHARGE

The club was suffering from what Darnell imagined to be good husbandry. Having splashed out on player salaries, including that of Chapman, when Northampton got into the Southern League, the chairman thought enough was enough. For all the euphoria of the FA Cup run, he reasoned that the town could not support a spending club; hence Town had never paid a transfer fee. Chapman set about doing repair work accordingly. His initial five recruits came on free transfers. One was himself. Fred McDiarmid and George Badenoch, both Scots, had been clubmates at Tottenham. Fred Lessons was from Nottingham Forest but perhaps the most impressive capture was that of yet another Scot,

David McCartney, whom several clubs had been interested in taking from Chelsea, for the key position of centre-half.

These were not Darnell signings. These were Chapman signings. Chapman was starting as he meant to go on. Even at 30 he had developed an unshakeable view that the manager must be in sole charge of the team. Long before the birth of Alex Ferguson, Chapman had decided to live by the principle that became Ferguson's mantra. But he did not expect any chairman, however well he knew Darnell, to have his power blatantly usurped. Darnell, the local coroner and a charismatic figure in the town, had been accustomed to making decisions. So Chapman worked subtly. He let Darnell appreciate the improvement in both the team and gate receipts before asking for the purse strings to be seriously loosened. He also relieved his boss of the chore of overseeing team selection.

'In all the positions I have held,' Chapman wrote while at Arsenal, 'I have accepted the responsibility of choosing the team. It is not one, in my opinion, which can be shared.' The scepticism this evoked about his early years in management underrated his powers of persuasion. Reading between the lines of his reminiscences, you have their flavour: 'In every case, too, I have been loyally supported by my directors, and I recognise that this has largely contributed to any success I have achieved. I have always believed that a club should be like one big family, with all the members sticking and pulling together under one head.'

In dealing with Darnell he adopted an approach that might be compared with his elder brother John's non-confrontational style in negotiations with colliery owners and managers. Herbert spoke with politeness and a minimum of regional accent, wanting to be as classless as possible. He explained team changes in advance and created a climate in which his requests for funding seemed logical. He was a bridge between field and boardroom – and articulate in both spheres.

The role of player/manager helped him to get his ideas across, just as it had helped Cameron initially at Tottenham. Chapman had also learned from his time at Sheffield United the value of physical conditioning and injury diagnosis and, to these ends, hired Dick Murrell as trainer. A settled team, with Chapman at inside-right, recovered from defeat on the opening day and banished the hangdog air of the previous two seasons, performing with speed and panache. The local press immediately bought into Chapman's motivational powers and portrayed the side, correctly, in his image. No complaint from Darnell was recorded either. The club pushed on with much-needed ground upgrading, which included terracing and a small grandstand, helping to counteract the impression that Northampton Town FC was little more than an appendage of the county cricket club.

Results took a turn for the worse, however, when Norwich won at the County Ground in November. Over the next few weeks injuries conspired in a slump to fifteenth place in a table of 20, one defeat being at the hands of Tottenham and, in particular, Woodward, whose Christmas present was two goals planted in the Northampton net. Chapman analysed the downturn in tactical terms. He concluded that Northampton had been attacking unimaginatively, throwing bodies forward without enough care. So he ordered the middle line of three to hang back and create space into which the opposing players might be tempted, in turn offering gaps behind them for the Northampton forwards to exploit. At that level, at that time, it was quite a sophisticated idea. And it worked.

Chapman also believed it would help if the full-backs did not merely clear the ball but aimed long passes forward. He had seen the great Aston Villa adopt this habit and, requiring at least one full-back capable of passing to a high standard, identified Lloyd Davies, who had been relegated from the First Division of the Football League with Stoke City the previous season but retained enough of a reputation to command a transfer fee of at least £200. Northampton historians reckon Darnell had to pay as much as £400 – bear in mind that the British record was £1,000 for Alf Common – but even the lower figure would have made the chairman's eyes water since he had never committed any sum on the club's behalf before. He nonetheless agreed to write the cheque for a player who, being only three months short of his thirty-first birthday, was nearly a year older than Chapman. Darnell, impressed by his manager and emboldened by the rise in attendances thus far, even found some of the money from his own resources. The supporters raised funds, too; there was a revivalist air that students of the early career of Ferguson would recognise, for in 1976 the fans of St Mirren were to prove equally enthusiastic about chipping in towards the signing of a key addition to their team, Jackie Copland.

Davies had already represented Wales four times. He was to obtain a further 12 caps during a Northampton career that continued until he was 42. He remains the club's most capped player. He lasted almost until 1920 when, eight years after Chapman's departure, Northampton entered the new Third Division of the Football League. But for Chapman the short term was what mattered and so well was it organised that by the end of Davies's first full season the team were champions of the Southern League.

They had done pretty well in 1907–8, too, almost immediately abandoning their status as a Southern League joke and finishing eighth, equal on points with Tottenham despite the setback administered by Woodward on Christmas Day. Although they emerged from the qualifying rounds of the FA Cup with a 10–0 thrashing of Sutton United in which Chapman scored twice – a visit to a spa in Bedford had harked back to Chapman's visits to the hot baths at Southend with Tottenham – the competition proved less of a distraction than they might have wished, for they lost at home to Bristol Rovers in the first round. A late-season crowd of 14,000 for the visit of leaders Queens Park Rangers emphasised the feeling of optimism around the club, especially as Northampton won 3–2.

Chapman had gone into management with the idea of seeing how it went for a season but there was no need for him to sit Annie down and make a quiet assessment; he could hardly leave now. Nor was there much doubt that Darnell would offer better wages, which Chapman accepted with all the more pleasure because Annie was pregnant. It was, however, a summer of mixed feelings because in July 1908 his mother died. Emma Chapman's funeral took place in Kiveton and, less than two months later, Annie gave birth to Kenneth Chapman in Northampton. So Herbert was a parent himself now. The celebrations were joined by his brother Harry, who was staying with him while being treated by Murrell for a knee injury. But at work Herbert was busier than ever. Any misgivings the Northampton board had entertained about letting him run the club had been well and truly swept away and the price of hands-on autocracy was inevitably going to be paid in hours.

He had to be a full-time manager and that entailed replacing himself in the team. He chose Albert Lewis, whose form with Coventry in the Southern League had attracted several clubs. Chapman is supposed to have all but kidnapped the player in his office and insisted on his signature as the ransom; it was the first of many such stories of managerial single-mindedness that were to surround Chapman's successors such as Ferguson and Brian Clough. At any rate Lewis did sign – and was to end the season as leading scorer with 32 goals. The rest involved developing players already at the club.

The intention was to make the attack more productive. McDiarmid was moved forward from wing-half and McCartney encouraged to make the play more from centre-half, his shorter balls complementing the long stuff from the full-backs. Moves were devised to pull opposing defences out of position. In the fourth League match, Watford came to the County Ground and were beaten 7–0, but consistency was to take a little longer and Northampton immediately lost by the only goal at Norwich, where the final whistle blew five minutes early and Chapman took so long to persuade the referee to restart the match that several players had to be hauled out of the bath. Next his men came from 2–0 down to overcome Reading 3–2. They went to the South Coast to take on the leaders, Southampton, and won there, too. Just after Christmas they took over at the top with 15,000 seeing a narrow victory over Southend at the County Ground. The local press hailed Chapman – and there was still the FA Cup to come.

Chapman changed his preparatory routine for the visit of Derby County, giving his team the vaunted air of Woburn Sands, a Bedfordshire village with pleasant pine woods, instead of baths, but they could only draw with the Second Division club, who won the replay. There was a further stumble in the League at Watford, where they lost 4–1. Injuries were a factor; Chapman had had to pick himself at Watford, where he made the final appearance of his playing career. But a return to form saw Northampton restored to the leadership in early April, facing a serious challenge for the title only from Swindon.

The penultimate fixture of the season saw the issue settled. Northampton were away to Queens Park Rangers and Swindon at Luton. Northampton had the advantage and by drawing 1–1 in west London made it necessary for Swindon to have won in order that the contest be taken to the final day and a further battle of nerves. There was no radio (though Marconi did receive the Nobel Prize in Physics that year for 'contributions to the development of wireless telegraphy') and therefore no means of finding out what had happened at Luton. Chapman's players made for the train back to Northampton in a state of suspense that was joyously lifted by the sight of hundreds of jubilant supporters greeting them at Castle station. Chapman himself had other thoughts, for he had been told that his father was gravely ill, so the train that he took after the match was heading in the direction of Kiveton Park.

John Chapman was still alive when Herbert arrived. He died several days later, on the eve of Northampton's final match, aware that he now had two successful footballing sons. Almost exactly two years after Harry had been the hero of an FA Cup final, Herbert was champion of the Southern League. His father was laid to rest beside his mother in the churchyard at Wales.

In fact the 2–1 home victory over Plymouth that took place while a dispirited Swindon were losing 6–2 at Southend was not quite Northampton's concluding fixture, for they had earned the right to new experiences and the first was the recently instituted

Charity Shield match between the Football League and Southern League champions (the forerunner to today's Community Shield between the champions and FA Cup winners). Newcastle United had won the First Division in 1908–9, and by quite a margin, even though their season had bizarrely featured a 9–1 defeat by Sunderland in a derby at St James' Park. They had gone on to knock Sunderland out of the FA Cup before reaching the semi-finals and, having completed a hat-trick of League titles in the space of five years, were accustomed to speculation about the Double, let alone individual honours. So it was useful for Chapman's players to measure themselves against some of the biggest names in the game: internationals such as Billy McCracken, Jock Rutherford, Peter McWilliam and Colin Veitch. For Northampton to lose 2–0 at Stamford Bridge was respectable. All the figures, indeed, testified to Chapman's efficacy.

He had kept the defence as tight as in his first campaign while designing an attack that produced 90 goals in 40 League matches, with Fred Lessons as well as Lewis exceeding the previous club record for an individual in a season. But it was the atmosphere around the club, as much as the technical aspects Chapman had engineered, that had made the difference, as Darnell generously acknowledged when he alluded to the 'family' ethic in paying tribute to the manager at the dinner held to celebrate the club's achievement. Chapman indeed had treated the players with almost brotherly care – he was still only 31 – but there was also a friendliness among the players, staff and directors for which Darnell deserved a share of the plaudits.

Chapman had developed a comprehensive style of management that, while not quite unprecedented – given Billy Sudell's benign dictatorship at Preston – had yet to be exercised by a mere employee. The extraordinary George Ramsay at Aston Villa and others had run their teams, but Chapman was running Northampton Town Football Club, having a say in how the ground should be modernised and the dressing rooms spruced and medical attention made sharper in order to make supporters as comfortable as possible and, more important, players committed to their surroundings. It was he who also took responsibility for keeping the club's affairs in the newspapers. He devised so many of the functions that were to be shouldered by the great managers of the decades following the Second World War that it is surprising, in retrospect, to consider that his methods did not immediately sweep through the game.

Perhaps it was partly because Chapman stayed in the Southern League until 1912, only two years before the first war, and did not maintain Northampton's rule over it, though they remained of high status, finishing fourth, second and, in Chapman's last season, third, only one win short of regaining the title on goal average. Or maybe few chairmen found managers with the personality of Chapman, let alone his hunger for responsibility. He took his team into Europe in the summer of 1909 to play Nuremberg, founded nine years earlier and already the leading club in the southern part of a Germany unaware of the horrors into which Kaiser Wilhelm II would impetuously lead it. And then Chapman returned to local priorities, helping to organise trials for youngsters from Northampton and its surrounds to find replenishments for the club's successful reserve team. Chapman knew Northampton, even with their increased attendances, would never be able to make a habit of spending substantially as on Lloyd Davies.

THE DECLINE OF WOODWARD

Meanwhile, Vivian Woodward was, as ever, the modestly unwilling talk of football society. He had been carrying all before him in 1908–9. In the first of those calendar years he had scored 20 goals and in the second he was to get 23 – and that was just for England. His utter disdain for limelight and lucre aside, he was a little like the David Beckham of a century on. Everything he touched seemed to turn to gold – almost literally in the case of Great Britain's Olympic participation. He was also captain of England and, having contributed an instrumental 19 goals to

Spurs' promotion campaign, led the national team on a triumphant summer tour of Austria and Hungary.

Upon his return, however, he announced that he would be retiring from top-level football in order to concentrate on architecture; he would play, but for Chelmsford in the South Essex League (the family's second home was at Clacton-on-Sea on the Essex coast), and only when work permitted. If this raised eyebrows, so did the news in the late autumn that he would, after all, be gracing the First Division – but in the blue shirt of Chelsea. He explained that he had once promised Chelsea's chairman, Gus Mears, that, if he ever left Tottenham, he would turn out should they need him, and that he had duly received a letter from Mears bemoaning the spate of injuries that had weakened his team's attack.

Mears had founded Chelsea with his brother Joseph and their descendants were to run the club until the sale for £1 in 1982 to Ken Bates, who in turn sold an equally rickety business – albeit for somewhat greater profit – to Roman Abramovich in 2003. In those early years the Mearses' Chelsea were able to draw vast crowds – England's biggest on average in some seasons – but when Woodward joined they were struggling on the field. They were in the relegation zone when the final fixture arrived, as if carried by Puck: a derby against Tottenham, also endangered in their first season at the level. Chelsea had to win. A draw would have been enough for Spurs. But Spurs won 2–1, the vital goal coming from a Chelsea reject, Percy Humphreys, whom they had signed in the wake of their star's departure.

So Woodward had been relegated by his former club, but he proceeded to help Chelsea to return to the First Division. At the outbreak of the First World War he volunteered and was sent to the 17th Service Battalion (1st Football) of the Middlesex Regiment as a second lieutenant. Woodward proved quite an aid to recruiting, for supporters as well as players were eligible for the Football Battalion and plenty of Chelsea followers were only too anxious to serve alongside him. When Chelsea reached the FA Cup final in 1915 – played at Old Trafford in Manchester in order to avoid disruption to travel in and around the capital and dubbed the 'khaki Cup final' because so many uniformed soldiers were among the crowd of 50,000 who saw Sheffield United win 3–0 – the army offered Woodward leave but he declined to take over from Bob Thomson, who had played in the previous rounds.

The following winter the Football Battalion reached the front line, where four men were killed and Woodward was among 33 others injured, sustaining a grenade wound to the right thigh. He returned to the trenches of the Western Front seven months later, in August 1916. The Battle of the Somme had claimed some 57,000 British troops in a single day and among the footballers who had died was Woodward's former England colleague Evelyn Lintott. After Woodward's return the Battalion suffered further heavy casualties but Woodward was lucky enough to finish his war as coach of the army football team.

Woodward had been the most distinguished player with whom Chapman ever shared a dressing room – Nudger Needham included. After the war he carried on playing at increasingly humble levels. He spent some years on the Chelsea board. He gave up architecture in favour of agriculture, moving to Essex, near the coast where he had spent much of his youth, to try dairy farming but became beset by financial problems in a period of recurrent depression.

He had never married. There were no children for him to nurture as he had been nurtured, especially by his mother, according to James Catton, who noted his manifest affection when she came to watch him play, as she often did; he would never leave her side to get changed for the match until sure she was seated comfortably. Catton recalled 'this courtly lady' who 'evidently followed football'. Woodward did his bit in the Second World War as an air-raid warden but he became increasingly lonely. Long gone was the society of fellow sportsmen. His health declined and in 1949 he was encouraged to leave the farm by kindly souls from the Football Association, who saw him installed in a nursing home at Ealing in west London.

There he was visited four years later by Bruce Harris, a

long-serving cricket correspondent of the *London Evening Standard* and touring companion of, among others, Neville Cardus and E. W. Swanton. Harris had discovered Woodward's whereabouts from a bus driver, Mr J. R. Baxter, who had served under Woodward in the Battalion. Harris and Baxter went to the nursing home together and Harris reported: 'We found Woodward bedridden, paralysed, infirm beyond his seventy-four years, well looked after materially. The Football Association and his two former clubs are good to him; relatives visit him often. "But," he told me in halting speech, "no one who used to be with me in football has been to see me for two years. They never come – I wish they would." The FA sent along a television set. It is little use to him, I fear, in his weak health. He gets more from the sound radio at his bedside.'

If he still listened to FA Cup finals, the last he would have heard was the Stanley Matthews final in 1953. He may or may not have been aware that England had lost at home to a continental team for the first time, and by 6–3, to the Hungarians. He died in the nursing home later in that winter of 1953–4, a season that culminated in the election as Footballer of the Year of Tom Finney, a man of honour and dignity as well as a player of sublime gifts, a successor to the England scoring record of whom Woodward – once awarded a goal because the referee had seen him wheel away in satisfaction and knew he would not cheat if the ball had not wholly crossed the line – would have thoroughly approved.

OSCAR WILDE, DR CRIPPEN AND FANNY WALDEN

The physical side of the game, whose rough edge Woodward had all too often felt, was causing concern as the 1909–10 season opened. By midwinter it would be the subject of a stern letter to referees from the Football League secretary, Tom Charnley, whose career had grown under Billy Sudell's wing at Preston and, since 1902, administered the League's affairs from an office in the town. 'Reports are continually being received,' he wrote, 'that the many unfair and unscrupulous tactics indulged in by some of the players engaged in League football are allowed to pass unpunished by referees . . . remiss in their duties . . . not taking cognisance of these offences, which they should penalise as to have a salutary effect on the offenders. Rough and dangerous play, likely to injure players, should be at once stopped.'

Into this hazardous environment, nonetheless, Chapman brought Frederick Ingram Walden, nicknamed 'Fanny', as those of slight build often were at the time. Walden, later to tease the even tinier James Catton, measured 5' 2" and tipped the scales at under nine stone. He looked more like a jockey than a footballer but was to be turned by Chapman from a physically struggling inside-forward into a winger of England class, a fast and tricky provider of goals by the bunch. Walden was 21 when Chapman signed him from nearby Wellingborough for a small fee and began preparing him for the first team. It took only a few months and Walden announced himself with a hat-trick in a 6–1 rout of Luton at the County Ground, which instantly took him to its heart.

Once, arriving with the team for an away match, he was assumed to be a young supporter and turned away until giggling colleagues intervened, but opponents always knew who Walden was after he'd played against them. Especially the weaker ones. Northampton ran up double figures against Croydon Common and Southend, while New Brompton were hit for seven. The retention of the title looked more than possible when the Cup provided its customary welcome diversion – more welcome than ever to Chapman in that the first-round draw brought his brother Harry to the County Ground. The Wednesday, with whom the younger Chapman had won the trophy three years earlier, were from the middle of the First Division and acquired numerical advantage as well when Davies was injured, leaving the home side with 10 men. The match ended goalless and in Sheffield the family feud went Herbert's way as he found the ploy for the occasion, moving McCartney from the middle line to the front; a 1–0 win was secured and once more the tactical nous of Chapman was noted. The next round saw Nottingham Forest, also of the top tier, visit Northampton, who had a player sent off after the Forest forward Enoch 'Knocker' West 'rolled over and over as though in great bodily pain' (*Northampton Daily Echo*). West played on and, although the match ended goalless, Forest won the replay 1–0. West proceeded to earn a transfer to Manchester United, with whom he won a League championship in 1911, but he was to suffer an infinitely more severe attack on his character than the *Echo*'s, for in 1914 he was accused along with three fellow United players and four from Liverpool of conspiring to fix a match and banned from the game for what turned out to be some 30 years, throughout which he maintained his innocence, at one stage bankrupting himself through a wartime court case during which one of the other players changed his story, undermining West's account.

The Cup exit was followed by a dip in League form and, although Chapman's team not only equalled their 90 goals from the previous season but conceded one fewer, they finished 11 points behind a defensively outstanding Brighton and Hove Albion. Elsewhere, the giants prevailed. Aston Villa won the Football League and Newcastle the FA Cup, requiring a replay at Goodison Park to see off Barnsley of the Second Division, whose players had celebrated their draw in the original match at Crystal Palace by accepting an invitation to watch filmed snatches of it at the Alhambra Theatre in Leicester Square.

Shortly after football had left the sporting stage to cricket, the country had in George V a new King. Edward VII, a heavy smoker, had died of bronchitis a few hours after being informed that one of his horses had won at Kempton Park. 'I am very glad' were his last words. He had been a popular monarch, with no aversion to pleasure but a serious side that led him fiercely to oppose the use of the word 'nigger', which he described as 'disgraceful'. This should be assessed in the context of the time: he espoused the view while society was absorbing Rudyard Kipling's imperialist poem 'The White Man's Burden' and it was some 40 years later that Agatha Christie had a detective novel published under the title *Ten Little Niggers*, which the purchasers of American serial rights tactfully changed to *And Then There Were None* (it also became known, in a second film version, as *Ten Little Indians*).

The American summer of 1910 featured yet another retention of the world heavyweight boxing championship by Jack Johnson, the first black man to hold the title and one whose supremacy evoked the term 'great white hope' for his opponents. It all culminated in the offering of a vast sum to the undefeated James L. Jeffries to come out of retirement and put Johnson in his place. The date chosen for the fight was the Fourth of July – Independence Day – and the venue an arena in Reno, Nevada, which could accommodate 20,000. Johnson won, and there followed race riots throughout the United States with several deaths among the celebrating blacks and resentful whites. It was unusual for them to mix, for there was official segregation in Southern states such as Georgia – where a posse was said to have gunned down three blacks in the aftermath of the bout – and unofficial in the north. This concept of civil rights was to persist until the mid–1960s and in Britain, too, while racial discrimination was hardly enshrined by law, it did not become illegal until 1976, a year after women had been assured of equality by a Labour government whose most prominent reformist was the Home Secretary, Roy Jenkins.

Homosexuality was also to remain illegal throughout Herbert Chapman's life and for decades after and, when Jenkins spoke to Parliament about the Bill that would legitimise it at least in private between consenting adults, he was to refer to 'this affliction'– the affliction that had brought the downfall of Oscar Wilde. Not that Herbert Chapman, who had been 20 and making his way at Grimsby when Wilde penned his last work, 'The Ballad of Reading Gaol', a poem about the privations of prison life, would have been expected to have much in common with the hedonistic playwright.

Wilde had been no follower of the movement towards team sports, scorning them as 'manly'; his idea of sport was more likely to involve a visit to a cross-dressing club or some such establishment at odds with the Methodist way and it might not have harmed him but for his habit of taking along Lord Alfred Douglas, son of the decidedly manly Marquis of Queensberry, a founding father of the Amateur Athletic Club (now Amateur Athletic Association) and supporter of boxing for ever to be identified, however flatteringly, with the rules of the ring. Lord Queensberry, having made no headway with his opening deterrent tactic of leaving a card at the Albemarle Club 'for Oscar Wilde, posing as a somdomite [sic]', decided to take part in a court fight against Wilde's charge of criminal libel and won, ruining Wilde, who would die destitute in Paris at the age of 46.

The move to the left might strike today's political students as painfully slow, but 1910 saw the new electorate begin to warm to the Labour Party in two general elections that produced hung parliaments, Asquith's Liberals forming minority governments in both January and December but Labour increasing its Commons presence from 29 to 42 of the 670 seats. The instability had been caused by a Budget introduced by David Lloyd George which had sought to appeal to the working class. Lloyd George had called it 'a war budget . . . raising money to wage implacable warfare against poverty and squalidness'. This would be funded by increases in the income tax paid by relatively high earners – those receiving at least twenty times the £200 a year to which Chapman's footballers were officially restricted – to a scarcely eye-watering 6 per cent. Yet this, combined with provisions for more tax on land ownership, convinced the Conservative-dominated House of Lords that the thin end of the socialist wedge was being driven into the economy and peers made their protest by delaying the measures for a year.

A census indicated that the richest 1 per cent of England and Wales had 70 per cent of the wealth (a century later the latter figure was estimated at 23 per cent) and among the millions whose lives Lloyd George was pledged to improve was John Beckham, a 'scavenger' (refuse collector) who lived in Walworth, south-east London, with his son and daughter-in-law and their children, one of whom was the great-grandfather of David Beckham. Coal mining still employed nearly a million people and discontent among them was expressed in strikes which also affected the docks and railways. Agriculture provided jobs for 1.2 million but the highest total of workers in any activity was 1.3 million: the number of domestic servants. Most of those subjected to the 6 per cent tax would have had at least two servants. But, if the heads of those households felt squeezed, they could at least reflect on the relief extended to the slums through sick pay of 10s. a week and unemployment benefit of 7s. It was hardly social security, but it was a start.

The newspapers, as ever, spiced a diet of royal mourning and affairs of state with more than a dash of crime and there was the classic case in 1910 of Dr Crippen – Hawley Harvey Crippen, a practitioner in homeopathic medicine from the United States who lived in Holloway, north London – whose wife had disappeared. She had gone back across the Atlantic, he said, and died there. Meanwhile his lover, Ethel 'Le Neve' Neave, moved into the former marital home. The police searched it but found nothing untoward. Crippen and Le Neve fled nonetheless to Antwerp, where they boarded a liner to Canada, Le Neve attempting to disguise herself as a boy. Not very well. The captain had never seen such curves on a boy. He worked out who 'he' might be and, after checking Crippen's appearance, had a telegram sent from mid-ocean to the British authorities. It was the first instance of wireless telegraphy helping to resolve a crime. A detective from London took a faster ship than Crippen's and was waiting in Canada with handcuffs. The news would have been received by Herbert and Annie Chapman as they prepared for the birth of their second child, another boy, a brother for Kenneth whom they were to name Bruce. He arrived just before the start of the new season and two months later, as the last of the leaves fell, Crippen was condemned to death by hanging for murder; Le Neve was acquitted of a lesser charge and set free.

In the meantime there had been an extraordinary event at the County Ground. Northampton were due to kick off against Coventry at 3.30 but there was no sign of the visitors. They were still on the train. They had cut things fine in order to take advantage of a cheaper service and the engine had broken down. Chapman brought his players off the field and waited along with a bewildered crowd. Coventry arrived at nearly 5 p.m. and the match began, but the light was fading fast and the referee had no choice but to abandon it. Chapman sent a letter to the local paper thanking the spectators for their patience and, when the match was replayed to a conclusion two months later, Northampton won 4–1.

After beating Luton 5–1 in an FA Cup first round whose surprises included a 2–0 win by Chesterfield at Bolton, a town coming to terms with the loss of 344 men and boys in a pit disaster, Northampton drew the holders, Newcastle United, those giants with whom they had been proud to contest a Charity Shield. Chapman took his men to the North East two days in advance and, staying at Tynemouth with its windswept beaches, they were drilled in the tactics to be used at St James' Park. His modest declaration to the press on arrival – 'I hope my boys will give United a good game' – had hidden the seriousness of his intent, in the manner to be written in the managerial textbook.

He wanted to limit the effectiveness of Newcastle's offside trap, organised by McCracken, and the idea was to attack with direct individual thrusts. Northampton duly wove no patterns but went straight for goal from the wings. If blocked, they would switch the ball from flank to flank and someone else would try. It kept McCracken and his fellow full-back Tony Whitson occupied and, after Newcastle had led, an equaliser came from Frank Bradshaw, a team-mate of Harry Chapman's in the 1907 final whom Herbert had signed in the summer. In the second half, the vast majority of a 42,000 crowd and even McCracken became frustrated in the face of Northampton's relentless discipline, their pressing and their patience; it became 'like a game of chess', as the *Echo*'s correspondent admiringly reported, and it ended in stalemate only because Walden's attempt to snatch victory in the final minutes came back off the crossbar. Yet there was to be no replay at Northampton.

The *Echo*'s joy over the result turned to dismay as Darnell entered into negotiations – and Chapman cannot have been opposed to them – to sell home advantage to the First Division club. This was hardly unprecedented and Northampton may have thought they had done well to raise Newcastle's opening offer of £400 to £900. But the *Athletic News*, by now the national voice of football enthusiasts, joined a chorus of disapproval by asserting that the club had let down their supporters, indeed the cause of football in their community. Darnell – and again there was no hint of dissent from Chapman – responded that the only alternative would have been to sell players. They had bought again, spending £250 on Bradshaw and £150 on Fred Clipston, a right-back from Portsmouth. Even if the 21-year-old half-back Jack Hampson from Oswestry represented less of a strain on resources, this was a substantial outlay by a club in debt, it transpired, to local tradesmen as well as the financers of the ground improvements Chapman had advocated.

On their return to St James' Park, his team lost to a disputed penalty. 'We were robbed' was Chapman's uncharacteristically angry comment. And so it was back to the Southern League campaign. The previous season had featured much entertainment and a new darling for the crowd in Walden, who also played cricket for Northamptonshire and went on to become a Test umpire. But Chapman had resolved to tighten the defence and, while this was impressively done, Northampton would have needed to turn six of their twelve draws into wins to snatch the title from Swindon, who deserved it. The manager moved to resolve this shortage of penetration by acquiring Walter Tull from Tottenham a few weeks into the next season. But there were underlying questions for him and Darnell, such as: were there enough people in the Northampton area to keep pace with Chapman's ambitions? While the chairman pondered afresh, Chapman sought a means of advancing the club towards the game's potentially more lucrative mainstream.

Like most people in the Southern League now, he wanted a bridge to the Football League and in late 1911 he called for automatic promotion to the Second Division instead of the election system that had favoured Tottenham, Chelsea and a few others. Once again, however, he found turkeys unwilling to rally behind the notion of Christmas dinner. But by now he was in the season that was to prove his last at Northampton.

The summer of 1911 had been long and hot and seaside resorts, above all Blackpool with its Tower, were packed; the working class had arrived on the pleasure scene. Those of more generous means had plenty to contemplate. A few cars had begun to appear on the roads – in America, Ford's Model T had sold more than 10,000 – the first non-stop flight from London to Paris had been made by Pierre Prier in just under four hours (Henri Seimet was to trim an hour off the journey in making it in the opposite direction 11 months later) and, as if to establish the luxurious primacy of the ocean liner as a means of travel, the *Titanic* was launched at the Harland and Wolff shipyard in Belfast; it thus became the biggest vessel afloat.

In August, while Chapman had been readying his players for the new season, a temperature of 98 degrees had been measured at Raunds, north-east of Northampton. A nation fanned its brow unaware that the Prime Minister, Herbert Henry 'H. H.' Asquith, had held a secret meeting to discuss British strategy in the event of war with Germany.

The heatwave receded and football resumed. Walter Tull, prospering under Chapman as he never had at Tottenham, scored nine goals in his first 12 matches and the team's output improved as the manager had hoped. They won more matches, drew fewer. The trouble was intense competition at the top of the Southern League, especially from Queens Park Rangers and Plymouth Argyle. It was difficult to pick a favourite as the annual break for the Cup came. Perhaps if Northampton had gone out in the first round, as proved the fate of both Rangers and Argyle, they would have benefited. But Chapman's club had their best Cup campaign to date, reaching the last 16.

They started the competition proper by beating Bristol City and were then drawn against Darlington, mighty minnows from the North Eastern League, the champions of which were to be Middlesbrough's reserves. Chapman did not make the error of underrating Darlington. Indeed, he took his team to the coast, as before the original match with Newcastle a year earlier. Saltburn, however, was in the grip of a terrible frost and, having shivered through the night, the players did well to return home with a draw. The replay was duly won but a trip to Fulham saw the Second Division club prevail by 2–1. It was back to the title campaign – and more disappointment. Queens Park Rangers took the honour.

It looked as if Chapman had driven Northampton as far as he could. They were perennially buoyant in the Southern League and now accustomed to making some impression on the FA Cup. Football was established in the area with all its familiar features, such as terracing, a grandstand – and a debt. But there was no sign of the Football League accepting Chapman's bridge. It was to be built with the creation of the Third Division in 1920 and Northampton to get in then, along with Southampton, Queens Park Rangers and all the other main clubs from the south. But Chapman could not wait another eight years. He took his step into the Football League right away, returning to Yorkshire to take over a depressed and dispirited Leeds City.

The approach came in April and it was a sombre time for many – not just the supporters of a football club finishing second from bottom of the Second Division. The nation was coming to terms with a spring of tragedy.

In January the expeditionary group led by Robert Falcon Scott had reached the South Pole only to find a tent and a note from Roald Amundsen, the leader of the Norwegian participants in the race, who announced in March that he had got there a month before the British. Worse was to follow, for Scott's men were unable to return to safety. Their progress across the snow was slowed by the injuries and frostbite encountered by Lawrence 'Titus' Oates, a holder of the Victoria Cross from the Boer War, who heroically resolved to sacrifice himself, limping from his tent to certain death with the words: 'I am just going outside and may be some time.' Scott and the others died before March was out.

In April the *Titantic* left Southampton on her maiden voyage to New York. She hit an iceberg and sank with the loss of 1,517 souls, from some of the richest on earth, including Benjamin Guggenheim and John Astor IV, to poor emigrants in steerage. Dai Bowen, the Welsh lightweight champion, and his fellow boxer Leslie Williams were among those below decks; they had been engaged to fight in the United States. Another victim was the campaigning journalist W. T. Stead, whose crusade against child prostitution had not only prompted legislation but inspired George Bernard Shaw to write *Pygmalion*, naming the lead character Eliza after the 13-year-old daughter of a chimney sweep whom Stead had intended to 'buy' for £5 for a night in order to draw attention to this scourge of late Victorian times; although Stead spent three months in prison for abduction, he and colleagues having neglected to obtain the father's permission for the 'sale', the government had responded with measures including a rise in the age of consent from 13 to 16. That was in 1885. In 1912, as Shaw worked on *Pygmalion*, later to be adapted to the musical *My Fair Lady*, Stead perished in the freezing Atlantic. He had been on his way to a conference on world peace at the Carnegie Hall, New York.

LEEDS CITY

TITANIC TASK

The offer from Leeds City was to replace Frank Scott-Walford, a man whose dress sense – as sharp as his waxed moustache – belied the earnestness of his approach to the job of secretary-manager. It had, according to a dignified letter of resignation, made inroads into his health as well as his bank account, which had often been tapped to pay wages and even transfer fees. There was no suggestion that any residual debt to him be repaid. Although the chairman, Norris Hepworth, was extremely rich, Scott-Walford knew he had already put more than £15,000 into the club.

Chapman, at his interview, took an instant liking to Hepworth. This was a very successful man, one who shared the work ethic of his father, Joseph Hepworth, who had left school at 10 to work in a mill and eventually set up a wholesale clothing company. It became J. Hepworth and Son when Norris joined and together they built the business which, since 1986, has been called Next. But towards the end of the 1911–12 season Norris Hepworth, having reflected on nearly eight years in which he had been the only chairman of a club in recurrent deficit and now under pressure from its bank for the return of a £7,000 loan, called in a receiver, Tom Coombs, who was to oversee affairs at Elland Road for three and a half years. Norris nevertheless had enough faith in Chapman to offer an improvement on his Northampton salary, plus incentives. Only potential – Leeds, though their crowds had averaged 8,500 in the season just finished, could attract 20,000 or more if performing well – can have attracted him to the club. There was the prospect of doing for Leeds in the Football League what he had done for Northampton in the Southern.

From Hepworth he would have obtained the assurance of a free hand in team matters; even Scott-Walford had picked the side. Scott-Walford's difficulty had been in holding on to his better players and he could afford replacements only by recruiting cheaply in Ireland during the summers. The *Athletic News* was optimistic that Chapman could fare better. 'Leeds City can congratulate themselves,' wrote Catton or one of his assistants, echoing the valedictory tributes to Chapman of the Northampton press, which referred to 'the winning personality that makes him very popular', his tact and abilities both to judge and coax the best out of a player. Chapman declared: 'I am here to get Leeds City into the First Division.' But first he had to keep them in the Second, for they faced re-election and he had to chase up votes from the other clubs. Enough materialised at the Football League meeting in early June, which also heard that £696 had been collected for the families of *Titanic* victims.

GARBUTT, PENTLAND AND HOGAN

The couple of years leading to the outbreak of war in 1914 were also to prove significant in the careers of three of Chapman's contemporaries, each of whom was likewise to exert a memorable influence, albeit not in the country of his birth but on a European mainland destined to be ravaged by war.

Chapman had encountered Willie Garbutt while in his first spell at Northampton, then at Tottenham. Garbutt was with their Southern League rivals Reading. The son of a carpenter, he came from a village near Stockport, Cheshire, and in his youth had joined the Royal Artillery. After Reading he had played for Woolwich Arsenal and Blackburn Rovers and done well enough to earn selection by the Football League for the annual fixture against the

Scottish League. He retired through injury at 29 and moved to Genoa to work on the docks. There was plenty of English company in the city and from James Richardson Spensley, founder in 1897 of the football section of the Genoa Cricket and Football Club, came an offer to be Italy's first professional manager.

Garbutt immediately changed the club's training methods much as Chapman had done at Northampton, introducing more emphasis on fitness and tactics. He also arranged to pay transfer fees, which had never been done in Italy before, and, having thus augmented a team already featuring Luigi Ferraris, the captain whose name the club's stadium (shared with Sampdoria) still bears, guided Genoa to the national championship in 1915. He was a popular and charismatic figure, always smoking a pipe. The players called him 'Mister' and the title remains Italy's version of 'Boss' or 'Gaffer'. It is also used in other countries. When Sir Bobby Robson arrived in Portugal in 1994, the interpreter Porto had engaged to assist him – one José Mourinho – greeted him as 'Mister'. Garbutt was to win two more titles with Genoa and later, in the 1930s, one with Athletic Bilbao in Spain. Had Chapman's dream of European competition been realised during the coincident span of his managerial career and Garbutt's, they might have renewed their Southern League rivalry in the Champions' Cup.

Another expatriate whom Chapman knew from the Southern League was Fred Pentland, who became renowned in Spain and especially Bilbao. 'El Bombín' – the nickname celebrated his bowler hat – had been in the Queens Park Rangers side that won the title. Pentland had progressed to the First Division with Middlesbrough and encountered Garbutt, then of Blackburn. Pentland even played for England, alongside Vivian Woodward. Some 18 months after Garbutt's career had been ended by an abdominal tear – among those who saw him fall in agony at Ewood Park was an Italian student of English and the game called Vittorio Pozzo, who had squeezed himself on to a football special train from Manchester with thousands of fellow United followers – Pentland himself succumbed to a knee injury.

In 1914 he went to Berlin to coach Germany's Olympic team and was interned at the start of the war at nearby Ruhleben, where other inhabitants of a vast detention camp included his former Middlesbrough team-mate Steve Bloomer and Chapman's old boss at Tottenham, John Cameron. After spending the whole war there, Pentland began his managerial career in Santander but soon went to Athletic Bilbao, with whom he was to enjoy two successful periods.

Jimmy Hogan was even more of a coach than a manager. Indeed, Jonathan Wilson wrote in *Inverting the Pyramid* that he was the most influential coach of all time, his credits including contributions to the style of great Austrian and Hungarian teams as well as the football idioms of Holland, Germany and, indirectly, South America.

Yet Hogan might have been lost to football at the age of 10 when, walking along the cobbled streets of his native Nelson in Lancashire on the lookout, as ever, for a bit of rubbish with which to hone his shooting skills, he spied an old hat and instinctively kicked it, not knowing that it had been mischievously placed in waiting for a football-mad kid like him. Under the hat was a large stone. So badly were his toes damaged that for several weeks it seemed he might never walk properly again, let alone play the game to a decent professional level.

Hogan would have been with Fulham when he first met Chapman, who was at Tottenham; Fulham were on their way to retaining the Southern title. But the manager who had signed Hogan and shared his belief in the subtleties of the old Scottish style, Harry Bradshaw, was no longer happy with his form and let him go to Swindon. From there he went to Bolton, whose preparations for a season included a trip to Holland. They beat Dordrecht 10–0 but the willingness of the young Dutch players to learn impressed Hogan, who had always felt at odds with the over-physical aspects of the English game. Later he heard from his friend James Howcroft, a referee who often officiated abroad, that Dordrecht were looking for a coach and he applied. Hogan preached the passing game so successfully that he was asked to prepare the national team for a match against Germany, which Holland won 2–1. And then, missing his old life as a player in England, he returned to Bolton for a while. Again Howcroft intervened. After refereeing a draw between Austria and Hungary in Vienna, he responded to Hugo Meisl's disappointment with the home performance by declaring that, if he wanted help, Hogan was the man. Hogan was to stay in Austria until the outbreak of war.

UNFINISHED BUSINESS

Chapman spent the two years leading to war doing what his Northampton achievement had promised: Leeds City rose from nineteenth in the Second Division to fourth, only a couple of points from promotion.

He had begun by performing surgery on the team more radical than even Brian Clough was to attempt at Elland Road in 1974, albeit with more of Chapman's trademark tact. By the time Leeds City were ready to kick off the 1912–13 season, only four of the players handed over by Scott-Walford remained in the first team. These were Stan Cubberley at left-half, Hugh Roberts and Fred Croot on the wings and Billy McLeod at centre-forward. McLeod was one of the most coveted goalscorers in the League and Chapman, upon hearing that Northampton would listen to offers for Walden, tried to buy the winger to serve him. But Chapman's old fans at the County Ground held a collection to keep their little idol and Chapman was to describe this as the great regret of his Leeds years. When Walden left at the end of the season, it was to join Tottenham for £1,700, surely beyond Leeds's budget; the British record did not reach £2,000 until later that year when Sheffield United signed George Utley from Barnsley.

Chapman did, however, persuade Coombs to release a hefty £1,400 in January. That was for Jimmy Spiers, once of Rangers and now Bradford City, with whom the Scot had fallen out since captaining them in the 1911 FA Cup final, when his lone goal overcame Newcastle in a replay at Old Trafford. Spiers was a star and, with McLeod, did much to lift Leeds in the second half of the season. The first half had been a disappointment, at least for those who had expected an instant acquisition of the mechanical qualities of Northampton. How could it be otherwise, with so many new players? Even internationals – Billy Scott, the Ireland goalkeeper, George Law, a Scotland full-back and Evelyn Lintott, the ill-fated former England centre-half whom Chapman made captain – needed time to knit. Over Christmas they started to lose home matches and the crowd was down to 8,000 for the Boxing Day disappointment at the hands of lowly Blackpool. It was time to splash out on Spiers. The receiver's confidence in Chapman was remarkable; it appears Coombs and Hepworth succumbed to the persuasive powers the manager had used on Darnell. If so, they were vindicated when Leeds announced a £400 profit at the end of the season.

It would have been more but for a £125 fine imposed by the League as a result of Chapman's dealings with Scott, Law and Lintott. When signing them, Chapman had agreed to pay a full year's salary of £208, but on contracts expiring at the end of April, thus exceeding the maximum wage of £4 a week. Several weeks into the season, Chapman told his directors about the error and asked them to tell the League. No doubt he hoped for a slap on the wrist. Instead came the fine, plus costs, and censures for the players and Chapman, who was warned as to his future conduct. If any at Leeds thought the last bit could be safely ignored, they were to be proved wrong.

For now, though, they lived the dream, oblivious. Despite a Cup knockout by Burnley in a tie initially abandoned in a blizzard, the cash flow had been helped by the late-season surge. A McLeod hat-trick against Bury meant he had struck in seven consecutive matches. He extended the sequence to nine in a win over Nottingham Forest watched by 20,000. A draw in the concluding fixture at Huddersfield left a mood of optimism and an average crowd of 13,400, nearly 5,000 up on the previous season.

A rudimentary analysis of how Leeds reached eleventh place

showed that, while they had scored plenty of goals – more than anyone except second-placed Burnley – their defensive record was what you might expect from a struggling side. Chapman could see his assets and liabilities. McLeod, with 27 goals, and Spiers, with 10 in 19 matches, were key men along with Croot and the ever-present Lintott. Those who left included Chapman signings, some after mere months.

A significant summer arrival was Chapman's former Northampton centre-half, the rugged Jack Hampson. To accommodate him, Lintott was moved to right-half but injury affected the captain's season so badly he played only six matches. The last he would ever play. For a nation split by the cause of the suffragettes and disturbed by their tactics – Emily Davison had died after stepping in front of George V's horse at the Derby – fate was preparing an annihilation of men. Emmeline Pankhurst and her daughter Christabel were to suspend all militant activity when war broke out. And after the guns stilled the cause was to gain gradual acceptance. But Lintott was long gone, lost in France.

As his final season began, few conceived the scale of tragedy to come. The summer of 1913 had been, for Chapman, just another close season in which to try to steal a march on rivals. He endeavoured to keep the players fit and bonded by arranging golf tournaments and cricket matches. The football pitch painted on the desk of his office was used so that players could see clearly any points he was making, whether to the group or in individual meetings. It was an extension of the blackboard habit, or precursor of the PowerPoint presentation. Not that the discussions were one-way, for Chapman listened to ideas and, having been impressed by the ferocity of the players' arguments during card games, encouraged them to debate aspects of the team's play. 'Although in the frank discussions a player may feel a little hurt at being singled out for some fault,' he later said, 'a little tact and good humour quickly removes this.' Even on the morning of home matches, he would have them assemble at a hotel and, after a light meal, discuss the imminent contest. Results seemed to benefit.

'In future football,' he said, 'there is no doubt that brains, personality and character in the players are going to be more predominant. Our present Leeds players are the best set I have ever known for intelligent application to the game. We make a study of it together. General tactics and individual play are discussed. We go over the good points and mistakes of the previous Saturday's match, not forgetting the prospects for the next.'

Chapman, having brought Hampson for the defence, improved the attack by signing Ivan Sharpe, whose crosses for Steve Bloomer had helped Derby County to take the League title in 1912. Sharpe, an amateur international who had won Olympic gold alongside Vivian Woodward, was a football journalist as well as player and joined the *Yorkshire Evening Post* at the same time as City. He was to form a classic partnership with Spiers on the left. For the right wing, Neil Turner came from Petershill in Scotland.

Hampson and Sharpe appeared on opening day, in a routine 3–0 win over Glossop at Elland Road, where 23,000 then watched a 5–1 triumph over the neighbours from Bradford Park Avenue. Almost as many saw Leeds lose, surprisingly, to a Hull City managed by Harry Chapman, who had retired as a player after a single season there. But Leeds were soon back in form. There was competition for places now, as was shown when Lintott deputised for Hampson or Croot for Sharpe, or in a draw at Huddersfield secured by Turner on his debut in place of Simpson Bainbridge (most of the crowd would have learned the identity of the scorer only the next day, for the match was completed in a rainswept, mist-shrouded twilight). Against bottom-of-the-table Nottingham Forest, Chapman's men struck eight without reply, McLeod getting four.

The next fixture took them to Highbury to play Arsenal, who had moved only that summer, shedding their 'Woolwich' prefix. Chapman's first gaze met an incomplete stadium: the original East Stand was in the course of construction. He noted its proximity to the Gillespie Road underground station and settled down with 18,000 others to watch a 1–0 defeat that, at least from the Leeds point of view, said as much for the performance of the home goal-keeper, Joe Lievesley, as the relative merits of these promotion candidates. Chapman knew Lievesley from his season at Sheffield United. Lievesley had been the understudy to Fatty Foulke, whom he later supplanted. He came from quite a football family. An uncle and two brothers also played professionally, and three sons were to follow. One, Leslie, became a coach in Holland and Italy, where he worked with one of the greatest teams ever, the Torino of the late 1940s, and died along with most of its members when their aircraft hit a hill overlooking Turin; his name is engraved on a huge monument visible from the city.

On Christmas Day there was a vast convergence on Elland Road for the visit of Fulham. Many, arriving late because of a tram strike, pushed into the ground and Leeds had difficulty in deciding how much of the takings should be paid to the away club. There was a dispute and the next day, when Leeds went to London for the return fixture, Fulham held some money back. The matter was referred to the League, which, when it reported in February, was broadly sympathetic to Leeds.

In this month Norris Hepworth died. His last contribution had been to sanction the paying of more than £1,000 for the stylish full-back Fred Blackman from Bradford City. The club's debt to Hepworth had risen from £15,000 at the time of Chapman's appointment to £18,000 in less than two years. The manager attended the funeral along with McLeod, Spiers, Law and Croot, their black top hats clustered by the chilly graveside at Lawnswood Cemetery. Also in attendance were the other Leeds directors. But there was little doubt that Chapman and Coombs, the receiver, now ran the club.

Leeds had gone through a sticky patch and been knocked out of the Cup by West Bromwich Albion in front of nearly 30,000 at Elland Road. Hence the recourse to Blackman. The day after the funeral, he made his debut at Hull, where Leeds lost 1–0, Harry doing the double over Herbert on the last occasion when football would pit the brothers against each other. The rest of the campaign suffered from poor away form. It might have been a bit better, Chapman argued, but for Leeds's experience at Clapton Orient, where they played a rearranged fixture on a Monday and the home club fixed the kick-off for 4.30 p.m. in the hope of attracting more spectators. After Leeds objected that the light might fail, Orient agreed to 4.20, but the referee and linesmen arrived late and there was a further delay when Billy Scott, the goalkeeper, was asked to change his jersey; its plain blue was deemed too similar to his team-mates' blue with gold chevron. Midway through the second half, Leeds were leading 1–0 but, according to the *Yorkshire Post*'s subsequent report, 'it was practically impossible to distinguish players in midfield' (note the term 'midfield', associated with more modern football). The referee consulted his linesmen and played on.

In the gathering gloom, Orient equalised and Scott claimed he could not have seen the two shots that subsequently passed him. The officials disagreed and Chapman called it an 'insult', telling the referee an appeal would be lodged. A fortnight later the League ruled that Orient had set the kick-off time too late and fined them 25 guineas (£26.25), out of which Leeds's expenses would be paid. But the result stood. And there was no excuse for the subsequent defeat by lowly Forest. If Chapman's team had won that, they would have been promoted ahead of Park Avenue on goal average. Only a point came from the return against Arsenal, for whom Lievesley kept another clean sheet. Had a claim for a goal not been rejected because of a foul on him, Leeds would have crept above the Londoners into third place. But it was still the club's highest finish. The average attendance was also a record at 18,000, which meant it had doubled in the two seasons since Chapman's move from Northampton.

Notts County and Bradford Park Avenue went up and Preston, their Invincible days a fond memory, came down for the third time, along with Derby, for whom Bloomer had stopped playing at 40 before deciding to begin his coaching career in Berlin. By August, war having been declared, he was in the Ruhleben camp, where he remained until 1918. So had it been an ill-advised decision to follow Cameron and others to Germany? By comparison with many footballers, Bloomer, Cameron and their fellow inmates were lucky. Teddy Hodgson, having played for Burnley in their FA Cup final victory over Liverpool, went to the war and developed a kidney disorder from which he died in 1919. And even he was luckier than some of Chapman's acquaintance.

THE WAR BEGINS

Evelyn Lintott came from a prosperous middle-class family in Surrey and initially, like Woodward, resisted the notion of turning professional. He went to the West Country to study teaching at St Luke's College in Exeter and made a couple of appearances for Plymouth Argyle in the Southern League before moving to London to become a master at a school in Willesden and play for Queens Park Rangers. He became an international alongside Woodward and received an offer to graduate to the First Division with Bradford City. Now he did turn professional, but only so Queens Park Rangers could receive a transfer fee of £1,000. He soon returned to teaching. He became a leading spokesman for the players' union and, on Sundays, a lay preacher. By the time of the 1911 FA Cup final, however, Lintott was considered past his best and did not feature in either the initial match or the replay. He had made what was to be his final England appearance in an 8–2 victory over Hungary two years earlier. Yet Chapman believed there was something left in him and tendered that dodgy 52-week contract to the experienced half-back.

Amid the disappointment of Lintott's second season at Leeds, the injuries and the loss of both his place and the captaincy (to Spiers), he decided to retire. Chapman engaged the rest of the squad for the 1914–15 season. With the players he played golf, which he had incorporated into their training routine, and cricket. He took a short holiday. And then, on 28 June, as Chapman prepared to welcome his men back for serious training, Franz Ferdinand, Archduke of Austria, and his wife Sophie were assassinated in Sarajevo by a young Serbian nationalist. The chain reaction that led to the Great War had begun. Within a month, Austro-Hungarian bombs were falling on Belgrade. Within a further week, Germany had invaded Belgium and declared war on France. It was now time, as Asquith's staff had foreseen, for Great Britain to declare war on Germany. This happened on 4 August.

On 22 August, British troops engaged their German counterparts for the first time. The Germans made gains and at one stage Paris seemed acutely threatened. Then the long battle lines were drawn for what proved a shedding of blood on a scale unprecedented in Europe in which 'lions led by donkeys', a phrase dating from the Crimean War, would be applied to the British infantry. Few understood what was in store. Lord Kitchener, the new Minister of War, understood better than most. He knew that the general British concept of war as a matter for regular soldiers might have to be varied. He told the nation's young men: 'Your Country Needs You.' Lintott did not hesitate.

He still lived in Bradford, near the Valley Parade ground, and volunteered in the city. But there were delays in recruitment and so, in September, he tried at Leeds and was successful, joining the 15th (Service) Battalion (1st Leeds) of the West Yorkshire Regiment on the day it was formed. Clearly officer material, he was soon promoted to lieutenant and waited for the call to action. With thousands already falling on the muddy fields of Flanders, it seemed unlikely to be much delayed. But Lintott was to take a long and circuitous route to his death.

His battalion, known as the 'Leeds Pals', included other footballers as well as Yorkshire cricketers. But, while cricket and the amateurs of rugby union had been widely praised, professional football was in the dock. Newspapers, politicians and even members of the clergy felt the game was not doing enough to replenish the forces and the point was vividly made by a letter to *The Times*: 'Every club that employs a professional footballer is bribing a needed recruit from enlistment, and every spectator who pays his gate money is contributing so much towards a German victory.' The FA had asked the War Office for advice on whether or not to suspend play and had been told to make the decision itself.

Talks produced a compromise under which matches would continue but with a rousing recruitment campaign at half-time; this led to at least one debacle in which there were no volunteers. A few people friendly to football, suspecting that its working-class character was being maligned, vainly argued that the sport of kings – horse-racing – continued to offer diversion. The *Athletic News* preached stridently to the converted: 'The whole agitation is nothing less than an attempt by the ruling classes to stop the recreation on one day a week of the masses.' The poor were giving their lives in thousands and yet they 'should, according to a small clique of virulent snobs, be deprived of the one distraction they have had for over thirty years'.

In these circumstances the 17th Service Battalion (1st Football) of the Middlesex Regiment was formed at Fulham Town Hall in December and immediately became known as the Football Battalion. The first wave of recruits included the entire Clapton Orient team which had beaten Leeds in the dark the previous season – Heart of Midlothian had already enlisted en bloc in Scotland – and Walter Tull, whom Chapman had rescued from Tottenham to score goals for Northampton. One whom Chapman might have remembered from his playing days there was Bernard Vann, now chaplain of Wellingborough School and about to be commissioned into the Sherwood Foresters. Among those alongside Lintott was the big, muscular defender Donald Bell, who had secured his release from contractual obligations to Bradford Park Avenue; he had turned professional after teaching at a school in Harrogate. Jimmy Spiers remained in Chapman's team for one more season, before heading for his noble fate across the Channel.

Midway through Spiers's final year at Leeds, a fleet of German battleships approached the north Yorkshire coast, about 60 miles away. It was early on a December morning and Scarborough took the first bombardment, its castle and three churches among the buildings hit. The guns were then turned on Whitby before the ships moved north to Hartlepool, where steel factories, gasworks and rail lines were battered along with more churches and hundreds of homes. In all the assaults lasted nearly one and a half hours, killing 137 people and injuring 592 more. The nation was aghast, blaming the government and Royal Navy for lack of readiness as well as the German admiral responsible, Franz von Hipper, whom newspapers called a 'baby killer'.

As the controversy over football's contribution to the war effort raged, many supporters, like players, voted with their feet. Half the national audience had deserted the game by the end of the 1914–15 season and its khaki Cup final in which Chelsea, without the principled Woodward, lost 3–0 to Sheffield United. Everton had won a First Division cast into disrepute by the match-fixing between players of Liverpool and Manchester United. Chapman's Leeds City had regressed in the Second Division, never so much as threatening to repeat their promotion campaign, slipping from fourth to fifteenth in the 20-club table as their average attendance sank to a record low 7,000.

It was the last season before the League, letting go of the notion that people needed relief from the war, closed down along with the FA Cup. For Leeds it began with four defeats. Many newspapers were refusing to print football reports, though they were soon to relent. Their main pages were grim and Kitchener, warning that the war might last three years rather than three months, renewed his appeal for volunteers, ominously coupled with a reduction in the height and chest-measurement requirements.

When the war began, the phrase 'over by Christmas' had played on optimistic lips. But on Christmas Eve the citizens of Dover contemplated the dubious honour of having received the first bomb to fall on British soil; hurled from a German aircraft in the general direction of the harbour, it instead fell in the grounds of a rectory, causing the gardener to fall from a tree. By the end of the war, 27 were to be killed in the town.

On Christmas Day, matches more remarkable than Leeds's concurrent win at Glossop were taking place between the trench lines. Details are, understandably, sketchy but one account had a football being propelled from a British trench into no-man's-land during the famous truce that began at dawn, when at various locations the soldiers exchanged gifts of cigarettes, cake and drink. Some took the opportunity to recover and bury the bodies of comrades. Some took part in kickabouts with – as one letter home put it – 'the men we were trying to kill yesterday'. The truce was never repeated.

The carnage resumed and, in the new year, England having emerged from a carpet of snow, the last FA Cup to be contested for five years saw Leeds go unfancied to Derby yet triumph, Sharpe giving a brilliant display on his former ground. At Hull, McLeod struck five times in a 6–2 win clouded for Chapman by the reflection that the opposition were no longer managed by his brother, whose health was failing. But a Cup exit at Queens Park Rangers was followed by the most dismal days of Herbert's reign at Elland Road: 5–1 defeats at Wolverhampton and even Leicester and, in the final match, a 2–0 loss at home to Barnsley watched by only 5,000.

At least the club was alive. At one stage it appeared Tom Coombs might sell to the Leeds rugby league club but a consortium was formed by the local businessman Joseph Connor, who, as secretary of the West Riding FA, was seen as a safe pair of hands (this turned out to be somewhat optimistic). Connor would have to run the team in the old-fashioned way because Chapman was resolved to turn his back on football in the national interest. His last season for the duration had been by far his least impressive: one of too many team changes. But it was over and a couple of the statistics could be surveyed with pleasure. McLeod led the scorers' list as usual, albeit with a reduced tally of 18, while Spiers had chipped in with 10. McLeod went to work in a factory. Spiers went to the war.

FOOTBALL'S HEROES

Jimmy Spiers first returned to his native Glasgow with his wife and children. Although the status of a family man meant he would have been exempt from the conscription to be introduced the following year, he enlisted with the Cameron Highlanders. A fellow Scot was already among the forces in France. Willie Angus had been released by Celtic when war broke out. He had a new club, Wishaw Thistle, but as a member of the Territorial Army he was mobilised and became one of Kitchener's replenishments at the front. In June 1915 he left his trench and defied bombs and bullets to reach a wounded officer lying yards from an enemy position; Lieutenant James Martin was from Carluke, also the home town of Lance Corporal Angus, who, in completing an apparently suicidal rescue, suffered 40 injuries from bursts of fire. He was taken to hospital in Boulogne and, after a few weeks, returned to London – minus an eye and part of a foot – to be presented with the Victoria Cross by the King at Buckingham Palace.

Spiers was also to be awarded a medal for bravery. While he signed up, the brilliant goalkeeper Dick Roose was already seeing action, in the picturesque Dardanelles, in the ill-fated Gallipoli operation whose intent had been to capture Istanbul yet whose effect was mainly to fill the Turks with confidence. George Holley, who had played with Roose at Sunderland, received a letter from him in June: 'If ever there was a hell on this occasionally volatile planet then this oppressively hot, dusty, diseased place has to be it. If I have seen the fragments of one plucky youth whose body ... or what remains of it ... has been swollen out of all proportion by the sun, I have seen several hundred. The bombardment is relentless to the extent that you become accustomed to its tune, a permanent rata-tat-tat complemented by bursting shells ... and yet at night the stars are so bright in this largest of skies that one cannot help but be pervaded with a feeling of serenity, peculiar as that appears.'

Roose was the footballer with whom Marie Lloyd had an affair. A celebrity in his own right, he was tall, well-built, good-looking and charismatic; the *Daily Mail* had named him one of London's most eligible bachelors. Born in North Wales, the son of a Presbyterian minister, he had kept goal for London Welsh football team while briefly studying medicine at King's College. He discovered that he could retain his amateur status while making a good living through 'expenses' – some more legitimate than others – paid by a succession of clubs. Because almost his entire career of 12 years was spent in the First Division with Stoke City, Everton, Sunderland, Aston Villa and Woolwich Arsenal, he and Herbert Chapman would not have crossed paths often; they inhabited the same division only between 1902 and 1904, when Chapman was with Sheffield United and then Notts County. But Roose was often the talk of football, as well as a man around London, in whose fashionable centre he lived.

While with Stoke, he was said to have missed a train from the capital to Birmingham for a match against Villa. Knowing that private trains were kept in sidings for hire by the prosperous or the use of VIPs, he had one take him to the Midlands – Roose was the only passenger – and asked for the bill of £31 to be sent to the club. He was accustomed to reimbursement, even for expensive suits and shoes. When at Sunderland, he was the subject of an inquiry by the FA, who had received complaints from other clubs about overpayment of expenses. Asked to list his claims for an entire season, he began the document: 'Pistol to ward off the opposition – 4d. Coat and gloves to keep warm when not occupied – 3p. Using the toilet (twice) 2p . . .' The FA failed to discover any irregularity and dropped the case. But Roose was not all laughs. He had a foul-mouthed rant at FA officials after being injured against England during one of his 24 appearances for Wales and once, after a 1–0 defeat when with Stoke at Sunderland, responded to the taunts of a home supporter at the post-match dinner by pushing back his chair, crossing the room and punching the man in the face. On this occasion the FA suspended him for two weeks.

Assessments of his goalkeeping style sometimes spoke of 'genius'. He was bold and brave and, in an age when keepers were regarded as fair game for rough challenges, liked to get his retaliation in first, as in his debut international when he raced more than 50 yards to shoulder-charge an Irish winger over the touchline, rendering him unconscious. Roose was all for mind games, too. Once, facing a penalty against Manchester City, he wobbled his knees in an attempt to put the taker off; it was the first known instance of the 'spaghetti legs' trick used by Bruce Grobbelaar in the European Cup final of 1984 and copied by Jerzy Dudek, also of Liverpool, in 2005. Having saved the kick, Roose raised his arms in glee to the City supporters, who pelted him. But Roose was also clever tactically, especially in leaving his goal to take advantage of the law allowing a goalkeeper to handle anywhere in his own half as long as he did not carry the ball. He overdid it occasionally and among those who found an empty net with long shots was Nudger Needham. But overwhelmingly Roose prospered. At times he doubled as a sort of libero, initiating attacks with his basketball-style advances, but he also used his territorial privilege to break up promising opposition moves in their early stages, diminishing the game as a spectacle according to complaints from rival clubs to the FA; in 1912, the law was changed to restrict handling to the penalty area.

In that year, Roose hung up his distinctive white gloves and started giving after-dinner speeches for £50 a time. He also returned to his medical studies. When war broke out, he joined the Royal Army Medical Corps. He was sent to treat soldiers at a hospital near Rouen, returned to England and then sailed for Gallipoli in the spring of 1915. 'If ever there was a hell . . .': Roose may have revised this definition at the Somme the following year, before he, too, died a hero.

Back home there was a chance for Chapman to do something for his country. He and a few Leeds players had joined some sort of 'civilian army' of which details are vague. They were also to 'attest', along with chairman Connor, to their willingness to be called up under a scheme administered by Lord Derby on behalf of a government anxious to avoid, if at all possible, conscription. Chapman was sharing Elland Road with troops for the purposes of their training. He would have heard from his family about the exodus from Kiveton Park, where cheering residents had lined the streets to wave the young volunteers off. The village now had a cinema – perhaps showing Charlie Chaplin's new film, *The*

Tramp – for which Herbert's brother John was partly responsible, as with many other community assets. At the end of the war, John Chapman was to shoulder another burden: he organised the building of a memorial to the young men lost. But, in the summer of 1915, Herbert was 37 years old with a wife and two children, soon to become three because Annie was heavily pregnant. The call, when it came, was to help as a civilian.

But first there was football to supervise. Such a show as could be assembled went on. The League was replaced by regional divisions – the Midland, into which Leeds went, and Lancashire – and a London Combination, with existing players on nominal wages, supplemented by earnings from outside jobs, and guests who happened to be stationed or working nearby, appearing for expenses only. Fanny Walden, who was employed by an engineering firm in Leeds, became a member of a Chapman team again, much to the ire of Tottenham, who had paid so much for his services.

More important football was taking place across the Channel. The Battle of Loos, from late September to mid-October, saw the first British use of poison gas. The Germans had used chlorine gas in April at Ypres, on the French, who initially thought the yellowish green cloud drifting towards them was smoke. It tasted sweet and peppery. And then they felt the throat and chest pains that were the first signs of damage to their means of breathing. A slow death often followed. And now the British were ready to send 150 tons of chlorine gas to the Germans. As their commanders waited for optimum wind conditions, men of the Royal Irish Rifles planned to dribble and pass six footballs across no-man's-land in the wake of the lethal cloud and 'score a goal' into a German trench. When the officers discovered this, they had the footballs shot. But they found only five. Sergeant Frank Edwards, captain of the Regiment team, had deflated and hidden his ball. He kept it out of sight as the gas was released. And then the wind briefly changed, causing some gas to blow back and affect the British as they hurriedly pulled on their goggle-eyed masks. Edwards still puffed away at the valve of his ball and eventually hurled it out of the trench. It was chased until it punctured on the barbed wire of the German lines. Edwards had lost possession; during the advance, he had been shot in a thigh.

Most regiments had a team and football tournaments helped soldiers to relax. The internees in Germany, too. Italy, where Willie Garbutt had guided Genoa to the championship, was different – it had renounced alliance with Germany and thrown in its lot with the British – but Fred Pentland, Steve Bloomer and fellow expatriates had been contained from the outset at Ruhleben where in May 1915 an 'England' team took on the 'Rest of the World', prominently featuring Scots such as John Cameron. There was also a league in the camp, and no shortage of stars with whom to stud the teams. The inmates included Fred Spiksley, the Wednesday dazzler of Chapman's youth. Spiksley had coached AIK Stockholm to a national title in Sweden before moving to Germany to work with first 1860 Munich and then Nuremberg. He escaped after a few months and, from England, sailed for the United States, where he spent the rest of the war working in a munitions factory.

Hogan was arrested in Vienna. Shortly before he was due to be sent to an internment camp, a wealthy Austrian stepped in as his guarantor. Hogan coached tennis, tended gardens, did odd jobs. He was then engaged to coach MTK in Budapest on the condition that he reported regularly to the police. He won the Hungarian championship and did not return to Britain until the war was over.

The 1915–16 season began joyously for the Chapman family with the arrival of Molly, their third child. But it was one of mixed fortunes for Leeds City. The club finished tenth out of 14 in the Midland Division and in the spring, while Chapman's old captain Lintott was being transported across the Mediterranean, won a tournament for six Yorkshire clubs. Lintott and his unit had initially sailed to Egypt to protect the Suez Canal, leaving a few weeks after a regional controversy over Billy McLeod, who had left Leeds for Bradford Park Avenue, causing supporters of the former to complain that it was a bit soon – two years – after his testimonial. By the time Lintott and his brothers in arms had embarked on their voyage back to Europe, the mood around Elland Road had been lifted by further distinguished guests. Clem Stephenson, an outstanding inside-forward from Aston Villa, was to play nearly a hundred wartime matches for the club. And to be a key figure in the rise of Herbert Chapman at Huddersfield; in this sense Chapman's last full season with Leeds might be reviewed as significant, even though it was utterly overshadowed by events elsewhere. Recruiting had declined as the casualty figures rose; Britain had conceded defeat in its resistance to conscription.

But Dick Roose needed no letter. By now he had joined the Royal Fusiliers as a private. He was sent to the trenches. So was Spiers. Two more Chapman signings, Tull and Lintott, were also converging in readiness for the conflict on the Somme, along with Bell from Bradford Park Avenue and the Clapton Orient and Heart of Midlothian contingents. As the regiments gathered, they competed in a cup competition, often to the sound of distant artillery. Sometimes not so distant; Charlie Buchan, who ran the Grenadier Guards team, recalled in his memoirs that once they changed pitches after a shell landed next to their original venue. Major Frank Buckley, an England centre-half, was in charge of the Football Battalion side, which beat the Field Artillery 11–0 in the final.

On 1 July, the first day of the Battle of the Somme, Lintott was killed. He was reported to have led his men over the top and, when hit by fire, to have stayed on his feet, drawn his revolver and called for redoubled effort. He was hit again but not brought down until a third machine-gun burst. His body was never found. Also on the first day, three of the Hearts players – Harry Wattie, Duncan Currie and Ernie Ellis – died. Four days later, Donald Bell saved many British lives by attacking a machine-gun position under heavy fire. He was awarded the Victoria Cross. And he, too, was to be killed, a year later, while carrying out a similar act of extreme valour. The Somme claimed Willie Jonas of Clapton Orient, who died instantly when clambering out of a trench. His last words were posted home by his team-mate and boyhood friend Richard McFadden: 'Goodbye, Mac. Best of luck, special love to my sweetheart Mary Jane and best regards to the lads at Orient.' McFadden survived only until October when a shell hit him. Another Orient player, George Scott, was fatally wounded and taken prisoner. Roose was awarded the Military Medal in August but in October he was dead. Even Tull, who recovered from shell-shock after the Somme to fight in a sixth major battle, was to die, late in the war, though not quite as tragically late as Bernard Vann.

CHAPMAN'S WAR

The task of making weaponry for the front was too much for the Arsenal alone – the real Arsenal, the one that stayed at Woolwich while the football club moved – and so factories had to be built. A vast operation for the filling of shells with explosive grew across 400 acres of former farmland at Barnbow on the outskirts of Leeds, and that was where Herbert Chapman came into the national effort in 1916.

A salary was negotiated that enabled him to leave Leeds City – he remained a 'consultant' to the club – and become a senior manager of this vast enterprise, which was not only to employ 16,000 people, all but 1,000 of them women or girls, but to have a farm with dairy, abattoir and butchery, an electricity sub-station and medical and dental centres. It was hard and unhealthy work but many of the women, who became known as 'canaries' because their skin turned yellow with prolonged exposure to TNT, were glad of wages that enabled them to leave domestic service. Danger was inevitable. In December 1916 the first of three serious accidents took place at Barnbow, killing 35 women, and Chapman had to keep production moving in these tragic circumstances. Among his ideas was incentivised pay. By the end of the war, Barnbow had sent more than half a million tons of munitions to the front, at a cost substantially lower than other factories had achieved.

It was only a few months after Chapman started at Barnbow that his brother Harry died. Harry had been moved from Kiveton Park to a nursing home in Hampshire but Herbert recognised that his fight against tuberculosis was being lost and drove him back north to stay with himself, Annie and the children at their home in the pleasant suburb of Oakwood, next to Roundhay Park. Harry died in September, leaving three children to be taken in because his wife had died a year earlier. Herbert and Annie decided to take care of the eldest, Harry Jr, who was in his teens (he eventually found his way into football management, taking charge of Shrewsbury Town for a season after the Second World War). Herbert had done everything he could to make his brother's last months comfortable. These were such sombre times that he must have leant heavily on the Christian faith with which he had grown up and which was never to leave him.

Prayers for those at the front must, to many, have seemed vain to the point of emptiness. The heroism and the horror went on. Roose, despite suffering from trench foot, a fungal infection that thrived in the cold and unhygienic mud, ran full pelt at the German trenches firing his gun; his body was among those never found. Fred Wall wrote later that it had been his final impetuous dash (the long-serving FA secretary and former Royal Engineer had a gift for the brutally pithy, as Hogan was to discover when he returned to England at the end of the war). Some bodies came home in disgrace and that of Bob Whiting, a goalkeeper with Chelsea and Brighton, might have been one of them, for, having seen action in 1916, he could not face a return from leave. Arrested and charged with desertion, he stood trial in France. He might have faced a firing squad but the tribunal offered an opportunity to return to the front. Two months later, while assisting a comrade under fire, he was killed by the Germans. As winter turned to spring the toll included Eddie Latheron, whose goals had helped Blackburn to be champions in 1914, and Sandy Turnbull, of Manchester United; he would not live to receive a pardon or even have, like 'Knocker' West, the dubious privilege of his dismal day in court.

Walter Tull still had a year to live. And it proved a magnificent year, one that merited a place in the history of not just football but British society.

His father had come from Barbados and settled in Folkestone, Kent, where he worked as a carpenter and married an English girl. But both died when Walter and his brother Edward were young and the boys were sent to an orphanage in Bethnal Green, London. Despite their disadvantages, they were to achieve much. Edward, after being adopted by a family in Glasgow, became the first person of mixed race to qualify as a dentist in Britain while Walter made his mark on football, overcoming difficulties at Tottenham which included crowd abuse on away grounds and improving so sharply after Chapman signed him for Northampton that the mighty Rangers were reputed to be on the verge of taking him to Scotland. Instead he had answered Kitchener's call and enlisted in the Football Battalion. He was the first Northampton player to join up. But that was only one of his firsts. Tull had risen to sergeant by the time of the Somme and fought there from the start, only to encounter his shell-induced illness in December and be sent home. But he had convinced senior officers of a greater potential and, instead of returning to France, he was directed to an officer training school in Scotland. Despite military regulations forbidding 'negroes' or 'mulattos' from exercising command in the British Army, he was commissioned as a second lieutenant in the late spring of 1917.

He was sent to Italy, where the going was hideously tough. The Italians had joined Britain and its allies in the hope of gaining territory but soon became deeply involved in trench warfare with Austro-Hungary. In one day towards the end of 1916, some 10,000 soldiers were killed in the Dolomites by avalanches alone. Among the hundreds of thousands lost before the end of the war were, inevitably, footballers and those from Genoa were to include Luigi Ferraris. Tull and his men arrived in the spring of 1917 and he was soon cited for 'gallantry and coolness' in leading a night raid across the fast-flowing Piave river. Further action saw him recommended for a Military Cross. He stayed in Italy until the following year, the last of the war, when he was transferred to France and gave his final service in the spring offensive. He had started to fight in the first Battle of the Somme and died in the second. Despite repeated attempts to recover his body, enemy fire forced his men back. But there is a memorial to Walter Tull in a garden of remembrance at Northampton Town's Sixfields Stadium, with an epitaph written by Phil Vasili, the author of a history of black footballers in Britain. It describes him as 'a man, though rendered breathless in his prime, whose strong heart still beats loudly'.

Imagine the pride and sorrow of Chapman as Tull's story became known. Imagine his thoughts as Spiers, once captain of Leeds City with a key role in the push towards the First Division, had been awarded the Military Medal for bravery at Arras in April 1917 only to die at Passchendaele four months later. Imagine how Chapman had felt about the loss of his first Leeds skipper, Lintott. As the Americans' effect on the conflict began to tell, the Germans were forced further and further back and still heroic deeds were required. With exactly six weeks of the war to go, Bernard Vann, now an acting lieutenant colonel in the Sherwood Foresters, led his men through heavy fire and proceeded, alone, to rush a field gun, killing three enemy soldiers. He won the Victoria Cross but never received it personally because, three days later, a sniper picked him off. And then the Germans had surrendered and were signing a peace treaty. It was 11 a.m. on the eleventh day of the eleventh month and all, at last, was quiet on the Western Front.

BANNED FOR LIFE

Two months later, in Munich, the German Workers' Party was formed. It had few members but the defeated nation's government, sensitive to reaction to the Versailles treaty, had asked the army to keep an eye on any potential boat-rocking and so a young corporal, who had been wounded and decorated at the

Somme but was now assigned to intelligence duties, was sent to an early meeting. It was unashamedly anti-Jewish but the corporal didn't mind that; his objection was to the poor quality of argument, as he saw it, being put up by some academic during the course of a debate about how to curb capitalism. He intervened so impressively that an invitation to join followed. Upon acceptance, he became the fifty-fifth member of the German Workers' Party. His name was Adolf Hitler and by the end of 1920 his oratorical skills had helped to swell to more than 3,000 the numbers of what would become known as the Nazi Party. In Italy, meanwhile, Benito Mussolini had formed the Fascist Party. Once more, peacetime could be measured by the ticking of a clock.

Willie Garbutt contemplated Genoa without Ferraris and others. Jimmy Hogan turned his thoughts to home. He had sent his wife and children to England at the outset of war and now planned a journey from the humbled central bloc of Europe to join them. It took him from Budapest to Liverpool, where he found work as a foreman with a tobacco company. Money was tight and Hogan, upon hearing that the FA were offering postwar grants of up to £200, went to London. He was received by Fred Wall, who began by saying that the money was intended for people who had fought. When Hogan replied that he had been interned, Wall handed him three pairs of khaki socks with the observation that 'the boys at the front were very glad of those'. Hogan spent most of his remaining career on the Continent and, after the Hungarians had beaten England 6–3 at Wembley in 1953, Sándor Barcs, president of their FA, declared: 'Jimmy Hogan taught us everything we know about football.'

Chapman had worked except for his cherished Sundays – worked even on most afternoons when Leeds played in the Midland Division – in his efforts to provide shells. And, as Mrs Spiers and her children mourned the fallen hero, Chapman hadn't been taking too much interest in the relative irrelevance of the football club Jimmy had left behind. At least there is little evidence of it: just an old team photograph from 1917. For what the Midland Division was worth, Leeds City won it in both 1916–17 and 1917–18. They also beat Stoke, who had finished top of the Lancashire Division in the second of those seasons, over two legs in a play-off for the unofficial championship. In those terms, they appear to have fared better without Chapman's direct involvement than in the final season before the League was suspended. An examination of the chain of command that was supposed to replace him renders this explicable only by the quality of players Leeds could use as guests, such as Fanny Walden and Clem Stephenson (Charlie Buchan, maybe the best of them all, played only once, in 1918).

The extent of Chapman's involvement with Leeds City at that time was to become a matter of eternal conjecture. But how influential he was as an 'adviser' is perhaps best judged from the chaos of the succession. Upon leaving for Barnbow, he recommended that at least the administrative side of his job be filled by the assistant manager, George Cripps. But Cripps and the chairman got on like oil and water and there followed a tale of Yorkshire intrigue that led eventually to the club's demise and the expulsion of Chapman, among others, from football.

It started when Connor told Cripps to concentrate on paperwork while he, the chairman, took charge of the team. Some accounts have it that he shared this duty with another director, John Christian Whiteman, which would have been fun for the players because J. C. Whiteman was a singer of comic songs with plenty of stories to tell from his time as theatre manager of the Leeds City Varieties in the heyday of music hall when an adolescent Charlie Chaplin was just one of the 'Eight Lancashire Lads' dancing troupe and Harry Houdini ready and willing to defy handcuffs either side of the Atlantic. Whether Whiteman helped or not, the team seemed to fare well enough. But below the surface lay decay. So dismayed did Connor become about the state of the club's finances that in 1917 he declared that either Cripps went or he did. Cripps blamed the difficulties on a period of illness during which he had handed responsibility to a clerk. Accountants were summoned to have a look at the books and it is hard to make sense of what happened next, for Connor relented and the team was turned over to Cripps, except that the players didn't like him and preferred to travel to matches separately from him. The only record of Chapman intervening in the wrangles is that he is said to have advised the players to be tolerant.

After the war Chapman, his Barnbow duties receding, redirected his thoughts to football and the club he still hoped to take into the big time. By early 1919 he was ready to manage as before. But Cripps was not prepared for demotion to his old role as assistant. Not without compensation at least. And the sum mentioned after discussions with his solicitor, James Bromley, a former Leeds City director, was £400. It was a lot. But Cripps gave it a link with reality by threatening to reveal details of illicit payments made to players during the war; this would be done, if necessary, in the context of a case for wrongful dismissal.

The question of what would have constituted an illicit payment was not simple: at length the pre-war maximum wage had given way to an emergency system under which clubs, naturally receiving much less than before at the gate, were supposed to pay 'token' wages plus 'expenses' – in other words, two vaguely defined entities. But Leeds, with their big names, might well have stretched any definition. At any rate, the club's accounts soon disappeared into a strongroom, never to be seen by the inquisitors from the FA and League who, in the end, took secrecy as an admission of guilt.

Oddly enough, the club seemed to have survived the feud between Connor and Cripps. The chairman said a deal had been done under which Cripps took £55 and signed a confidentiality agreement while handing over the accounts, chequebooks and letters to the club's solicitor, William Clarke, who had locked them away. Cripps's solicitor, Bromley, confirmed the handover but said it was on condition that the club donated £50 to Leeds Infirmary; whether this was in addition to or instead of the £55 settlement with Cripps was not specified. So Cripps may have appeared to fade from the scene as Herbert Chapman prepared his players for the 1919–20 season and the resumption of the League, out of whose Second Division his club aspired to bound.

But another of Bromley's clients now advanced to the centre of the stage.

Charlie Copeland was a full-back with a belief in his negotiating power that the club – whether represented by Connor or Chapman as the contracts were sorted out for the forthcoming campaign – did not share. He asked for the new maximum of £6 a week; the club offered £3 10s. (£3.50) for weeks when he was in the reserves, as he usually had been, plus a bonus for first-team appearances. Copeland refused; the club said the only alternative was a free transfer. Copeland now threatened to reveal the details of the suspect payments; he was duly transferred, to Coventry City. And then, in late July, he wrote to the FA, who in turn got in touch with the League. The twin administrations considered what to do and it took them two months. The game had restarted – Leeds had played their first six matches, winning three and drawing one – when club officials were called to a commission of inquiry in Manchester. They were ordered by Charles Clegg, chairman of the FA and of the commission, which also featured 'Honest John' McKenna, the League president, to produce the relevant documents for the financial years from 1916 to 1918. William Clarke, on the club's behalf, declared that these could not be made available.

No reason was given. A deadline of 10 days was set for their provision and, during that time, Leeds drew at home with Wolverhampton and then went to Molineux and beat the same opponents 4–2 with Billy McLeod, back from Bradford, scoring a hat-trick. It was the last match Leeds City ever played. Because of a rail strike, they travelled by charabanc (a basic form of early motor coach, often used for outings to the seaside or horse-racing) and returned in a state of high-spirited ignorance. Chapman, if he suspected how firmly the authorities were to act, transmitted little of his anxiety. And then the club vanished. Leeds City were thrown out of the Second Division in favour of Port Vale, who fulfilled their remaining 34 fixtures, finishing in mid-table. Connor and his fellow directors were banned from football for life – and Chapman, too, even though he protested to the FA that he had been absent at Barnbow during the time of the alleged payments.

The early indications about his last Leeds team were that they would have finished in the top four or five without getting close to the second of the promoted sides, Huddersfield, let alone the emphatic champions, Walden's Tottenham. It was academic. The club had been disbanded and the players, along with the club's kit and equipment and even a billiard table, auctioned at the Metropole Hotel. McLeod fetched the top price of £1,250, paid by Notts County, others went for a few hundred; Lincoln City picked up Francis Chipperfield for £100. A local-paper headline gave the club a fitting farewell: 'Going, Going, Gone!' Within a few weeks, however, Leeds City's reserve fixtures had been taken over by a new club called Leeds United.

The thoughts of Frank Scott-Walford can only be imagined. He had got back into the game, but at the wrong place – the perennially failing football state known as Coventry City – and time. He took over their Southern League Second Division team in 1914 and, after steering them to fifth place out of 13, lost his job as the club was wound up. Again Scott-Walford was owed money: £100. At least at Leeds City he had enjoyed a farewell dinner and been presented with a silver flower bowl. He carried his memories to the grave in 1935.

The questions about Leeds City remained. Why was the club allowed to die? Why were those documents not provided? Was it to protect Connor and his fellow directors? Was it part of whatever deal was struck with Cripps? Was it to protect players who had received illicit payments? Or did it suit all concerned? Perhaps it would be carrying conspiracy theory too far to point out that, within a couple of years, Leeds had a League club again, the League went into the post-war period looking clean and tough – 'We will have no nonsense,' said 'Honest John' – and the players, from Stephenson and Buchan to the humble Charlie Copeland, played on. Copeland had one season with a reconstituted Coventry, who had been elected to the Second Division and stayed out of its bottom two only after colluding with Bury – according to an inquiry that slapped a life ban on their chairman and other officials three years later – to obtain a win in their final fixture. While Coventry so shamefully avoided relegation, Copeland submitted himself to it by joining Merthyr Town of the new Third Division, where he had a handful of matches and retired at the age of 32.

Whoever took final charge of the documents never revealed their secrets and therefore the questions eternally linger. The morality of the affair is hardly worth judging, given the background against which it took place: the hypocrisy born of the game's initial refusal to accept professionalism; its prolongation by the maximum wage, whose good intentions were constantly undermined by the wish of one club to pay a little more for a player also coveted by a rival. The late Dick Roose had not been the first to mock the futility of the authorities' attempts to check expenses, nor was he the last. Some players had phoney jobs on the side. Illicit payments were rife and McKenna all but conceded as much a few years later when he said: 'Perhaps others have escaped being found guilty of malpractices.' The apparent harshness of Leeds City's punishment could have been ascribed to a general feeling that overpayment was more truly reprehensible during the war.

Chapman may not have been guilty at all. Before the war he may have behaved according to his conscience – as adapted to the demands of his chosen profession. During the war he may have done nothing at all. He was certainly innocent in the technical sense, for Leeds City were punished not for making illegal payments but for failing to provide documents and Chapman had no power to override his employer by doing this.

And yet there was the photograph from 1917. It was part of a series of official team pictures taken at the start of each season. The early ones show Chapman and his faithful trainer, Dick Murrell, at the ends of the standing row, each in a suit with Chapman further distinguished by his oddly frivolous choice of headwear: a boater. He then changes to a bowler. He is missing in 1916–17, his place taken by Cripps, but returns in 1917–18, joined by not only Cripps and Murrell but Connor, Whiteman and the other directors. He is wearing a felt homburg now, but the sartorial detail matters less than Chapman's presence among the chevron shirts at the start of the second Midland Division season: slap-bang in the middle of the period in which the commission was assured he had too much on his plate at Barnbow to devote time to Leeds City's affairs. Maybe he just popped in for the photograph – who knows? At any rate, his appeal having been rejected by the FA, he appeared to take banishment on the chin and started looking for work outside football.

GAP YEAR

TAKING STOCK

It was coming up for Christmas 1919. Annie had given birth to the Chapmans' fourth child, Joyce, six months earlier and the boys had become boarders at St Peter's in York, a school so old that Guy Fawkes had attended as a pupil (out of respect for his memory, 5 November always came and went without blazing effigies). Herbert reviewed the family budget and, while there were savings that would last for a while, at least one unpalatable decision was made; Ken stayed at the school while Bruce, the younger and less able son, was temporarily withdrawn. Herbert was not to be unemployed for long and he had more than his engineering qualifications and experience in football – no great stigma seems to have attached – to thank.

At Barnbow he had come to the attention of Joseph Watson, an industrialist of such weight that he vied with William Lever for supremacy in the soap market. Watson had been asked by the government to help to establish and operate Barnbow. He had also started, with Lever, a factory to produce margarine, supplies of which the government was anxious to maintain, and all this would be recognised by his elevation to the peerage in the new year list of 1922. Watson had been Baron Manton for little more than a year when he died from a heart attack while fox-hunting. But late in 1919 he needed a good manager for the Olympia Oil and Cake Works at Selby, 22 miles to the east of Leeds. Chapman moved the family there upon his appointment as 'superintendent of labour'.

A year later, he was out of work again, but it had been a refreshing year at Selby. The world had changed and there had been time to think about matters other than football; under the terms of his ban, he was not technically allowed even to be a spectator. There was plenty to think about, too, much of it gravely. Herbert's brother John had been prominent in the efforts to repair the morale of Kiveton Park and Wales. When the memorial to the dead of the twin communities was erected, 52 names were engraved on it. The plaque on a wall of the colliery offices listed 61 miners, some of whom had lived outside the parish boundaries.

Miners had been in great demand because so much of the war was conducted below ground level. Walter Blackwell, a renowned tunneller, was one. He had enlisted along with 88 other young men at a meeting in St John's Rooms, the local church hall, where recruiting sergeants dispensed tots of rum to discourage last-minute wavering. Then Blackwell and his fellow recruits had walked through Kiveton to the railway station, led by the village band. They had trained at Winchester before being taken across the Channel in July 1915. There they had lived the hell described so vividly in Sebastian Faulks's *Birdsong* and other terrifying novels. Herbert Chapman would have known Blackwell, who loved his sport and played for both the cricket and football clubs in Kiveton. And the shortage of weaponry Chapman had helped to address was mentioned in Blackwell's recollections: 'It was nothing for our artillery to fire about six rounds and then be finished for the day.' By November heavy rain was filling the trenches, which collapsed, forcing men to emerge, in many cases to be picked off by snipers. But Blackwell had survived until the following month, when a gas-filled shell landed among his group of four. Three were killed. Blackwell awoke in a hospital in Boulogne. He had back and leg injuries and was suffering from the effects of the gas. He had a further year in hospitals in Sheffield and Liverpool before being discharged on a small disablement pension and was to continue to decline until his death in 1926.

Another with whom Chapman would have been acquainted was Harry Osborne 'Os' Checkley. His father, like Herbert's, had been an early miner at Kiveton and Os, like Herbert, was a muscular Methodist whose weekends were divided between sport and the church, where he was a Sunday school teacher. He had also followed in Herbert's footsteps by travelling to Sheffield to study engineering. Os had enlisted on New Year's Eve 1914 with Albert Lamb, alongside whom he worked in the High Hazel seam. Five months later, he had seen Albert die near Ypres and less than a month later Os himself had been killed.

It was not just the humble families who had suffered. Asquith had lost a son, Raymond, at the Somme. He had lost, too, much of his reputation; Asquith was no longer Prime Minister at the end of the war, having quit and been replaced by Lloyd George after being heavily criticised over the conduct of the conflict. The dearth of shells that Herbert Chapman did his bit to remedy had been one fiasco, Gallipoli another, and the introduction of Conservatives to a coalition government had not relieved the pressure. Nor, as an opponent of votes for women, would Asquith have much enjoyed developments in that area since he left Downing Street. The general election at the end of 1918 had been the first in which women had been allowed both to stand and vote (if they were over 30 and either on the local-government register or married to someone who was). The election produced another coalition government under Lloyd George and among the anti-coalition Liberals who lost their seats was H. H. Asquith.

With so many young men away, women had had an opportunity to be more than home-makers or servants: at Barnbow and many other places, they had done valuable work normally associated with men, bus and train driving included. Many women were determined never to go back to domestic service. Although Britain had been in the vanguard of opposition to the slave trade, conditions for many of its women and girls could, at worst, be miserable, with the hours almost interminably long and the pay, especially for those who lived and ate in, barely existent. It had nevertheless been the most widespread form of employment across the sexes. And for the lucky ones it could be closer to the world portrayed by Julian Fellowes in *Downton Abbey*, whose fiction was set in the North Riding of Yorkshire, perhaps 70 miles from Kiveton and half as much from Selby (though Highclere, the fine house used for filming, stands in Berkshire).

That the war, at least, had been no respecter of class is painfully illustrated by the story of Isie Russell Stephenson, great-aunt of Fellowes and the inspiration for Maggie Smith's acid matriarch the Dowager Countess of Grantham. Isie Fellowes was born in 1880, two years after Herbert Chapman, and entered a life of privilege. On visits to London from her native Kent, she would be accompanied by a maid. She was presented to society in 1898, married Hamilton Russell Stephenson, known as 'Bertie', and lived in a house with a butler and other staff. Bertie went to the war and in 1918, informed that he would be returning, she went with eager anticipation to meet his boat. He came off it on a stretcher, mortally injured. She was in her late thirties, with a son (he would be killed in the Second World War). Life had to go on and at length she accepted an invitation to a dance. When she arrived, she wondered if she had misread the invitation; was it some kind of hen party? Everywhere she looked there were women, alone, bereaved. Eventually she noticed a few males. Perhaps one in ten. The ranks of the eligible, like the workforces of collieries and the terraces of the football grounds, had been thinned out.

The 1921 census was about to reveal a 1.75 million surplus of women over men. They had to go to work. Or somehow find a provider; advertisements appeared in the newspapers offering lonely hearts to invalided officers. And sex, when it burst on the literary scene, was not entirely ignorant of a woman's point of view. Nearly a century before E. L. James wrote *Fifty Shades of Grey* came E. M. Hull with *The Sheik*. Edith Maude Hull, born in Hampstead, was the wife of a gentleman pig farmer and lived on an estate at Hazlewood in Derbyshire, about 30 miles south of Kiveton Park. While her husband was away at the war she dabbled in writing and, no doubt drawing on some impressions gleaned while in North Africa on holiday during her teens, came up with a romantic tale of an English woman who is kidnapped in the desert by a sheikh. Over a period of months, while he is sexually dominating her, they fall in love. It became a best-seller and the ensuing film, to be released in 1921, was to launch Rudolph Valentino as the world's leading film star.

NORRIS GETS HIS WAY

In football the developments of Chapman's year out at Selby had included the promotion to the First Division of Huddersfield Town – while Arsenal made the most of a controversial retention of such status. At the end of the last League season before the wartime shutdown, Chelsea had been second to bottom of the First Division. They would have been automatically cast with Tottenham, the only club below them, into a Second Division containing Chapman's ill-starred Leeds but for the complication caused by the fix involving players of Liverpool and Manchester United. United had obtained two points from that – and only one point separated them from Chelsea. But there was no appetite for any punishment of United, whose officials, supporters and, in the main, players had, it was felt, been let down by the errant few. In February 1919, the management committee proposed an extension of each division from 20 clubs to 22. Derby and Preston had earned promotion and would get it. Chelsea would be reprieved. Which left one First Division place to be filled when the League resumed in September. Tottenham had an obvious claim to it. Barnsley, having finished third in the Second Division, might have argued for a play-off with Tottenham. Both appeared to have a stronger case than Arsenal, who had finished sixth. But Arsenal had Sir Henry Norris.

Norris was a big fish. Born in Kennington, he had worked for a solicitor before going into property development in his early thirties. He built houses, many in Fulham, where he made a lot of money and became both mayor and chairman of the football club, which won consecutive Southern League titles while Chapman was playing for Tottenham and got into the Second Division of the Football League. In 1910, however, he had also become a director of Woolwich Arsenal and exerted effective control of both clubs. He even attempted a merger. During the hostilities he worked for the War Office as a recruiting officer, reaching the rank of colonel and, in the summer of 1917, receiving his knighthood. In the election of late 1918 he won Fulham East for the Conservatives. But football threatened to erode at least the margins of his wealth, for the war had come at a bad time for his Arsenal project. He had moved the club to north London and started building a big ground. The debt was around £60,000 and even Norris would have found that a bit perturbing with attendances showing little sign of resurgence and the club in the Second Division.

So he got to work on his fellow chairmen, including John McKenna. Norris was a tall, thin man with a walrus moustache and hard, penetrating eyes and, if his aura were insufficient to impose his will, he had clout. He had *Athletic News* on Arsenal's side and that helped to remind everyone that the club had been London's first in the League (in 1893). The fact that Arsenal had helped to sustain the League with contributions during wartime got about, too. He was a master at calling in favours and the chairmen would think twice about disappointing a knight and parliamentarian. It was resolved to put the matter to a straight vote at a special general meeting in Manchester in March. Seven clubs applied for the remaining First Division place but Tottenham, the men in possession, Barnsley and Arsenal seemed the only plausible candidates. Barnsley received five votes and Arsenal eighteen to Tottenham's eight. Norris thus became the first and only man to win promotion off the field. His fate, though, was to be brought down spectacularly. But at least Arsenal justified their First Division presence with a top-half finish in 1919–20. Tottenham joined them after winning the Second Division title while Barnsley fell back into mid-table.

Also during Chapman's year at Selby, Huddersfield Town

reached the FA Cup final, the first since the war, with both sides captained by a returned soldier: Huddersfield by Fred Bullock and Aston Villa by Andy Ducat. Although Huddersfield lost 1–0 in extra time, it was quite an achievement for a Second Division team, albeit one which had just overcome near-extinction to clinch promotion as runners-up to Tottenham. The season was cutting well into May now and starting before August was out, in order to accommodate those extra fixtures conveniently provided by the League expansion, but Chapman spent his summer in the world outside.

There was excitement about new things such as radio sets appearing in shops in the United States and infant airlines starting. But at Selby things were not working out quite as planned. The business in which Joseph Watson was engaged – that of crushing linseed oil into cakes – was not being kind and in the autumn he decided to sell the factory. As Christmas 1920 approached, new ownership and management took over and Chapman was out of work once more. But this time his wait to discover the new direction in which fate would take him was even shorter. It was the middle of the football season and circumstances were drawing him back to the game. He and the family would not have to travel far either. Huddersfield was only 20 miles the other side of Leeds. And the apparent ease with which his return to football was conducted left an impression that, in the case of Chapman's suspension, the authorities had never really intended 'life' to mean life.

HUDDERSFIELD TOWN

BACK IN THE GAME

The ascent to the First Division of Huddersfield Town had been quite a flight over adversity. The club had been formed only in 1908 and in sporting terms the textile town, with its acclaimed neo-classical railway station facing St George's Square, was better known as the birthplace of rugby league. In 1895, a group of Yorkshire and Lancashire clubs had broken away from the Rugby Football Union – partly because it was rigidly amateur – and Huddersfield boasted an outstanding team which had won both the last Challenge Cup before the war and the first after it. The football club had gained election to the League's Second Division in 1910 and even finished fifth, a place above Chapman's early Leeds, in 1913. But its problem was lack of support. Although the chairman, Hilton Crowther, a wealthy mill owner, and his brother Stonor had financed a stadium expansion to accommodate 50,000, there were seldom as many as 5,000 at matches. A couple of months into the 1919–20 season only 2,500 saw a 3–0 victory over Fulham; the rugby team, on a good day, could draw ten times as many. For Hilton Crowther, enough was enough.

He announced an intention to move the club to Elland Road and amalgamate with the newly formed Leeds United. He wanted some of the family's money back and said that, if he didn't get £25,000 by the end of the year, the plan to relocate by 20 miles – Huddersfield lies in the Pennines, equidistant from Leeds and

Manchester – would be enacted. To the diehards' dismay, he backed this up by taking the manager, Arthur Fairclough, to Leeds for a public meeting. He relinquished the chairmanship and his successor, William Hardcastle, appeared two days later at Huddersfield's stadium – its name of Leeds Road can never have seemed so ominous to the 3,000 who gathered – with the stalwart captain Fred Bullock, who made the first of many speeches tapping the community's latent enthusiasm for the round-ball game.

Things were happening quickly. The League, whose officials sympathised with the Crowthers and were keen to see a thriving club in Leeds, called the parties to Manchester and Hilton Crowther put the case for a merger while Huddersfield representatives pleaded for time. They were given a month. Almost immediately the popular forward Jack Cock was transferred to Chelsea for £2,500. It must have been agony for the regular supporters. They had a team looking a good bet for promotion and a ground more than big enough to take First Division crowds – but both would have to be sold to raise £25,000 in time.

Between then and Boxing Day the team led by Bullock displayed splendid professionalism, winning seven of 10 matches and drawing another to move into second place. Meanwhile there was frantic fund-raising. The deadline was extended amid renewed pleas to the business community. Shares were sold singly for £1. Crowds rose sharply, the Christmas attendance of 26,000 for the visit of Rotherham County demonstrating the potential for a challenge to rugby. The Crowthers were persuaded to settle for £17,500 plus a block of shares and they promptly invested the money, and a bit more, in Leeds United, where Hilton duly became chairman and Fairclough manager.

They were to miss out on a great deal. The second half of a thrilling Huddersfield season, for a start. Fred Bullock deserved it more than most. Born in Hounslow to the west of London, he had been with the club since its entry into the Second Division nearly a decade earlier and lost part of what should have been his career's peak to the war; he had been wounded on the Somme but fought on until near the end. Now he had contributed much towards the winning of Huddersfield's battle for survival.

The new manager was Ambrose Langley. He had played for The Wednesday, gaining an FA Cup winner's medal and getting to know Harry Chapman, whom he had taken to Hull after going into management. Langley had not only the remainder of the promotion campaign to supervise but an FA Cup run, for after Brentford had been beaten 5–1 at Leeds Road the team went to Newcastle and won 1–0. There were further home victories, over Plymouth Argyle (attendance a club-record 35,000) and Liverpool (a new record of nearly 48,000), before the first of two trips to Stamford Bridge. Bristol City were overcome there in the semi-final but Aston Villa with Clem Stephenson proved too strong in extra time, winning by the only goal in front of 50,000; it was too soon after the war to expect a packed house.

Huddersfield would be seeing plenty more of Villa. They had booked their place in the First Division. Leeds United, about to be elected to the League, would begin the new season in the Second. Langley, having so impressively completed the first stage of Fairclough's work with Huddersfield, would have a chance to develop the team in front of bigger crowds; the average had already risen to nearly 11,000 in the League and the Cup takings were heady. Langley, however, was not to last long at the higher level.

His team won five of their opening six matches in the 1920–21 season, conceding goals in only a 3–0 defeat away to champions-to-be Burnley. But then they won only one of 12 and, as Christmas approached, were disturbingly close to the relegation zone. The directors concluded that Langley needed assistance. In the new year they resolved to get Herbert Chapman, who was available for work thanks to the sale of the Selby works. Although his ban from football notionally rendered pointless an approach to him from Huddersfield, there must have been an awareness that the FA would mercifully set the punishment aside in order to let him back. It was probably always going to be a temporary rather than permanent exile for Chapman, as opposed to his employers at Leeds City; he may even have received a nod and a wink to this effect before going to Selby. And this seems to have become a common assumption, for, after he had spoken to the Huddersfield board, there was a rival offer to him from Chesterfield, ambitious champions of the Midland League. He was not swayed; Huddersfield had been the first to demonstrate faith in him, to show a belief that the promise Chapman had shown at Northampton and Leeds before the scandal could be richly fulfilled. All that remained was for the ban to be lifted.

Chapman duly went to the FA and reiterated that he had not even been working for Leeds City when any offences took place. He went through all the other arguments advanced on his behalf at the time of the hearing, and, after the FA had accepted them, Huddersfield confirmed his appointment as Langley's assistant on 1 February. His salary would be £10 a week – £4 more than Langley – and he was invited to board meetings, unlike Langley, who never had been. It was not a happy arrangement from the incumbent's point of view and results, if anything, got worse at first, five consecutive defeats including an FA Cup exit at Villa Park. An upturn followed the signing – by Chapman, not Langley – of Clem Stephenson from Villa, whose former club were beaten 1–0 on his first appearance, watched by 25,000. Those people were witnessing the start of the greatest era in the club's history, one that would fill a Prime Minister with such pride in his Huddersfield origins that he, Harold Wilson, carried a photograph of Chapman's team in his wallet throughout his time in 10 Downing Street.

Seven wins in the final 10 matches, starting with Stephenson's debut, banished the threat of relegation and left the club with an average League attendance of nearly 23,000. During that concluding phase of the 1920–21 season Langley declared himself 'not comfortable' and asked the club to settle his contract. Having been given £550, he went to Sheffield to run a pub. Herbert Chapman was officially manager of Huddersfield Town. To be pedantic, he was, like most managers, still described as 'secretary/manager'. But he was in charge as before and, while his relationship with the board might not always have been as simple as with Darnell's Northampton Town, he was more than capable of working his wiles on the directors when cash was needed for players.

Operation Stephenson had been conducted with typical craft on several fronts. Chapman told the board the team was not short of promise but lacked an experienced head. Stephenson was the man he had in mind: at 31, not the youngest inside-forward in the League but a goalscorer, still averaging one every three matches, as well as playmaker whose passes were 'as sweet as stolen kisses' (the author of that phrase remains, sad to say, anonymous) and very clever at beating the prevalent offside trap by staying just in his own half until the ball was sent forward: in other words a master of Chapman's counter-attacking game. Chapman had wanted to build a team around him at Leeds but Stephenson had gone back to Villa after the war. Now, however, Villa had a rising star in Billy Walker; they were also known to be tired of vainly attempting to persuade Stephenson, who was from a mining family, to move to the Midlands from his native County Durham. Chapman did further homework by paying a call on George Stephenson, Clem's much younger brother, who had been a teenage reserve at Leeds City when the club closed. Villa had paid £250 for George at the Metropole Hotel sale and reunited him with Clem and another brother, Jimmy. He was out on loan at Stourbridge of the Birmingham and District League. Chapman went to see him and returned with a conviction that now was the time to bid for Clem.

One of his tactics in dealing with the directors was to give them a list of players who might fill a particular position, putting forward the name of the one he truly wanted at the opportune moment, sometimes the very end. In the case of Stephenson he went straight to the one name on his list. The chairman was now Joseph Barlow, who, with his fellow directors, may have reckoned Chapman over-optimistic in suggesting a move for such a big name. But Villa quoted a price. It was £4,000: only £600 below the British record and much more than Huddersfield had paid before. But crowds were hinting at potential again – 30,000 had seen the visit of Newcastle – and the coffers were duly opened.

A second signing was almost as significant, for Sam Wadsworth, who came in to replace the ageing Fred Bullock at left-back, also won a lot at Leeds Road, proving extraordinary value for £1,600; he had gone to war at 19 and returned, physically and psychologically damaged, to be released by Blackburn, but had rebuilt his career at Nelson and was eventually to become England captain.

At least Bullock had received international recognition. He had been picked for England at the age of 32 against Ireland in October, taking part in a 2–0 victory at Roker Park, Sunderland. Bullock also made 31 League and Cup appearances in that 1920–21 season but fitness problems took their toll and he gave way to Wadsworth for the concluding matches. Bullock was never to play again. He became landlord of the Slubbers Arms on Halifax Old Road.

That season the League title went to Burnley and the Cup to Tottenham. They, having beaten Wolves, received the trophy from George V, who, though his natural sporting preference was to shoot birds and animals, had become the first monarch to attend a final in 1914: evidence that football's place in society had healthily survived the war, even though times were hard and unemployment about to reach two million in June, double the figure of a few months earlier. Football reflected this by reducing the maximum wage, which had risen to £9 since the war, by £1. But the mood at Huddersfield was buoyant and Chapman only too eager to enhance it by ordering various improvements – a new pitch and dressing rooms for the players and a better view for the press – before taking the team to Paris for a tournament also featuring Red Star, Olympique and Clapton Orient. Huddersfield, having beaten Red Star 2–0, won the final against Orient by a single goal. The party did plenty of sightseeing and returned with a £400 cheque for the club's account and a bronze lion for the trophy room.

Newspapers on the long journey by boat and train back to Yorkshire would not have made entirely light reading. The coal mines had been returned to private hands – both they and the railways had been controlled by the government during the war

– and miners unwilling to take reduced pay were locked out by the owners. The response varied. At Kiveton Park most men stayed out but the colliery still found enough hands to fill lorries that, according to reports, were overturned by angry pickets when their convoy arrived at a steel works in Sheffield. Such was the poverty in Kiveton that events were held to raise funds to feed children and a local pub – the village now had at least one – became the beer equivalent of a soup kitchen for unemployed pit men. There was worse to come in the decade leading to the Great Depression and it affected communities all over the country. In some, riots broke out that summer; there was trouble as far apart as Bristol and Dundee as demonstrators demanded more relief for the jobless and their families. In Huddersfield, some 3,000 marched to the offices of the local authority to call for £1 for adults and 7s. 6d. for children, plus a rent allowance; they were met by the Salvation Army and offered not only food vouchers but left in peace.

Chapman was well off now, his £10 a week up to £15 and a £65 bonus banked, and working hard to secure an even brighter future for himself and the club. A tip sent him to Northumberland to sign George Brown, not quite 19, straight from his colliery team for a fee of just £75 (and what a deal that proved, for 'Bomber' Brown was to score 142 goals in 213 matches for Huddersfield before being sold to Aston Villa for £5,000). As if acknowledging that big outlays for the likes of Stephenson could not be routine, he also addressed means of producing players from within and developing them, forming a youth as well as reserve side and appointing an ex-player to coach each of them, following the style and tactics of the first team, encouraging them to stay solid and hit quickly on the break, using the flanks.

Having taken the first-teamers by charabanc to Harrogate, where their pleasures included a game of bowls, he went into the 1921–2 season with more or less the side that had finished the previous one. Nor, eight months later, when Huddersfield won an FA Cup final, was it to be with many changes from the team who had lost one under Langley two years earlier. The basis of the building had already been done; Chapman needed only Stephenson, to guide and inspire, Wadsworth, to fill the worthy boots of Bullock, and Billy Smith, a goalscoring left-winger already at the club.

The season began with a 2–1 home defeat by Newcastle in front of 25,000 and, although Huddersfield reversed the score at St James' Park a week later, the 50,000 crowd there emphasised how far the Town had come in a short time. Over the season, almost every pair of fixtures was to be marked by a bigger audience on the away ground than at Huddersfield, where the public seemed fickle; a few weeks after 25,500 had seen a 1–0 victory over Burnley, only 8,000 saw West Bromwich beaten 2–0. Or maybe the basic admission price of 1s. (5p), the subject of unsuccessful requests to reduce for the unemployed, meant people had to pick their matches. An improvement on Huddersfield's early results – suddenly they won six matches in a row – had helped to take Chapman's team into the top six. They fell back, however, and, at one stage in April, soon after a 6–2 thrashing at Everton, found themselves nineteenth out of 22, worryingly close to the relegation places.

CUP OF JOY

Both team and public seemed by now to be concentrating on the Cup. Drawn away to Burnley, Town forced a replay and won it in front of 35,000; such had been the interest that factories closed for the afternoon. Further successful replays, against Brighton and then Blackburn, pulled in 28,000 and 32,000 and, when at last Huddersfield were drawn at home, nearly 47,000 cheered them to a 3–0 triumph over Millwall. As many converged on Turf Moor to see Town beat Notts County 3–1 in the semi-final in late March, leaving Chapman and his players to turn their thoughts back to First Division status, to which they were unable to lay strong claim until the end of April, when fate had prepared for them a double assignment with Preston North End, first in the

League at Leeds Road and then, a week later, in the Cup final at Stamford Bridge.

Preston were, like themselves, a mediocre First Division side, but maybe North End felt more secure in their status. Or maybe they were saving themselves for the Cup. They were certainly in a poor vein of form when they arrived for the League fixture and lost 6–0, Billy Smith and Ernie Islip each completing hat-tricks. This gave Huddersfield 35 points; they were all but safe as they returned to Blackpool, where Chapman had taken his players for a fortnight of concentrated preparation for the season's climax. The Cup campaign had started there, the team having prepared by the Irish Sea for the Burnley visit. Now they were back, basking in salt baths and their status as final favourites, having fun at the music halls but keeping fit on the sands.

They travelled south on the same train as their adversaries. They and their supporters knew the final routine better than their Preston counterparts, for North End had not contested a final since the Invincibles prevailed at the Kennington Oval in 1889. Now the Yorkshire folk clambered on trains that ran from Huddersfield through the night, or arranged themselves on charabancs for the long and less comfortable journey down the newly designated A1 road to London. They wore no club colours, by and large, let alone replica strips – those were at least half a century off – but Sunday best, almost every man sporting a smart flat cap or homburg and either wearing or carrying an overcoat. Some whirled noisy wooden rattles – based on the ratchets police officers had used in the previous century to summon assistance – that added to the atmosphere as the northerners took in the sights of the capital and sampled its beer, many no doubt comparing it unfavourably to their local brews. Gradually they made it to Stamford Bridge, where a substantial but sub-capacity crowd of 53,000 saw probably the roughest FA Cup final ever.

Even the Chelsea and Leeds United sides whose rivalry was to typify the naughty 1970s would have winced at some of the off-the-ball chopping that brought a censure for both clubs from the FA (Huddersfield innocently asked the authority to be more specific, only to be told that they should know thuggery when they saw it). The FA also saw fit to instruct goalkeepers that henceforth they must not move to save a penalty until the ball had been struck. This followed the kick that won the final. Midway through the second half, Billy Smith was attacking when fouled by Tom Hamilton. The referee gave a penalty despite protests from Preston players – understandable in the light of newsreel film evidence – that the offence had been just outside the area. As Smith walked up to take the kick, the goalkeeper, James Mitchell, kept jumping in an effort, reminiscent of the late Dick Roose, to put Smith off. Clem Stephenson told Smith not to worry, adding: 'Just shove it in the net.' Which Smith duly did. Huddersfield Town, founded only 14 years earlier, had won their first trophy.

Preston's disappointment may have been slightly reduced by news that neither they nor Huddersfield could be relegated thanks to an Arsenal win that afternoon away to Bradford City, who would thus be going down with Manchester United. Later, at the Huddersfield celebration dinner in their Marylebone hotel, Chapman ascribed the Cup triumph to 'a happy team and a happy board of directors' and certainly, as far as the players were concerned, you could not mistake their bonding – enhanced by those trips to places as disparate as Blackpool, Harrogate and Paris – in group film sequences which involve a fair bit of pinching, giggling and general boys-will-be-boys levity.

Each received a commemorative gold watch and, all told, the expense of Chapman's way of running the team helped to swell the club's loss for the season to £1,700. But the effect of the breakthrough was priceless.

The manager's football philosophy that defence came first could be gauged from statistics still to be completed. Chapman and his men did not arrive back in St George's Square until the Monday, when the crowds reassembled and cheered their open-top bus through the streets. The destination was Leeds Road, where it was straight back to business with a match that afternoon against Middlesbrough, who were beaten 2–1. At half-time the Cup had been paraded before a hoarse 29,000 and that night there was a civic reception at which Chapman promised not to rest until the club had won the League championship. The concluding match was also at home and a 2–0 victory over Chelsea permitted the final League figures to be assessed. They showed that Chapman's team had scored few more than relegated Bradford City. On the other hand, they had defended like a top-six side. This had enabled them to finish fourteenth, a rise of three places. The taste for trophies acquired at Stamford Bridge was further indulged by a 1–0 victory over Liverpool in the Charity Shield match at Old Trafford. But it was the League in which Huddersfield were truly to distinguish themselves, and to continue to ride high, even after Chapman had gone. St George's Square was to become accustomed to victory parades.

THE TRAGEDY OF FRED BULLOCK

Bomber Brown had been blooded in the 1921–2 season, four goals on his six League appearances hinting at what was to come. The teenager got six in twelve in 1922–3, all towards the end of the campaign, as Chapman concentrated on other areas of the team, starting in goal, where a replacement had been needed for the veteran Sandy Mutch, now of Newcastle. Chapman's target had been Ted Taylor of Oldham Athletic. The manager had travelled across the Pennines by taxi with director Dick Parker and, on the way, explained the tactics he would use. He would pretend to be negotiating for Oldham's other goalkeeper and, knowing how popular he was with the board, let them deliver repeated rebuffs before appearing to concede and compromise by switching to Taylor at their suggestion. It worked perfectly and the fee was set at under £2,000: not bad for a man who would make eight appearances for England.

Chapman had already paid Bristol Rovers a joint £2,500 for the winger Joe Walter, who was to prove little more than a squad player, and David Steele, for whom the cheque had no doubt been principally written: the tough-tackling Scot duly strode from the

Third Division into Chapman's team at right-half and remained there throughout the club's greatest days. Another change was made at right-back, where Ned Barkas, plucked, like Brown, from the coalfields of the North East, also settled well. But as effective a signing as any saw Chapman present his former club Tottenham with £3,000 for Charlie Wilson, who was to be his centre-forward and top scorer in this and the ensuing two seasons. But it was not so much Huddersfield's goals that lifted them as the scarcity of goals they conceded.

A modest start left them just below mid-table on 15 November, the day of a general election in which victory went to the Conservatives under Andrew Bonar Law and Labour more than doubled their representation to 142 seats, edging the Liberals into third place. The new parliament was to assemble without Sir Henry Norris, who had declined to contest Fulham East over the issue of tariff reform; he was a protectionist, believing, along with many of the unemployed, that British industry needed a defence against growing competition. This was a view shared by Oswald Mosley, who had been elected a Conservative at Harrow in 1918, when he had been 22 and just back from serving as an officer at the front, but crossed the floor and now retained the seat as an independent. Huddersfield kept faith in a Liberal, Sir Arthur Harold Marshall. But, if the economy and other election issues had engaged Chapman and his players, they were soon overshadowed by a tragic event on their own doorstep.

Maybe Fred Bullock had not truly survived the war; Frank Buckley, an early enlister in the Football Battalion, was later to estimate that 500 of its 600 members were dead by the early 1930s, those who escaped the bombs and bullets having fallen to the lingering effects of gas inhalation or other injuries or suffered from depression. Bullock, who had served alongside Buckley and played for his battlefield team, had hardly seemed diminished when, megaphone at the ready, he hurled himself into the fight to save the club from extinction; but now, running the pub with his wife Maude, he may have felt on the margins of his former life in football. It is impossible to say with any conviction what had been on his mind as the nights of 1922 lengthened. There are even conflicting reports of whether his retirement from the game a year and a bit earlier had been enforced by injury or illness. All that is known is that Fred Bullock was found dead on election day in the Slubbers Arms; beside him was a beer bottle in which Maude had kept cleaning fluid. The funeral was attended by Chapman and the entire squad. The town had lost a treasure. But life and the campaign went on.

KEEPING IT TIGHT

Results took a turn for the better, Charlie Wilson performing a hat-trick in a 4–0 win over Birmingham City on Boxing Day, the time of year enticing nearly 28,000 (only 10,000 had come to see Arsenal a few days earlier, for money remained short in many households). Huddersfield were in third place and stayed there for almost the whole season. In the Cup they had beaten Birmingham and then, after a replay, Millwall, before going out in the quarter-finals, again after a replay, to Bolton, whose Burnden Park housed nearly 62,000 as a single-goal victory over the holders edged David Jack and his Lancashire team closer to the historic experience awaiting at the newly built Empire Stadium, Wembley.

Huddersfield could concentrate on the League and did so with staggering efficiency, conceding only three goals in their last 12 fixtures. On the day they bade farewell to Leeds Road for the season with a 1–0 win over Tottenham, the Cup final took place. So concerned had the FA been about filling Wembley – its initial capacity was for 125,000, or more than twice as many as had seen Huddersfield's success at Stamford Bridge a year earlier – that they all but advertised for support. Little did they suspect that the gates would be closed on an estimated 200,000, with so many milling outside that the Bolton players had to abandon their coach and walk to the stadium.

Naturally many of the spectators spilled on to the pitch, which was cleared with the help of police horses, including a grey destined for immortality as the 'White Horse', and West Ham United of the Second Division soon trailed to a goal from David Jack, who had scored in every round. After half-time Jack Smith made it 2–0. Meanwhile, a mercifully low figure of 22 people received hospital treatment. During the subsequent parliamentary debate, Oswald Mosley, speaking on behalf of Harrow constituents, spoke of 'the hooliganism imported' to Wembley, but the general view was of inadequate organisation and other MPs praised the good humour of the crowd.

For Huddersfield there remained one more match. The return with Spurs was drawn, yet another clean sheet completing their impressively sustained response to a 5–3 home defeat by Villa in March – it was as if Chapman had ordered an end to such frivolous entertainment – and confirming a rise from fourteenth place to third over the season. It was all based on the now-familiar resilience at the back. They let in just 32 goals in 42 matches. Only Liverpool, the champions, were tighter – and then marginally. The signings of Ted Taylor, Ned Barkas and David Steele had helped to form a truly solid team. Of 23 clean sheets (a surviving club record), 10 were kept away from home. This was a side with backbone.

Inevitably Huddersfield were acquiring a reputation for negativity. It had been noticed that Tom Wilson, the centre-half, had played deeper than usual in the Cup final the previous year – not the first example of 3–2–2–3 being used as an alternative to 2–3–5, but a sign of the way Chapman's thoughts were turning – and security was certainly being put above flair.

Not that anyone at Leeds Road minded. Chapman and his board were united. The directors noted that, quite apart from the progress of the first team, the reserves and youths were also doing well. They were again to bank the proceeds of an end-of-season tour – this time the Danish hosts paid £1,000 – and Chapman had been active in the market as a seller of players, raising an estimated £4,000 over the year. Although he took an opportunity to consolidate his position by having it minuted in a board meeting that he alone would pick the team and consultation would be at his discretion, he was later to pay tribute to the directors for their 'enlightened and courageous' work against the conventional wisdom that football would never truly grow in the rugby town.

The crowds must still have been a slight disappointment to Chapman. At times they seemed to mock the Crowthers' vision of 50,000. They were down over the season from 18,900 on average to 16,500 (a drop of 13 per cent). It was, however, part of a national trend. That attendances away from home had fallen from 29,600 to 21,300 (28 per cent) showed that Huddersfield had suffered less than most, as befitting FA Cup holders on the way to their highest League position. The community did its best: a year earlier a bus service to the stadium had been provided and now tracks were laid for the trams. There was a sense of Chapman the messiah around the town and the board must have felt a little as Manchester United's were to do once Alex Ferguson had won his first trophy, especially as the youth development was likewise about to bear fruit: among those who would take the Leeds Road stage in the season to come would be the 18-year-old Harry Cawthorne and another defender, Roy Goodall, who would become one of the club's – and England's – most significant players.

There was already rich promise in the scoring feats of young Bomber Brown. And then along came George Cook. He was another from the North East, an amateur inside-forward from Bishop Auckland who had joined Rotherham County but was found to have been financially induced. The club were held responsible, fined £50 and deprived of Cook's registration. Chapman, alert to the situation, stepped in and signed Cook, who played in more than half Huddersfield's matches in the coming season, scoring nine goals.

As usual, the pre-season routine had involved other sports, with Chapman taking enthusiastic charge of the cricket XI. But the campaign began without the consistency that had marked the end of the last. Having beaten Middlesbrough at home, Huddersfield lost at Ayresome Park to a side who would finish bottom. They also went down away to the promoted Notts County, who then arrived at Leeds Road and took part in a match even wilder than the 1922 Cup final: one that prompted Chapman not to plead innocence on the club's behalf but to discard one of the culprits. Maybe County started the trouble, but Ernie Islip took it over the edge when he felled Albert Iremonger off the ball. This was brave – the County goalkeeper was 6' 6" and so passionate that he once caused a match against Woolwich Arsenal to be postponed when, upset by a decision, he sat on the ball and refused to get up – but foolish because Islip was seen and sent off. Later Billy Flint, the opposing half-back, also went for a lunge at Billy Smith's ankle. There were no goals but plenty of other incidents and Huddersfield, to their credit (or Chapman's, because the decision would not have been made without him), asked the FA to conduct an inquiry, stating: 'If what we served up on Saturday is football, well, the sooner its death knell is sounded the better; may we go further and say that never do we wish to see anything like it again.' Islip and Flint were suspended for a month and Iremonger censured. Islip never played for Huddersfield again. He had won promotion and the FA Cup and, as recently as 1921–2, been the club's leading scorer, but now he was expendable. He was sold to Birmingham for £1,500 and the message had been sent; the name of Huddersfield Town was not for tarnishing.

The team then found a rhythm and even led the League for a week at the end of October, until a point was dropped at Liverpool in a match watched by Stanley Baldwin, who had become Prime Minister when Bonar Law fell victim to throat cancer. Not until late March was the leadership regained and then it became a two-horse race between Huddersfield and Cardiff City for the title. Stephenson, in the weeks before and after his thirty-fourth birthday, had played a vital role, scoring in single-goal victories over Blackburn, Chelsea and Newcastle, and then young Brown took on the match winner's mantle. As long as the defence kept those sheets clean, enough could be done.

At the penultimate hurdle, however, Chapman's rearguard let in three at Aston Villa, with Billy Smith's retort inadequate. The title was Cardiff's to secure. They led by a point. If they won their final match at Birmingham, where the home side had only pride to play for, nothing Huddersfield did to Nottingham Forest at Leeds Road would matter. If Cardiff drew, however, it would come down to goal average, so Huddersfield needed to score at least three. In hope more than eager anticipation, 19,000 turned up and saw Cook, with two goals, and Brown meet the target in seeing off Forest. Then there was a tense wait for the result from Birmingham.

Most of the crowd stayed outside the ground instead of hurrying to squeeze into the trams. In a small room where the results were received by telephone, a group held their breath and stared at the silent black object, its earpiece dangling by a cable. Suddenly the door burst open and in strode a beaming Chapman. The result had reached him and the sums had been done. As if there were any lingering doubt, he proclaimed: 'We've won!'

The drama, which would have made gripping television, had turned on a 10-minute spell. At the same time as Cook had put Huddersfield 2–0 up, Cardiff were awarded a penalty for hands by Percy Barton at Birmingham. Who would take the kick that took the title to Wales? Two players, buckling under the pressure, declined before up stepped Len Davies. His effort lacked conviction and Dan Tremling saved. At Leeds Road 10 minutes later, the winger Ted Richardson, making his only appearance of the season, freed Brown, who ran on to score the goal that won the League. Huddersfield also owed it to poor Davies and his failure from the spot. He didn't let it ruin his career, going on to become Cardiff's all-time leading scorer and putting one over Chapman when the Welsh club met Arsenal in the FA Cup final of 1927.

Meanwhile, Arsenal flirted with relegation. They finished only a point above Forest and conceded nine goals in their matches against Huddersfield, for whom Charlie Wilson got a hat-trick each time. They were going to struggle again the next season and yet, because they were among the many clubs who attracted bigger crowds than Huddersfield, were to end up with Chapman at their helm. Hindsight defines Huddersfield under Chapman as a little like Derby County or – to be more precise – Nottingham

Forest under Brian Clough: punching above the weight of bottoms on seats. The average crowd in the first championship season was 17,100, a rise of less than 4 per cent. To ascribe this to low scoring would be simplistic, for they were acknowledged to be briskly skilful as well as mean. In the FA Cup, they drew 31,000 for the victory over Birmingham but more than twice as many saw them beat Manchester United 3–0 at Old Trafford and even Burnley, a town of even more modest size, mustered 55,000 for the despatching of Chapman's team from the game's oldest and most popular competition.

The season ended with Ramsay MacDonald the first Labour Prime Minister, his party having started to move the Liberals to the side of the political stage, and Mussolini's fascists swept to power in Italy. Mussolini was to use football as a symbol of Italy's vigour but, for the moment, it was an Englishman who organised it best there, Willie Garbutt supervising a second successive title triumph with Genoa despite taking time off to help Vittorio Pozzo to prepare the national team for the 1924 Olympics. Meanwhile, Jimmy Hogan preached his progressive gospel in Austria, Hungary and Switzerland. Hogan was to make quite a mark in Germany, too. There, Hitler was making less steady progress than Mussolini. He had no trouble pulling 50,000 crowds amid the hyperinflation and panic of the Weimar Republic but an attempt at revolution in Munich led to his arrest and sentence to five years for treason; he was to serve less than nine months and the subsequent publication of *Mein Kampf* emphasised that he had not wasted the time in futile contemplation.

SAME AGAIN

The first Huddersfield championship proved that Chapman's methods worked. While it was the Cup that captured the public's imagination, the League was the true test and in 1924–5 Huddersfield set out to emulate Preston's Invincibles, Aston Villa, The Wednesday and Liverpool by retaining the title. Along the way they would experience the frisson of a rather special local derby: one against the phoenix that had arisen from the ashes of Leeds City.

Arthur Fairclough, having left Chapman a few key men – Wilson and Watson at half-back, Smith for the wing – had assembled a Leeds United good enough to win the Second Division championship while Huddersfield were winning the First. He could not elicit much from the directors in the way of a budget for reinforcements, however, and Leeds were struggling. Yet Elland Road held 42,000 when Huddersfield drew there in September – and the return fixture, admittedly in bitter January, was to draw only 10,500, an extraordinarily small crowd for champions and title contenders, to Leeds Road. Huddersfield were nevertheless to remain the more successful club, despite the greater population of Leeds, until long after the Second World War. Leeds, indeed, were to be relegated in 1927, after which Fairclough resigned.

Such was Chapman's confidence in his squad that he had made few changes in the summer of 1924. The reserves and youths had won their respective competitions and merited encouragement. But the right wing had no occupant as reliable as Billy Smith on the left and so Chapman signed Joey Williams for £2,000 from Rotherham County (by now Fanny Walden was 36 and on his way back to Northampton to combine a career-ending stint in the Third Division with cricket for the county). The season began with a 3–1 win at Newcastle and Huddersfield were unbeaten after 10 matches. Then they lost to Birmingham. Taylor, injured and unlikely to return quickly, had been replaced in goal by Len Boot, whose erratic displays persuaded Chapman to invest another £2,000 in the 36-year-old Billy Mercer from Hull City. The problem was solved and, although Huddersfield suffered an instant knockout from the Cup at Bolton, they were lying a handy second when Leeds visited and succumbed to goals from Smith and Brown.

A hat-trick from Brown saw Villa beaten 4–1 and next Charlie Wilson took his turn to score three in a 5–0 rout of Arsenal at Highbury. Brown was sharing the burden with Wilson now, competing in a friendly and productive rivalry. Huddersfield were back at the top and on a run of 17 matches without defeat that was to last to the season's end. With three to go, another Brown hat-trick at Preston made them odds-on favourites to deny West Bromwich the title. They needed one more point and got it at Notts County, turning the final fixture at home to Liverpool into a celebration. Early on, Tom Wilson put through his own goal, but Harry Cawthorne, on a rare appearance, came forward to equalise. The championship trophy was paraded and at the end thousands flooded on to the pitch to hear speeches from, among others, chairman Barlow and captain Stephenson. Then the players were carried shoulder-high.

There is no record of a speech from Chapman. He would have been happy to watch his players – above all Stephenson – lap up the adulation. But maybe he already knew of Arsenal's interest. Maybe the tip-off had already come from James Catton. Given Arsenal's low ebb – they had endured a second narrow escape from relegation in as many years – it was inevitable that Sir Henry Norris would be casting around for an alternative to Leslie Knighton and any list without Chapman at its head would have been strange.

In the space of three years he had won the Cup and consecutive championships with a club of moderate size – the average home attendance of 18,500, though 8.3 per cent up on the first title season, still compared unfavourably with toiling Arsenal's 29,500 – and the team was still improving. In the season just ended, Huddersfield's goals scored had gone up from 60 to 69 and their defence conceded five fewer, a mere 28, the best figure recorded by a First Division rearguard since The Wednesday in 1903–4, when there were eight fewer fixtures.

Whether Chapman had spread happiness by organising success or organised success through the spreading of happiness could hardly be judged from the outside, but it was clear that this man stood for stability and good relations as well as the astute application of tactics. He had a head for business and such an eye for a player that Huddersfield were now supplying the national team as well as their own. Goodall and Brown were among several players who would distinguish themselves with England.

One of Chapman's most masterly deals came towards the end of his time at Leeds Road. He got permission from Aberdeen to talk to an outstanding young winger who had played in the United States a year earlier and threatened to go back if not granted his wish for a transfer to England. Alex Jackson, though not quite 20, had attracted much interest and, as soon as Chapman had made his move, Sunderland and Liverpool followed suit. Aberdeen gave Liverpool the first chance to meet Jackson officially but Chapman was in no mood to join an orderly queue. Ascertaining that Jackson would be in Glasgow, he arranged for him to be approached by a private detective – it happened in Sauchiehall Street – and taken to a boarding house to await the Huddersfield manager's arrival the next day. Chapman then accompanied Jackson to his parents' house in Renton, Dunbartonshire, and agreement was struck. The fee was said to be £5,000, a record for Huddersfield (and only £500 below the British record set when Warney Cresswell had moved from South Shields to Sunderland a couple of months earlier), and Jackson was to waste no time in giving his new club the benefit of their investment, scoring 16 goals as he and Bomber Brown, with a sensational 35, led the club to English football's first unbroken trio of titles. Even Villa had never done that. The manager who completed the hat-trick was Cecil Potter, who had come to Leeds Road after twice going close to promotion with Derby County, but the team was Chapman's. And Harold Wilson was pinching himself. He had been five when Chapman had settled in and brought Clem Stephenson to Leeds Road. In the few years it had taken young Wilson to obtain his scholarship to a local grammar school, Huddersfield had not only won the FA Cup but made a glorious imprint on League history.

MANAGEMENT'S NEW WAVE

The new style of management was not entirely Chapman's copyright. Nor, unless the directors of the new Leicester City in 1919 had remembered his early work with Leeds City, was it the model envisaged when they appointed Peter Hodge to look after the phoenix that had risen from the ashes of Leicester Fosse at the end of the war.

Hodge, who had managed in his native Scotland, was given charge of most club affairs. While Chapman was winning the First Division title in 1924–5, Hodge's Leicester were clinching the Second and he left Filbert Street with a side good enough to finish seventh, third and second – in each case above Chapman's Arsenal – under the supervision of Willie Orr. By then Hodge was with Manchester City, whom he also guided into the First Division as champions.

Another for whom the description 'secretary' was not so much inadequate as misleading was Frank Buckley. His rise in management did not quite match his progress to the rank of major in the war, during which lung and other wounds had ended his peripatetic playing career. His managerial debut at Norwich was inauspicious but, after three years as a travelling salesman, Buckley was to resurface at Blackpool and then, in 1927, join Wolves, where he became a manager in the Chapman sense, laying down a style, attending to youth development, making use of the press and even calling for numbers on shirts.

There were others who thought ahead and always had done, to a degree: George Ramsay at Aston Villa, most notably. But what set Chapman apart was that the boundaries of his influence were wide and clear, at least to him; any blurring was a matter of semantics. What he could not demand he manipulated, and an indication of his power is that Sir Henry Norris, before whom the luminaries of the Football League committees had shrunk, submitted to it. Norris covered his pride with words, speaking and behaving as if he ran his club – or clubs, though his interest in Fulham was waning – but knowing from the start that only Chapman could realise his ambition of making Arsenal the leading force in London football and thereby London the capital of the game.

ARSENAL: THE FIVE-YEAR PLAN

THE NEWCASTLE OF THE SOUTH

Chapman and Arsenal converged gradually. Chapman, so impressed with Highbury and its Tube connection when he visited with Leeds City before the war, had told Ivan Sharpe: 'What a chance there is in London. I would like to build a Newcastle United there.' He meant the Newcastle of 1905–11, when they completed a trio of titles and reached five FA Cup finals, despite being frustrated by Chapman's Northampton at St James' Park in the last of those seasons. On the most recent occasion when Chapman had visited Newcastle with Huddersfield, no fewer than 47,000 had been present and he yearned to create such an atmosphere in London, which had only just been eclipsed by New York as the most populous city in the world. His aspirations thus coincided with those of Norris and when, on 11 May 1925, the following advertisement appeared in *Athletic News*, only its somewhat exclusive and precious tone would have raised Chapman's eyebrows.

'Arsenal Football Club', it stated, 'is open to receive applications for the position of Team Manager. He must be fully experienced and possess the highest qualifications for the post, both as to ability and personal character. Gentlemen whose sole ability to build up a good side depends on the payment of heavy and exhorbitant [sic] transfer fees need not apply.' The address supplied was Norris's by the Thames.

No letter came from Chapman. He had been told about the impending vacancy by James Catton, who was also close to Norris and his fellow director William Hall. He knew that Ivan Sharpe was friendly with the Arsenal director Sir Samuel Hill-Wood and asked him to transmit the message that he saw Highbury as 'the place for me'. So Norris had had no need to place the advertisement. He may have done so out of deference to whatever period remained on Chapman's contract with Huddersfield, or a sense of propriety, or in case he and Chapman failed to reach agreement, or all of those. Who knows? But Catton made no secret of his role as an intermediary. It was simply arranged that Chapman should meet Norris, who, understanding that Chapman's achievements at Huddersfield had given him not only the status of a leading player but the market value of a star, offered to double his Huddersfield salary to £2,000 a year, making him the highest paid manager in England. When Chapman told the Leeds Road board, they offered to match it, but his mind was made up. He wanted to tap the potential of London: for himself as a football man, and for his sons, who would have a wider choice of career. Chapman had found the capital congenial when playing for Tottenham and was happy to leave Yorkshire behind for what turned out to be ever. The journey from Kiveton Park was over.

The Highbury he found in 1925 bore little resemblance to the Highbury he was to leave behind in 1934, let alone the place delivered to property development in 2006; Chapman did not live to see the so-called Marble Halls (in fact they were paved with terrazzo) in which his bust was to stand in perpetuity, even after the club's move to the Emirates, because it and the halls and bust therein were included in the Grade Two listing and therefore had to be incorporated into the new development. The Highbury at which Chapman arrived had been built to the customary Archibald Leitch format, with a two-tiered grandstand and three banks of terracing. It was a big ground – the stand held 9,000 – and crowds were already healthy enough to justify the subsequent assertion of Bob Wall, a long-time Arsenal employee and Chapman confidant, that the move from Plumstead to north

London in 1913 had been 'the most astute single decision ever taken by the club'.

It had naturally been opposed by Tottenham and Clapton Orient and, although there was the precedent of Manchester United's abandonment of Newton Heath for Old Trafford three years earlier, the concept of clubs uprooting was no more popular then than when Wimbledon were taken to Milton Keynes. Residents and the Islington council also protested, but in vain; a 21-year lease on playing fields owned by St John's College of Divinity was purchased for £20,000 and Leitch, whose previous works had included stands for Tottenham, Chelsea, Everton, Liverpool and Rangers in Glasgow, supervised the construction of an unusual multi-span roof, with the letters of the club's name, plus 'F. C.', painted on the nine gable fronts.

After the war, with the club's liabilities perturbing Norris – it may have been an astute move to Highbury, but he was unlucky with the timing – the team had been starved of funds, but at least the stadium proved successful. It staged internationals, including England's first at home to a foreign country – a 6–1 win over Belgium in March 1923 – and even more significantly it appealed to Chapman, stimulating his imagination.

As he settled in his office at the back of the original East Stand, he took out a blank sheet of paper. This was going to be a new Arsenal. The club had no trophies. It had been in the League for longer than Tottenham, but Spurs had won their second FA Cup in 1921. Chelsea had been to the final in 1915 and West Ham United taken part in the first one at Wembley in 1923. In the 1924–5 season, there had been three London clubs in the First Division. Spurs and West Ham had finished in mid-table, Arsenal third from bottom.

That it was not entirely the fault of the manager, Leslie Knighton, was widely accepted. Indeed, it was surprising that he had lasted six years in the job, so tense was his relationship with Norris, whose preoccupation was with reducing the debt. Knighton's playing career had been ended early by injury and he had become assistant manager to Arthur Fairclough at Huddersfield, helping to build the squad Chapman took over there. When Fairclough went to the embryonic Leeds United, Knighton was beckoned to Arsenal, after Norris had masterminded the dubious election to the First Division. Knighton's best season at Highbury had been 1920–21, when they finished ninth. He went on to have three years with Bournemouth and Boscombe Athletic in the Third Division (South) before returning to the First with Birmingham City, whom he guided to the FA Cup final in 1931, and Chelsea. Finally, the Chapman connection was to be re-established when Knighton, having spent three seasons with Shrewsbury after the Second World War, was replaced by the late Herbert's nephew Harry Jr.

As far as his Arsenal legacy to Herbert Chapman was concerned, Knighton deserved credit for having not only got rid of the debt but signed at least three players from whom the new regime would benefit. Just as Tom Wilson, Billy Watson and Billy Smith had been handed over to Ambrose Langley and, in turn, Chapman at Huddersfield, Chapman was to be glad of Bob John, Jimmy Brain and Alf Baker at Arsenal. So, given the right conditions, Knighton could manage a football club. Chapman made the conditions right.

He had the muscle to enforce it. The warning about budgetary constraint in Norris's advertisement turned out to be so much hot air (although he could have highlighted the word 'solely' and pointed out that Chapman's work was about more than the market). The first deal was done by Chapman and Norris together. The manager's priority, as in his early days at Huddersfield, was to buy a creative player of quality and experience. Again he placed speed of thought above pace. Charlie Buchan was even older than Clem Stephenson – nearly 34 at the time of signing – but of even higher repute, the scorer of 209 goals in 370 appearances for Sunderland, considered by many the best forward in the country during a prime which, like Stephenson's, was assumed to be over. At least Sunderland assumed so. When Chapman had asked him to come to Arsenal, he had not believed Sunderland would let him go – and confessed to astonishment when a telephone call to the manager, Bob Kyle, confirmed it. He was not to know that in December the Wearside club would break the British transfer record for the second time in three years with the capture of Bob Kelly from Burnley for £6,500.

When negotiations began, Sunderland had put a price of £4,000 on Buchan. Arsenal eyebrows were raised but Kyle justified the valuation by saying he would score 20 goals for Arsenal in the ensuing season. Norris responded by offering £2,000 plus £100 a goal and Sunderland – wisely, as it turned out – accepted. Buchan asked for a day to think things over and, when Chapman and Norris arrived at his sports shop, agreed to return to his native London subject to conditions. One was that Arsenal would compensate him for loss of profits due to his absence from the shop. It had to be done unofficially – in other words, against FA and League regulations. But it was done and in this case, as opposed to the Leeds City affair, Chapman's later claims to ignorance stretched the bounds of credulity beyond breaking point. Perversely, this one he was to get away with. Norris escaped sanction, too. The League contented themselves with a new regulation banning such arrangements in future.

So Buchan, born in Plumstead and once a reserve with Arsenal in their time there – he left after a dispute over expenses – became the first signing of the Chapman era. The means by which Sunderland were to get the balance of their money became widely known and Chapman, who always saw football as part of the entertainment industry, welcomed the attendant publicity. The next capture, though the £4,000 paid to Hibernian was a record for a goalkeeper, proved less exciting, for Bill Harper never truly convinced in his initial 18-month spell with Arsenal. But the spending demanded attention. While no one doubted the sincerity of Norris's opposition to 'exhorbitant' outlays – he spent each annual meeting trying to get the League to cap fees – here he was lashing out £8,000 in three months, unbalancing the books Knighton had so grudgingly put in order. In late February he was to release another £3,500 for the right-winger Joe Hulme, from Blackburn Rovers. But it seemed to make sense. Far from worrying about relegation as they had done nine months earlier, Arsenal were near the top of the table. Chapman had repeated his Huddersfield feat by bringing the heady smell of success to a club that had never known it – albeit with more than a little help from the opinionated Buchan.

The season had begun with the atmosphere Chapman craved: more than 53,000 were at Highbury to see a derby. Tottenham's centre-half, Charlie Walters, dropped back and helped to keep a clean sheet as Arsenal lost to the only goal. But it was their only defeat in eight matches. Then they went to Newcastle and lost 7–0. Buchan was scathing at a team meeting in the Royal Station Hotel before the train journey back to London; he said that playing for 'a team without a plan' tempted him to retire and take a shorter trip back to his Sunderland shop. Born of right-eous indignation – Buchan had been urging Chapman to alter the team pattern since the start of the season, when the change in the offside law was introduced – this was, fortunately, to prove an empty threat. And Chapman's response was constructive. He had indeed, for once, been slightly caught out by developments in the game and it was after St James' Park that he realised more had to be done to adjust Arsenal to the new law.

It had been designed to produce more open play and, in conse-quence, goals. Since 1867 a player had been onside only if three members of the opposing side were between him and the oppos-ing goal-line. As tactics developed and negativity lost some of its taint of poor sportsmanship, defences ruled; Newcastle became experts at catching forwards in Billy McCracken's offside trap and others followed, causing the flow of play to suffer. At Hud-dersfield, Chapman had taken the astute counter-measure of engaging an expert in springing such traps – but not everyone could have a Clem Stephenson.

So the FA resolved to do something. In late January 1925 they sanctioned experiments on the grounds of various clubs who had been knocked out of the Cup. Arsenal were one. They, under the doomed Knighton, played a friendly against Chelsea. It was a game of two halves. In the first, a line was drawn 40 yards from each goal, providing an offside-free midfield. In the second, the requirement for three defenders was changed to two. There was only one goal – for Chelsea – but a lot less whistle. The reaction to other experimental matches was also positive and the two-defender law came in with the 1925–6 season. The effect was immediate and most welcome.

In Chapman's two title seasons with Huddersfield they had, for all the wiles of Stephenson, averaged little more than 1.5 goals per game. Now, in the first season of the new law, Huddersfield would be just one of ten teams who averaged two goals or more in the top division. Chapman's Arsenal did it – even relegated Manchester City did it. But notions of more enjoyable fare for the fans were far from the thoughts of Buchan and his team-mates as they licked their Newcastle wounds. Week after week, Buchan had been suggesting that Chapman slot the centre-back in between the full-backs as a means of protecting Arsenal from newly liberated raiders. His thinking was that the 'third back' could organise the offside trap from a position just slightly behind the full-backs. The full-backs, meanwhile, would go wider to take responsibility for the opposing wingers, who had hitherto been policed by the wing-halves. Between or just in front of the wing-halves would be placed one of the inside-forwards, withdrawn to take over the former playmaking duties of the centre-half. This, if immediately instituted, would have been a sort of 3–3–4. Chapman preferred 3–2–2–3 and the variation of it that gradually emerged was to spread across not just England but Europe and farther afield. The days of 2–3–5 were numbered.

It is simplistic, however, to put the change down to the new offside law, and also misleading to suggest that Buchan's angriest lecture provided Chapman with a 'Eureka!' moment. He was well versed in the theory of the third back. In fact he had used one under the old law with Huddersfield, notably in the FA Cup final of 1922, when Tom Wilson's display had led the *Huddersfield Examiner* to hail him as a 'great spoiler'. There had been reports from elsewhere suggesting that the third back was on its way before the law change. Newcastle apart, Tottenham were among the clubs who had been experimenting. Chapman was simply waiting to see what the new era taught him before responding. Now that the lesson had been harshly administered, it was time.

Chapman agreed with much of Buchan's analysis. He moved the tall, elegant Jack Butler back from centre-half and gave the vacated midfield position to Andy Neil, having delved into the squad to find someone who, though 'slow as a funeral', could distribute the ball with the required accuracy. This linking role was eventually to be defined by Alex James. Buchan had volunteered for it but Chapman wanted him further forward, scoring as well as setting up goals. To accommodate Buchan at inside-forward, Jimmy Brain had been switched to centre-forward and that was already working well. Arsenal approached midwinter on top of the table and a sentimental journey took Chapman back to Huddersfield, where 22,000 braved icy conditions to see a 2–2 thriller in which Alex Jackson equalised twice. Buchan scored one of Arsenal's goals and vied with Jackson for man of the match. In all Buchan was to get 21 in League and Cup, guaranteeing Sunderland £100 more than they had bargained for, while Brain got a club record 33. Chapman had strengthened the defence while, through the new combination of Buchan and Brain, equipping the attack to take liberal advantage of the more favourable law. The club equalled their best Cup performance since a semi-final (as Woolwich Arsenal) in 1907, overcoming Wolves, Blackburn and Aston Villa to reach the last eight before falling at Swansea. Huddersfield's relatively early departure from the Cup at Manchester City may have cleared Leeds Road minds, for, with three consecutive wins, Chapman's old team leapfrogged the new. They never looked back in winning their third title under Potter, who was on £600 a year, less than a third of Chapman's remuneration. When they came to Highbury, they could afford to field an understrength team – on the same day, Jackson scored the winner for Scotland against England at Old Trafford, where Ted Taylor and Roy Goodall were among the vanquished – and lost 3–1. Chapman was unable to greet Potter; instead of congratulating old friends on their achievement and himself on second place, the highest in Arsenal's history, he was absent, scouting, searching for players who would take Arsenal to the very top.

They would have to sink, however, before they rose again. Chapman had asked for five years and that, it transpired, was exactly the time it took to endow Arsenal with a trophy. But first they had to find their way to Wembley. That required only one more year.

BACK TO SQUARE ONE

Chapman took the players for an end-of-season break across the Channel and then spent his first full family summer based at Haslemere Avenue, where a neighbour was the 4' 6" music-hall comedian Harry Relph, known as 'Little Tich'. Chapman began his preparations for the resumption by signing a captain. Tom Parker was a right-back who had recovered from a nightmare FA Cup semi-final with Southampton the previous season in which he had first scored an own goal against Sheffield United, then had a penalty saved and finally conspired with his goalkeeper, Tommy Allen, in conceding a second goal. At Arsenal he was to be a symbol of reliability over several seasons: a snip at £3,250. Another astute buy was the centre-forward Jack Lambert, a big and robust 23-year-old South Yorkshireman who would prove cheap at £2,000 from Doncaster Rovers.

It was the summer that began with the General Strike. In London the buses – the famous red double-deckers had just appeared – were driven by soldiers and volunteers from 3 to 12 May and then the miners, whom the Trades Union Congress had been trying to support, were on their own again. They were to remain locked out until November and the King saw fit to rebuke the chattering classes. 'Try living on their wages,' said George V, 'before you judge them.' Those in dispute had only parish relief and Kiveton Park saw its share of both poverty and bitterness, with confrontations over a breakaway by miners at nearby Waleswood to join a rival union. Chapman's brother John was, as ever, constructively involved, despite failing health that was to cause him to have two operations before his death at the end of the following year. He was said to have remortgaged some of the family's properties to raise money for food coupons for miners. Amid all this Elizabeth Bowes-Lyon, wife of Prince Albert, the King's second son, gave birth to a daughter – she was to become Queen Elizabeth II – and Rudolph Valentino died aged 31.

Joseph Stalin, edging close to absolute power in the Soviet Union with a ferocity that helped to explain the Western recoil from socialism, was to announce his first five-year plan in 1928. Chapman had been ahead of his time in choosing such a span, and he restated it at the start of 1926–7. There were four years to go and they involved no further challenge for the League championship. Arsenal had become a Cup team.

They were wildly inconsistent in the League, winning and losing by large scores. The defensive leaks that had been plugged the previous season reappeared as Butler struggled with his destructive duties in the middle of the back three; Chapman made a mental note to find someone more resilient. He also wanted a left-back and got one in December, ready for the Cup. This was Horace Cope, bought for £3,125 from Notts County. Another signing that month was to prove more significant. Herbie Roberts was one for the future; not quite 22, a gangling Shropshire lad playing part-time for Oswestry Town while apprenticed to a gunsmith, he was to be groomed for the key role in central defence. In the light of what he was to achieve, the fee of £200 verged on theft. While he went into the Arsenal reserves to learn Chapman's ways – as at Huddersfield, all of the club's teams were identically organised in order to keep the difficulties of a step up to a minimum – Cope joined the quest to reach Wembley.

It began in the familiar territory of South Yorkshire, where Arsenal beat Sheffield United 3–2. A fortnight later, United visited Highbury in the League and history was made, less by a 1–1 draw than the broadcasting of match commentary. It was no surprise that Arsenal should host the first radio commentary because Chapman, unlike some in the game, warmly embraced the new technology. The newsreels, for instance, he saw as a way of spreading the word. He had a link with radio through friendship with Gerald Cock, the BBC's director of outside broadcasts, and it was a pity that Chapman did not live to exploit television because Cock became director of that from 1935. But in 1927 radio was enough to be getting on with and people believed in it; television seemed more far-fetched.

In 1925 John Logie Baird had given demonstrations of infant television – he showed moving silhouettes at Selfridges department store in London and progressed to vague images of the face of a ventriloquist's dummy – but suffered a setback when, having arrived at the offices of the *Daily Express*, he rang the news editor and excitedly described the medium of the future. The news editor listened and promised to send someone down. The chosen underling later reported an assumption that he would be encountering a lunatic. 'Watch out,' the news editor had told him. 'He may have a knife.'

The cutting edge, for now, was radio and this was under the control – as television would be – of John Reith. Why Reith had been made general manager of the British Broadcasting Company, when it was set up in 1922 by a consortium of radio-set manufacturers, is hard to guess – the young Scot had a background, such as it was, in engineering – but he duly prepared a staff of four, Gerald Cock included, for the transformation that was to begin at the turn of 1927. The General Strike had been influential. With newspapers not available, the BBC's value as a news source had been emphasised. So had the fierce independence with which Reith was to become almost synonymous. During the strike, he had refused to let government ministers use the BBC as a mouthpiece for their position – all views were represented, including those of the TUC – and, when the Archbishop of Canterbury had requested a platform from which to call for a return to work, it had been denied.

Now there began the British Broadcasting Corporation: free of political interference, but with a warrant from the state to produce all sorts of programmes. Reith had little interest in sport.

Stern and domineering, he had a surprising idea of muscular Christianity. Surprising, at least, for one so overtly moralistic, in that it came to involve the bestowal of his affections on a long-running series of young women. He was nonetheless to become a heavyweight contributor to the character of the British twentieth century. And his instinct told him that sport must be integral to public-service broadcasting. He wasted little time in arranging for running commentary, to begin on 8 January with the rugby union international between England and Wales at Twickenham. Where Reith's staff got the name of Henry Blythe Thornhill Wakelam is not clear, but the phone rang and, after confirming that he was indeed 'the chap who used to play for Harlequins', Teddy Wakelam became the BBC's first sports commentator.

Wakelam was a former captain of Harlequins, the club for which both of Chapman's sons were to play. Although rugby was naturally his area of greatest expertise, he covered the historic Arsenal match too and held the microphone at various other events, including a military tattoo as well as cricket and the Wimbledon tennis. He received a swift but effective education in the new art, being taken to the hut chosen to serve as a commentary box at Twickenham, introduced to a blind man and instructed simply to describe the match to him. From that moment, sport became open to blind as well as sighted people in Britain, as it had done in the United States. Football was to continue to grow in popularity with the proliferation of the media. It was another development Chapman had foreseen, however vaguely.

The *Radio Times*, from which listeners could discover which programmes were on, contained a diagram in its edition current on 22 January, the day of Sheffield United's visit to Highbury. It was of the stadium layout and pitch, which was divided into eight rectangles or 'squares', each numbered. While Wakelam described the action, a co-commentator gave the number of each square as the ball entered it. This was the remarkable Cecil Lewis, one of the founding four executives of the BBC whom Reith had been hired to guide. An air ace with a Military Cross who went on to earn a share of an Oscar for adapting *Pygmalion* for the cinema,

Lewis would be hailed by George Bernard Shaw as a 'prince of pilots' and 'master of words', but at Highbury he was a man of few words, all of them numbers from one to eight. This is an extract from the commentary:

Wakelam: 'Oh! Pretty work! Very pretty . . .'

Lewis: 'Five.'

Wakelam: 'Now upfield . . .'

Lewis: 'Seven.'

Wakelam: 'Come on, Mercer! Now then, Mercer. Hello! Noble's got it . . .'

Lewis: 'One, two.'

Mercer, incidentally, was David Mercer, of Sheffield United, not to be confused with Joe Mercer, who would later become an outstanding left-half with Arsenal. The format received mixed reviews and is mainly remembered as the supposed origin of the phrase 'back to square one'. Given that the format was abandoned within a few years and that no use of the phrase was recorded until 1952, it seems unlikely. Other theories involve the first square on a snakes-and-ladders board – this is flawed by the appearance on it of a ladder but no snake's tail along which to return – and the children's game of hopscotch, forms of which truly do provide for a way back to square one.

Anyway, if Arsenal had been playing from left to right as Wakelam saw it, Charlie Buchan would have needed to enter square one or two before scoring the first goal on radio. Billy Gillespie equalised. And Arsenal minds turned back to the Cup. Next was a trip to meet Port Vale. A 2–2 draw brought the Second Division team to Highbury for a replay which Buchan settled with the only goal. Arsenal continued to look anything but trophy candidates as they lost 3–0 in the League at Anfield, but the Cup was different and two weeks later they beat Liverpool 2–0 at home, earning a quarter-final, again at home, with Wolves. This was less daunting than history might suggest – Wolves were in the Second Division – but a 2–1 win permitted dreams of Wembley for only another Second Division side, Southampton, stood in Arsenal's way. Yet what was the nation to make of an Arsenal who could, on off days, be like lambs to the slaughter, losing 7–0 at West Ham? And then, after the semi-final had been negotiated – Buchan and the flying winger Joe Hulme scoring in a 2–1 win – going down 6–1 at champions apparent Newcastle and 5–1 at Sunderland in the space of four chastening North East days? One obvious answer was the state of flux that had led Chapman to ask, publicly, for time. Another might have been tension between the manager and Norris behind the scenes.

Arsenal also lost 2–0 at home to Huddersfield in a match marked by two goals for the visitors' newly signed Johnny Dent and a broken leg suffered by Arsenal's tireless wing-half Billy Milne. Alf Baker came in for the concluding weeks of the season, in which the outside possibility of relegation was banished. But Chapman was later to tell friends that among his greatest achievements had been the guidance of that work-in-progress team to the Cup final.

Training for it was conducted not by the seaside but in the familiar surroundings of Highbury. At Huddersfield there had been the trips to bright and breezy Blackpool and at Arsenal there would be Brighton. But Chapman had his instinct and it kept him close to home.

A FUMBLED OPPORTUNITY

Arsenal went to Wembley as favourites even though Cardiff would have had the sentimental vote as bridesmaids twice over: losers to Chapman's Huddersfield on the last day of the League season 1923–4, when Len Davies had his potentially title-clinching penalty saved, and to Sheffield United in the 1925 final at Wembley, when Davies did not play. Davies was back for this one, to probe a defence that was Chapman's main concern. He had bought Cope to replace Andy Kennedy at left-back, but the new man had been lost to injury, so Kennedy would play on one side of Butler with Parker on the other. Baker and John were the wing-halves, Buchan and the long-serving Billy Blyth the inside-forwards,

Hulme and Syd Hoar on the wings and Brain at centre-forward. The goalkeeper, Dan Lewis, was one of eight players inherited from Knighton; the Chapman signings were Parker, Hulme and Buchan.

As they fought their nerves in the dressing room and Chapman gave his concluding instructions, the crowd entertained themselves. For the first time there was community singing, which became a much-loved Cup final tradition. It was the big new idea. The miners' dispute and General Strike had helped to create an impression of a nation divided and Lord Beaverbrook's *Daily Express*, which was winning a circulation war with the *Mail*, saw an opportunity to address this while (a) increasing its own visibility and (b) advancing the cause of conservatism. Beaverbrook, having served as Allied head of propaganda during the war, was an expert in this sort of thing. The newspaper had the band of the Welsh Guards play for the crowd at Fulham's home match against Reading in the Second Division on Boxing Day 1926 and a brightly dressed conductor led the singing of songs that had been popular during the war – 'Pack Up Your Troubles', 'It's a Long Way to Tipperary' – mixed with more traditional anthems.

It was repeated on a variety of other grounds, including Highbury, and Arsenal's semi-final at Stamford Bridge was preceded by a programme featuring the hymn 'Abide With Me' as sung to William Henry Monk's tune 'Eventide'. Crowds loved to sing and at least one tune had spread spontaneously when the Swansea Town supporters' rendition of the music-hall favourite 'I'm Forever Blowing Bubbles' was taken up by their West Ham counterparts. It had been heard at the first Cup final and the West Ham manager, Charlie Paynter, then arranged for the club band to play it before matches at Upton Park, where even now it precedes every fixture. Whether Chapman encouraged the adaptation of the wartime song known as 'Till We Meet Again' or 'Smile a While' at Huddersfield is not known, but the crowd there had begun to belt it out to new words – 'Often you can hear them say . . . Who can beat the Town today?' – around the time of his second championship campaign there.

The build-up to the 1927 final was organised by the *Express* with FA permission and it culminated appropriately, for 'Abide With Me' was a favourite of the King and Queen Mary. The nation listened; a million were estimated to have tuned in to BBC radio, for which George Allison, not Wakelam, did the commentary. The box numbers were entrusted to Derek McCulloch, later to become 'Uncle Mac' on the enormously popular *Children's Hour*. Allison, a journalist, was certainly an expert on Arsenal – he was a director of the club. A supporter from the Woolwich days, he had edited the match programme and contributed a column to it as 'Gunner's Mate' (Arsenal had long since become known only as the Gunners due to the fall from favour of their former Woolwich nickname, the Reds, after the Russian revolution). Allison had an interesting curriculum vitae. It included stints as greyhound specialist of the *Sporting Life* and London correspondent of the *New York Post* – a rare double – and he was destined for even greater things.

Allison described Parker, as captain, making the introductions to the King, and the bow-tied referee supervising the toss. More than 90,000 roared as the crisply attired teams – Arsenal's deep-red shirts had been kindly supplied by Buchan the shopkeeper – lined up and the match got under way, only to descend into scrappiness and physicality (if not quite the blatant excess that had marked Chapman's previous experience of the final) in which Hulme alone shone for Arsenal. The only goal, which came in the seventy-fourth minute, signalled a change in Cardiff's luck, for they had seen Parker make a spectacular stop on the goal-line and been denied a possible penalty. A throw from the captain, Fred Keenor, reached Hughie Ferguson just inside the penalty area and hurriedly he shot. The ball went low and straight towards Dan Lewis. The blame was variously attributed – some mentioned a sheen on the jersey of distinct hue that Buchan had provided for the goalkeeper, some a degree of moisture, some the challenge from Davies that seemed to prompt Lewis to rush, while Lewis himself reckoned a slight deflection off Parker had made the ball spin wickedly – but the newsreels were not kind to the Welsh keeper in showing him spill the ball, then knock it into his own goal with a panic-stricken elbow. No more benign were the cynical whisperers who wondered if national allegiance had caused him to err on purpose; Lewis threatened to quit the game when he heard that. But Len Davies was a winner at last and the Cup was heading out of England.

There were four League matches to go and Arsenal won three, losing only at Bury and finishing the season with a rousing 4–0 home win in a derby with Tottenham, whom they leapfrogged into eleventh place.

Huddersfield remained above such parochial issues. But they did at last have to settle for a step down into second place. Newcastle won the First Division, falling just four goals short of a century, and Middlesbrough the Second with no fewer than 122, of which George Camsell had struck 59. At Everton another scoring phenomenon, Dixie Dean, was warming up. Suddenly a golden age of goals had arrived. In time, Chapman's Arsenal would be its rulers. But first Chapman had to establish his own power to make all footballing decisions within the club. While Norris was around, it would always be challenged. But Norris was to go. And it would not be long before he did so.

NO MORE MR NICE GUY

A side of Chapman had surfaced in February. His ruthlessness would have been accepted – notably by any who recalled his expulsion of Ernie Islip from Huddersfield for a costly breach of on-field discipline – but the demise of George Hardy was something else. Chapman had never much rated the trainer, who had been the first employee taken on by Norris and Hall at Woolwich Arsenal. Chapman wanted someone less old-school: someone who would develop the players' fitness instead of just telling them when to jog round the track and how often. But Hardy had been with the club more than 17 years. He was popular, an extraordinarily powerful man who sometimes entertained the team at training by picking up two players, tucking one under each arm and setting off on a jog round the pitch. During the war there had been a player, a big ex-miner from South Yorkshire called Robert Benson, who worked in a munitions factory but agreed to make up the numbers in a friendly. He complained of feeling unwell and was taken to the dressing room, where he died in Hardy's arms. Hardy was part of the Highbury furniture. But Chapman, soon after arriving, had asked Norris to replace him and Norris had refused. So the issue had been around a long time. But it was about to disappear. The trainer whom Chapman wanted along-side him on the bench, a crocked Arsenal player by the name of Tom Whittaker who had been studying various forms of therapy, was to take Hardy's seat after a volcanic eruption by the manager that hastened the beginning of the end of Norris and the start of a new era in football.

It happened amid the tension of the Cup replay against Port Vale at Highbury. According to Whittaker's recollection, Arsenal were attacking without much success when Hardy thought he had discerned the problem. The next time the crowd went quiet, he rose, advanced, cupped his hands and shouted instructions to one of the forwards to play farther upfield. Chapman, furious at this intrusion into his domain, sent Hardy back to the dressing room and afterwards there was a row in which Norris's cohort Hall and another director, Sir Samuel Hill-Wood, felt obliged to intervene. Chapman then made the change he had long envis-aged, appointing Whittaker to train the first team and Hardy the reserves. Whether the moment had been chosen was an interest-ing question but Norris was indeed away at the time, perhaps on one of his visits to the South of France, and the task of restoring ultimate boardroom control fell to Hall, who backed Chapman, stating that the manager had authority over all football matters. It was never again questioned and Norris later claimed his position had been made 'untenable'. Chapman, by dividing, had ruled.

Hardy's service was recognised by a benefit match, but by then he had started work at Tottenham. Rather than work with the re-serves, he had left the club. Whittaker was established and, even more than Allison, would become a major figure in Arsenal's future.

Norris, meanwhile, offered the opinion that appointing Chapman had been the biggest mistake of his life. It was not that he deemed second place and a Cup final underachievement – they had been the two most successful seasons in Arsenal's history thus far, even if the team seemed to have stopped improving – but that he, Norris, had been usurped, cynically outmanoeuvred, to the detriment of the club and football as a whole. At the end of the season he quit as chairman. In truth, his troubles were only beginning and Chapman would play a leading role in their exacerbation until Norris was banned from the game with his reputation in ruins.

What had he done? Not a great deal that was against the spirit, let alone letter, of the company law around which he was accustomed to working – but a great deal in contravention of football's rules. When signing Buchan from Sunderland in 1925, for instance, Norris had compensated the player for his loss of sports shop earnings with what later became known as a 'bung'. He had come up with inducements to other players out of his own pocket; again this was prohibited. But where Arsenal ended and his pocket began was sometimes hard to tell.

In 1921, Norris and Hall had been using Arsenal money to pay their chauffeurs. Leslie Knighton learned of this in the spring of 1923 and advised Hall how hazardous it was, after which the practice stopped. Had it come to the newspapers' notice at that stage, a dash of devil would have been in the detail, for Norris's man, Ryder, notionally received £3 10s. (£3.50) but only £3 was ever handed over from the elegant leather of the Rolls-Royce's back seat because Norris kept 10s. for lodgings. It reads badly, but to Ryder it would have seemed perfectly reasonable. As, indeed, would the bungs to the players, which were commonplace in football. Norris reckoned that, with all he had put into the club – much in loans repaid by the time Chapman came on the scene, admittedly – a few pounds for Ryder's wages hardly equated to the family silver. He had got into bad habits, though, and the corner cut when he forged Chapman's signature was one.

Whether Norris suspected Chapman of letting the football authorities know, directly or otherwise, of his cavalier approach to book-keeping is unknown; there is evidence that he blamed former associates at Fulham FC. But he had already made far too many adversaries in football, the FA's Charles Clegg among them, and Chapman was certainly not an advisable one to add to the list. The relationship between them never recovered from the Hardy incident, which took place only a few weeks after Chapman found out about the faking of his signature on the endorsement of a cheque from the sale of the reserve-team bus – imagine how that was received by a man once exiled from the game for a year – and, when the time for transparency came soon after the end of the 1926–7 season, there was no holding back. Chapman had been the fall guy once and that was enough.

Norris, scorning advice from Hall to quit football completely – he remained on the board after his resignation as chairman – rather than answer to the League and FA, awaited their inevitable curiosity. The League came to him first, with kid gloves, offering a chance to go quietly without a scandal. He promised to resign but, before he did so, the FA began its own investigation in response to a lone attempt by Hall to clear himself (Norris must have felt surrounded by malign fools at this stage, for he appears seldom to have blamed himself for anything). The FA inquiry began in July and Chapman refused to support Norris's contention that they had jointly agreed the ploy to secure Buchan. One by one, Norris's defences crumbled and by late August the FA had decided that he and his closest associates would be permanently suspended from football. Given warning, Norris immediately issued a statement that both the FA and League should be abolished and replaced by a more just body.

As a shareholder, he was still entitled to attend Arsenal's annual general meeting, which took place early in the new season, and Chapman was there to hear him launch a personal attack on the manager, accusing him – and Norris was not wholly alone among shareholders in this view – of betrayal. Chapman did not respond in kind. He was just glad to see the back of Norris. Under the successor to the chairmanship, Sir Samuel Hill-Wood, his authority would never be questioned and he could operate, as at Huddersfield, in an atmosphere of trust.

Norris, meanwhile, fought on through his lawyers. The annual meeting had been conducted in the absence of the press and when, the next morning, a report of 'heated scenes and frequent interruptions' appeared in the *Daily Mail*, he was furious. He was especially concerned that his attack on Chapman had been reported – even more so by the information that he had been asked to refund £664 to the club in accordance with FA recommendations. Norris resolved to sue the FA for implying that he had taken money out of Arsenal and the *Mail* for portraying a report of a private meeting as if it had been rowdy. He was later to drop the action against the *Mail* but to pursue, injudiciously, the one against the FA, which went before the Lord Chief Justice in February 1929 and, to the FA's great satisfaction, established the principle that sporting bodies had a privilege to publish – as the FA had in the case of Norris and associates – the results of disciplinary proceedings. Norris was ordered to pay both his own costs and those of the FA.

He remained rich enough but somewhat broken, a victim of his own petty megalomania and football's hypocrisy; even Clegg admitted, as had 'Honest John' McKenna after the Leeds City case, that the punishment had been as much about deterrence as rigid enforcement. Norris did not entirely fade from football's view – he was reported to have arrived at the entrance of the board room of an unspecified club but been refused admission – before his death from a heart attack at home in the spring of 1934.

BROTHER JOHN

At the time of Sir Henry Norris's banishment from football, the Chapman family were mourning: Herbert's brother John had died in early August. By now Herbert's next birthday would be his fiftieth; John had celebrated his fifty-seventh in June. He had been in poor health and undergone two operations since the turn of the year and now he would follow his mother and father into the cemetery at Wales, leaving six children, the youngest in his early twenties and named after Herbert.

John, like the elder Herbert, was a man of achievement. They had had the same parental introduction to principle, the same mining-community background, the same basic education and love of cricket and football. They had shared a desire to help and organise their fellow man and such was the respect in which they came to be held that, when they died, thousands lined the streets, whether of a Yorkshire pit village – the procession through wet streets to St John's church stretched for three-quarters of a mile – or a manicured London suburb. Yet in some ways they were starkly different. While Herbert had seemed to travel as soon as he could, doing the Pennine rounds and gravitating south, John had lived in Kiveton all his life, working above ground at the pit, representing the miners through their union and the whole community at various levels of government from the age of 27. He had become a Labour stalwart but not excessively partisan. An obituary in the *Worksop Guardian* drew a picture of a noble man, 'patient and conciliatory' in his conduct of industrial relations, amiable with political foes and generous in his donation of time to good causes. Few men, the writer added, 'enjoyed so diverse a field of friendship as Mr Chapman'.

On the day he was buried, the pit lay idle. Rain fell incessantly into a blustery wind and yet the flower-bedecked coffin was watched by an estimated 3,000 as a pony drew it to the service at the Methodist chapel and on to the interment. John had been only 22 when he married Hannah, a teacher like Herbert's Annie, and they had lived in several homes before settling in one large enough for the six children: Clifton House on Wesley Road. It had become a family tradition to invest any spare money in property – one theory is that it had started with Emma resolving not to waste Battling Jack Booth's winnings – and John and Hannah bought four adjacent houses including Clifton, renting two to Harry and Ernest and giving the other to their eldest daughter Mabel. At least John, for all Hannah's grief, had not gone so tragically early as Harry. But Herbert had now lost two adult brothers and he, too, was never to contemplate the joys – or fears – of retirement, never to be able to present his wife, children and grandchildren with the gift of time.

One secret that was to die with him was his precise attitude to trade unions. It went to the heart of the big difference between the upwardly mobile Herbert and John, who never stopped nurturing his roots. John's coffin was given a guard of honour by Yorkshire Miners' Association members, Herbert's by Arsenal players, not one of whom was likely to have been paying a subscription to the players' union. Yet his first great team at Huddersfield had been solidly unionised. Clem Stephenson, his keynote signing, had played in a benefit match for the union in 1919 and in 1922, when the maximum wage was reduced to £8, the Leeds Road squad had offered to support industrial action. A prominent figure in the union's management committee at that time was Charlie Buchan – and that didn't deter Chapman from making him his first signing for Arsenal. Buchan promptly ceased union activities, however. Nor did his clubmates appear to have any enthusiasm for a body now boasting around a thousand members up and down the country.

This perturbed the union hierarchy. They were used to healthy membership at Arsenal, where Tom Whittaker and Joe Shaw had been staunch representatives in their playing days. But Shaw had retired three years before Chapman's arrival and injury was finishing Whittaker. Both were integrated into the club's coaching establishment. The union had hardly a member during Chapman's years in charge, despite the sprinkling of ex-miners in the ranks, and in 1933 there was the curious episode when Jimmy Fay, the union secretary, wrote to Tom Parker in his capacity as captain and asked if he had any explanation. When the reply came back, it had been dictated by 'H. C.'. Frustratingly, the union has no record of its contents, but it appears unlikely to have been an apologetic pledge to rectify this unfortunate oversight, for nothing stirred on the union recruitment front until Wilf Copping arrived from Leeds United a few months after Chapman's death.

Probably the simplest conclusion would be that John Chapman was a moderate socialist and Herbert a benevolent capitalist. He once wrote that the professional footballer should be remunerated as a talented specialist – 'he devotes all his time to training and the game; he must be paid' – and another time that he should take what his manager, i.e. Chapman, considered appropriate. 'The players think that they are not well enough paid. That is an idea which we all have. Whether the game can allow them to draw more from it, only the balance-sheets of the clubs tell. The Arsenal might, in their especially favourable situation, be able to pay their players more, but they are simply members of a big combination . . .

'It sometimes seems to be thought that the League is run for the benefit of the professionals. It would make for more contentment all round if it were fully realised that they are the servants of the game and of their clubs. They know the conditions, or they should do so, before they become professionals, and it is up to them to abide by them or – get out. I feel that it is necessary to write plainly on this matter. It is in the interests of the men that I should do so, because only by giving loyal service to their clubs can they hope to make the most of their opportunities.'

Around the time that he wrote that, a boy who had been born in 1928 to William Thomas Hill, a milkman from the London suburb of Balham, and his wife Alice Beatrice, was starting school. It is perhaps as well that Chapman's era was not affected by the revolutionary work of young Hill after he had grown up, become a professional footballer and been elected to the chairmanship of the union, whose title was changed to the Professional Footballers' Association. Jimmy Hill campaigned to have the maximum wage – it had reached £20 by the early 1960s – abolished and a series of further reforms brought about the elevation of star players and their agents into a new boss class. More than once, Hill was to wonder if it had all gone too far. Goodness knows what Herbert Chapman would have thought.

JACK AND THE LAD

Exactly three weeks after John Chapman had been laid to rest, Arsenal began the 1927–8 season with a 5–1 defeat at Bury. They then beat Burnley 4–1 and Sheffield United 6–1 at home and results never stopped fluctuating until after the FA Cup campaign had got under way (when they got worse but were at least consistent). It was that sort of First Division season: most teams could beat most of the others and only five points, ultimately, separated Derby in fourth place from Burnley, who were nearly relegated. Arsenal lost 2–1 at Huddersfield and didn't keep a clean sheet until the draw at Liverpool after Christmas. Meanwhile, Chapman, who had been unable to buy during the summer of turmoil, went to Kettering in October for the 19-year-old left-back Eddie Hapgood. This was a lad with his feet on the ground, a Bristolian who had moved to Northamptonshire because the Southern League club had no objection to his continuing as a milkman. He cost £950 and, after initially understudying Horace Cope, would become captain of both Arsenal and England. There were to be no further requests for Hill-Wood to produce the chequebook before the end of the season.

It was a winter of wild weather and, no doubt, speculation that 'climate change' (as it came to be known many years later) had set in. One day in December saw more than 1,500 people treated in London hospitals alone after falling on icy streets. A weekend in January, when Arsenal were fortunate enough to be in Sheffield taking on United in a 10-goal thriller (United won 6–4), brought floods to the capital, 14 drowning as the Thames overflowed, filling the moat at the Tower. In February various parts of the country were attacked by hail so heavy that 11 were killed. Football ploughed on. The game was resilient then, or perhaps foolhardy. Amid freakishly cold and wet conditions at Blackpool some years later, the Chelsea defender Peter O'Dowd collapsed at half-time with hypothermia. Chelsea finished with only six players but the match was completed and Blackpool, who won 4–0, were rewarded at the end of the season when they escaped relegation by a single point. At Blackburn on the same day, the referee succumbed to exposure along with two home players and three from Sheffield United but a linesman took over for the last 20 minutes.

So the FA Cup of 1928 was barely disturbed. The draw was kind to Arsenal in that it kept them at home for as long as possible. West Bromwich, now of the Second Division, were beaten 2–0. Next came Everton, whom Dean's goals were to make champions; they fell, too. And then it was Aston Villa in the fifth round, 60,000 turning up to see Chapman's men lay on their best display of the season, Jimmy Brain scoring twice in a 4–1 triumph. It was just as well for Chapman, this Cup run, for it overshadowed uninspired form in the League. Nine of the concluding 18 matches were drawn and only three won. There was no obvious sign of progress. Although the final position of tenth was one above the previous season's, Arsenal had taken two fewer points. The crowds were healthy enough in the circumstances – a League average of 27,500 at Highbury – but the Cup was still best for business and another 4–1 victory, this time over Stoke (now Stoke City in recognition of the borough's new status), saw Arsenal through to a semi-final against Blackburn, who won by the only goal at Leicester and thus went on to meet Huddersfield at Wembley, winning 3–1. Huddersfield, now under Jack Chaplin, were also runners-up in the League, but it was an ageing side, with Stephenson now 38 and fellow veterans Billy Smith and Bob Kelly in the attack.

The British transfer record, once held by Kelly, had been raised to £7,000 when Warney Cresswell joined Everton from Sunderland in 1927. Now it was about to be broken again. Indeed, it was to be smashed by Chapman. He had lost Buchan, who had retired at 36 in order to concentrate on journalism, and resolved to get David Jack from Bolton. Jack was graceful and creative as well as predatory, with a knack of rising to occasions: he had scored the first goal at Wembley in winning the 1923 final and the only one of the 1926 occasion. An England inside-forward, he averaged a goal every other match and, though 29, seemed fit enough to carry Buchan's mantle for a few years.

First, however, Chapman moved to find an alternative to Syd Hoar on the left wing. He went for the clever and tactically aware Welsh international Charlie Jones, who immediately displaced the ageing Hoar and went on to prove outstanding value at £4,800 from Nottingham Forest, initially at outside-left but especially after Chapman had switched him to right-half. Now, with the season well under way, it was time to go for the big one. Initially Bolton said Jack was not for sale, but, as usual, Chapman had done his homework. He knew the Lancashire club were short of money. When he persisted, they named their price. It was £13,000 – almost double the world record. So Chapman resolved to negotiate and his tactics, later described by the former Arsenal secretary and general manager Bob Wall, were to form one of the classic anecdotes about him.

Wall was in his early months with the club, aged only 16, working as a clerk with duties that included dealing with Chapman's correspondence. Chapman (Wall was to write 44 years later) had taken an instant liking to him and invited him along to the Euston Hotel, to which a Bolton delegation had been invited for talks. Chapman and young Wall arrived half an hour early and Chapman strode straight into the lounge, where he addressed the barman by name. 'George,' he said, slipping two pound notes into his hand, 'this is Mr Wall, my assistant. He will drink whisky and dry ginger. I will drink gin and tonic. We shall be joined by guests. They will drink whatever they like. But I want you to be careful of one thing. See that our guests are given double of everything , but Mr Wall's whisky and dry ginger will contain no whisky and my gin and tonic will contain no gin.'

When the people from Bolton arrived, Chapman ordered a round. He and Wall quickly disposed of their drinks and more were ordered. And so it went on until the Lancashire lot were merry enough to be tempted into dropping their price for Jack. Eventually it was settled at £10,890. Chapman was more than pleased. As he and Wall got into their taxi for the trip back to Highbury, he told the novice: 'That's your first lesson in football. You now know how to conduct a transfer.' And all done without breaking the law. If Wall's ginger had contained whisky, Chapman would have been conspiring in a breach of the 1923 Liquor Act, which prohibited the serving of alcohol to those under 18. Wall was to remain at the club for nearly half a century, assisting many managers, including the Double-winning Bertie Mee. But how reliable was his account, published in 1971? It certainly conflicted in many details with that offered in 1948 by George Allison, who wrote of negotiations conducted entirely in Lancashire.

Allison made no mention of young Wall. He said that he and Chapman had gone to Bolton one Wednesday, empowered to secure Jack. They had booked into a hotel in nearby Manchester and watched him play in a representative match. The next morning, they had met the Bolton board, who quoted that 'staggering' figure of £13,000 and refused to budge. Chapman and Allison returned to their hotel and decided to treat themselves to a lavish lunch of oysters and grouse, complemented by a fine wine. Afterwards they telephoned the Bolton chairman and invited him to tea. He arrived and was still there when the cocktail hour came, and stayed for dinner, then cognac and cigars. By now they had been joined by the Bolton manager, Charlie Foweracre. At midnight the Arsenal pair offered £11,500 plus an unspecified add-on and the deal was done. After Allison reminded everyone that the player had yet to be consulted, the group piled into a car and headed through the dark and deserted streets to find his house. A further detail by Tom Whittaker in yet another book might as well be included at this stage. It was that Foweracre had lost Jack's address in Bolton and could only remember that he lived near a baker's. At length they dragged him out of bed and he said he'd like some advice first from his father, Bob Jack, the Plymouth manager, whom he telephoned. Bob Jack said they should all meet the next day in London and there the signing took place.

By relating all this Allison provided the only known document of Chapman the bon viveur. Unless, of course, he went easy on the wine and drank cold tea instead of cognac as the negotiations reached their critical stage.

Wherever and however the fee was fixed, and whatever its precise size, Chapman's Arsenal had again raised football's eyebrows. But Jack arrived at Highbury with the team in trouble. They had won only two of their first 10 matches when he made his debut at Newcastle in October. Chapman was to describe it as a 'nightmare' for the new man, adding that the pressure of the five-figure fee and the succession to Buchan had crushed him, but Arsenal won 3–0 and results perked up a little, even if the defence still had its leaky days, conceding five goals to Villa in November, Blackburn in December and Sunderland on New Year's Day. Just in time for the Cup, Chapman made a helpful change, introducing Eddie Hapgood for Horace Cope at left-back. Herbie Roberts was also drafted in at centre-back, at last replacing Jack Butler. Stoke were eliminated by Arsenal for the second consecutive year, by 2–1 at Highbury, where Mansfield Town, bold standard-bearers for the Midland League, then succumbed 2–0. After a scoreless match at Swindon, they overcame this club from Chapman's past – now in the Third Division (South) – with a single goal, only to lose by the same score at Villa Park in the quarter-finals. That was to be Arsenal's last defeat in the Cup for a while.

Chapman had enough belief in the breakthrough's imminence to reject an opportunity to return to Huddersfield and take over from Jack Chaplin. It came around the beginning of April 1929 and, after some consideration, he rejected it. As the *Daily Mail* reported, he had been with Arsenal for nearly four years 'but so much of his time has been occupied by matters of an exceptional character [presumably the club politics involving Norris] that he feels the record of the club can be still further improved'. In addition, he had 'family reasons' for preferring to stay in London; Ken, now 21, was training to be a solicitor and Bruce, 19, making his way in the stationery business, while Molly, 14, and Joyce, 11, were at boarding school in Sussex. Huddersfield appointed Clem

Stephenson instead and he became their longest serving manager. Chapman went on to make the signings that led to the triumphant culmination of the five-year plan.

With the advantage of hindsight, a hint of improvement can be discerned in Arsenal's League form after they departed the Cup in that spring of 1929: three defeats in thirteen matches and a points tally that, if maintained from the start of the 42-match season, would have seen them challenge The Wednesday for the title. In a 7–1 home win over relegation-bound Bury, there were four goals from Jack: another encouraging sign. Arsenal edged up the table, again by one place, to ninth. Even so, the average home attendance suffered a slight fall, to 26,500. Meanwhile, Bolton proved they could win a Cup final without Jack when goals from Billy Butler and Harry Blackmore overcame Portsmouth at Wembley.

ARSENAL: ONWARD AND UPWARD

THE DAWN OF MODERNITY

Although times remained hard for many, and were to get much worse after the American stock market crash of October 1929, this might not have struck the visitor from another planet. In more ways than one, the Roaring Twenties had been a decade of electricity, with a growing sense of empowerment that extended to women. Not only had they obtained equal electoral rights – everyone over 21 now had the vote in Britain – but the rise of the 'flapper', initially on the other side of an ocean Charles Lindbergh had appeared to narrow with his historic flight, emphasised the emergence of a new confidence that women could drink, smoke and, with liberal make-up and skirts shorter than the pre-war norm, exude sex appeal. Music had become more evident.

In films *The Jazz Singer* had signalled the end of the silent era – 'Ain't She Sweet' and 'Blue Skies' were among its most popular songs – and Kern and Hammerstein's *Show Boat* become the first Broadway classic. Mickey Mouse cartoons had started and the short films of Oliver Hardy and Stan Laurel caused mirth to young and old alike. Cinemas were becoming bigger and more comfortable and in them you could eat chocolate; Cadbury's had diversified from Dairy Milk into Whole Nut. Slum clearance sent people to more comfortable homes where they could listen to radio – increasingly popular in Britain regardless of Reith's ban on accents other than 'proper' – and tend gardens. Nor was sport as entertainment just football: ordinary people flocked to the new speedway, for example, and greyhound racing.

It was the dawn of modernity and a greater variety. Things were becoming more affordable – the production lines at Cowley, Oxford, had slashed the price of a small car to £100 – and football had its stars, just like the cinema. The difference being that they seemed to represent their communities. So, for many people, football was not something to cut back on, certainly not for the north Londoners beginning to believe that David Jack's arrival might be the start of something big. Bear in mind that no team assembled in the capital had been champions of England, or even got within touching distance, despite Tottenham's second place in 1921–2 and Arsenal's under Chapman in 1925–6. In fact, that something big had already started.

Chapman had inherited the wing-halves Baker and John from Leslie Knighton. He had signed the full-backs Parker and Hapgood, and Roberts to plug the gap between them. He had bought Hulme for the right wing, Jones for the left, Jack for inside-right and Lambert for centre-forward. That left two positions and by the end of the summer they would be filled. Chapman was not convinced about Dan Lewis in goal, so he brought Charlie Preedy from Wigan Borough to challenge him. In the end he was to part company with both keepers. But the other capture was enormously significant: that of Alex James. In fact Chapman made two more signings and Cliff Bastin, like James, was to be one of Arsenal's very best.

James cost £8,750. It was time finally to sort out that playmaking role, to find someone who could turn defence into attack with the devastating speed Chapman craved. The process had started with the sure but slow Andy Neil, who had lasted a year before moving to Brighton and was now at Queens Park Rangers, and no one had truly carved the niche. 'King James', as the little maestro was known in his native Scotland – for whose national team he had starred with Alex Jackson, Chapman's capture for Huddersfield, in the Wembley Wizards' 5–1 triumph the previous year (James scored twice and Jackson three times) – would do it. There was no need for a friendly barman at Euston this time, or brandy and cigars in Manchester. Just a bit of collusion with Selfridges.

Preston, by now of the Second Division, had signed James from Raith Rovers for £3,000 in 1925 but realised they could keep him no longer. They put him up for sale at £9,000 and after Chapman had got close to that figure the deal was done. With so many other clubs, including Aston Villa, Manchester City and Liverpool, coveting James, the League did wonder how Arsenal had so easily won the race. Their inquiry discerned nothing untoward or underhand. There had certainly been no secret about how the question of wages was settled. Chapman's Arsenal, nothing if not creative, arranged that James should have the footballer's maximum plus an outside job, kindly provided by the Oxford Street store, in which he demonstrated sports equipment to customers in exchange for £250 a year. James was also engaged by the *London Evening News* to lend his name to a weekly column at £3 a time.

He had more demanding work to do at Highbury, for Chapman was asking him to change his game. James was 28 and an inside-forward accustomed to chipping in with more than the occasional goal; 53 had come in his 147 League appearances for Preston. At Arsenal his strike rate would drop sharply to about three a season as Chapman turned him into a provider. It was not an easy transition but in time James, whose nature was to entertain, would appreciate that there was more than one way of pleasing a crowd. He would always be hard not to notice with his deft control and brilliant passing, not to mention his unusually long and baggy shorts, which he wore to keep the cold from his knees.

But of all the gems Chapman unearthed, starting with little Fanny Walden in 1909, none was to sparkle more brightly than Cliff Bastin. Chapman had not known of the young Devonian, just turning 17, when he went to watch Exeter City play at Watford in the Third Division (South) towards the end of the 1928–9 season. Chapman had actually gone to check on the Watford inside-forward Tommy Barnett, but Bastin's skills and precocious understanding of the game riveted him. He travelled to the West

Country and, after City had accepted an offer of £2,000, went to speak to Bastin at his parents' home in a nearby village. Bastin was reluctant to leave City and the quiet life for London and a big club among whose stars he might be lost. He also wanted to continue to study electrical engineering. Chapman, however, proved persuasive, as Bastin later wrote: 'He cast me in the role of a sort of footballing Dick Whittington and took down the vases from the mantelpiece to represent my stepping-stones to fame.' At length Bastin agreed to sign – as long as he was allowed to study. Within weeks of his arrival at Highbury he was in the first team. The fans and the press hailed 'Boy Bastin'. Chapman's metaphor had hardly exaggerated and within a year the teenager, while not literally walking streets paved with gold, would have the precious metal awarded to the winner of an FA Cup final at Wembley.

THE FIRST HIGHBURY GREATS

As the 1929–30 season began, Chapman had all but assembled his first great Arsenal team. They were still not performing comparably with the unit he had left behind at Huddersfield, but the personnel were in place. It had cost the club upwards of £40,000 net and that made him the biggest spender in the game. He had offset a little with sales. A year earlier, Arsenal had received £2,000 from Everton for Andy Kennedy, and Syd Hoar now fetched £1,000 from Clapton Orient. Billy Milne had been retained despite the injury that had ended his playing career; he had become assistant trainer to Tom Whittaker, whose job he was to take when Whittaker moved up to manager in 1947. Milne, a Highlander who had joined the club from Buckie Thistle in 1921, was not to retire until 1960. Off the field even more than on it, Chapman was building a team that would last.

The season began as promisingly as the previous one had ended, with five wins in the first six matches including a 2–0 success away to Sheffield Wednesday (as they had been renamed), the champions. But then it all went wrong again and the new year was rung in with alarm bells; results truly were poor enough to suggest that the rest of the campaign would be about fighting relegation. The problem lay not in a defence which had tightened impressively since Herbie Roberts took the central role and Eddie Hapgood made the left-back's shirt his own – having cost a total of £1,150, they were young enough to see Arsenal through the rest of the Chapman years and beyond – but further forward, where James had not come to terms with his unfamiliar function. He seemed still to be chasing goals. But there was more to it, according to Chapman: 'He was seriously upset by the bitter criticism to which he was subjected.' The service to an attack featuring the expensive Jack suffered and in one 12-match sequence only 10 goals were scored. Chapman had tried the chequebook once more, paying Sunderland £6,000 for David Halliday, who had come south from Dundee to replace Buchan in 1925 and continued to score riotously. At Arsenal he edged out Jack Lambert (temporarily, it transpired), but the conditions were not right. Chapman had to go to the root of his team's difficulty.

With the Cup imminent and promotion-chasing Chelsea due at Highbury, he took a big decision. He dropped James. The reserve Len Thompson was brought in and Arsenal won through goals from Lambert and Bastin in front of a big crowd. The next tie, again at home, saw Thompson give way to the versatile Charlie Jones. Birmingham trailed by two goals but came back to draw. The replay looked a tough assignment for Arsenal. Yet Chapman judged it the right occasion for James to return. Three days beforehand, he arrived at James's house and, finding the player in bed, told him to get up and come to Highbury to start preparing for a comeback at St Andrew's.

The training that followed was detailed and assiduous and must have catered to James's needs because he responded with an excellent performance. Alf Baker scored the only goal from a penalty but the rest of the campaign was prominently to feature Jack Lambert. Was it the signing of Halliday that had stimulated him, or James's taking to the new playmaker's role, or both? Turning points cannot always be precisely analysed, but

'Bravo Arsenal' – note, bottom right, the civic pride of once-hostile Islington
(Personal collections of Lucas Pink, Andy Kelly and Mark Andrews)

Arsenal in 1930 *(top)* and 1932 *(bottom)*: at the far end of Chapman in both photos is his esteemed assistant Tom Whittaker *(Both Popperfoto/Getty Images)*

The Graf Zeppelin looming over Wembley Stadium during the FA Cup final between Arsenal and Huddersfield Town, 26 April 1930 *(Getty Images, Popperfoto/Getty Images)*

Herbert Chapman *(fifth from right)* and England players meeting Mussolini *(centre)* at the Palazzo di Venezia in Rome, 1933 *(The Print Collector/Heritage Images/TopFoto)*

Chapman and G.M. Foster, a member of the Corinthian club who helped to set up football classes for youngsters *(Personal collections of Lucas Pink, Andy Kelly and Mark Andrews)*

Arsenal continued to be champions after Chapman: Alex James lifts the FA Cup with George Allison in attendance after the 1936 final at Wembley *(Getty Images)*

The bust of Chapman, admired by his former players, continued to watch over all who pass through Highbury's Marble Halls *(both Getty Images)*

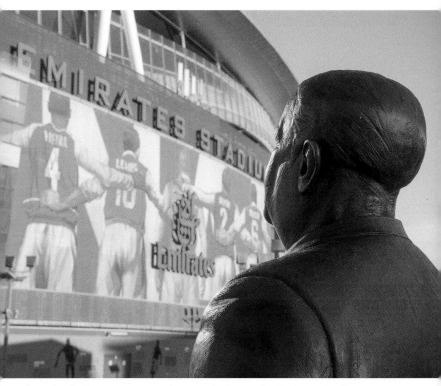

(and overleaf) Chapman's statue has watched over the Emirates Stadium since 2011 *(Julian Deghy for PhotographerLondon.com)*

later Chapman wrote with some bitterness of the crisis James had come through. It had been more prolonged than Jack's when he arrived. Barracking was always a pet hate of Chapman's and he said the treatment James had received had left no alternative but to 'allow him a rest' as the Cup began, then bed him back into the side on an away ground. 'Arsenal nearly lost him, and if the worst had happened, those who made the game a misery to him would have had to bear the blame.'

In the next round, Arsenal went to Middlesbrough, where Lambert and Bastin provided a 2–0 win, and in the quarter-finals they made the shorter trip to West Ham and prevailed by 3–0, Lambert now scoring twice. The romantic heroes of the Cup that season were Hull City under Billy McCracken, the old master of the offside trap. While they fought what was to prove a losing battle against relegation to the Third Division, they had managed to knock out McCracken's former club Newcastle, Manchester City and Blackpool, who were on their way into the First Division. And now Hull faced Arsenal. The venue, Elland Road, could hardly be described as Chapman's lucky ground and here it was that his season – the fifth season of his five-year plan – nearly died. With 10 minutes left Arsenal were two goals down and deservedly so. Then Jack scored one that turned out to be worth his entire transfer fee, for Bastin followed up with an equaliser and the replay at Villa Park saw Jack send a tense Arsenal through to the final. They were glad of the assistance of the Hull defender Arthur Childs, who got himself sent off for taking a kick at Lambert. But now all talk of imminent humiliation had been truly dispelled, for the big event at Wembley would be one in which Chapman above all could take pride, one that would grip the nation from north to south with Huddersfield, still a force to judge from their 2–1 defeat of double champions Wednesday in the other semi-final, pitted against Arsenal. Jackson and James, who had demolished the English at Wembley only two years earlier, would now be on opposite sides. Jackson's two goals had carried Huddersfield over the threshold. And James, too, was coming back to his best.

Of six matches in the month before the final, Arsenal lost none. There were five draws, but the performance that emphasised their right to continued First Division status was against Sheffield United, who were beaten 8–1, Lambert getting three, the reserve Bill Johnstone two and Hulme, Bastin and James one each. An even more remarkable match took place at Leicester, where Arsenal led 3–1 but ended up equally sharing 12 goals. Halliday got four of them, which showed how well the competition between him and Lambert was working. It also testified, however, to the absence of Herbie Roberts from Chapman's defence. Roberts had been injured. His place in the Cup final team would go to Bill Seddon, a former reserve captain. Lambert would be preferred to Halliday at centre-forward. But the unkindest cut was suffered by goalkeeper Dan Lewis, who missed out on what would have been his second final and a chance to atone for the infamous error of 1927. Lewis had encountered a recurrence of a knee injury during the 6–6 draw at Leicester, so Preedy got in. He was lucky; he had failed to make the most of an earlier opportunity to displace Lewis, and had also performed unimpressively in the initial semi-final against Hull. Lewis was disconsolate as the team prepared at Brighton for the big occasion. He was never to play for Arsenal again. Or, it appears, to piece together the fragments of his confidence as a professional performer. At the end of the following season, during which goalkeeping duties were shared among three others, starting with the 20-year-old Gerry Keizer from Holland, Lewis was transferred to Gillingham of the Third Division (South). He played only a handful of times there and appears to have disappeared from the game at the age of 30. He lived on for another 32 years, though, which was more than could be said for Hughie Ferguson, the triumphant beneficiary of Lewis's misfortune in 1927.

Ferguson had been a prolific goalscorer with Motherwell before joining Cardiff, where his feats had continued, and so much was expected of him when he returned to Scotland to join Dundee in 1929. There, however, he had struggled for goals and the jeers of the crowd contributed to a slump into depression. After a training session at Dens Park in January 1930, he had committed suicide by turning on a gas tap, leaving a wife and two children. No wonder Chapman despised barracking and spoke forcefully about those who had done it to James.

The little man in the baggy shorts was in prime form by the time Arsenal lined up at Wembley. The teams had run out together at Chapman's suggestion – a tradition that was to survive – but with the captains at the front, not the managers. In charge of Huddersfield was Clem Stephenson, the foundation stone of Chapman's edifice, and the fraternal nature of the occasion was to be emphasised by the players mingling afterwards in the victorious dressing room, then at a joint banquet at the Café Royal. It was a better than average match, too, on a late April day balmy enough to persuade the King to make a surprise appearance after 18 months confined mainly to home because of illness; the crowd appreciated it and cheered him warmly. After community singing to the band of the Welsh Guards, he was introduced to the teams by Tom Parker and Tom Wilson, the latter now in the eleventh of his 12 seasons at Leeds Road. George Allison was on the radio as usual and about to become the only commentator ever to describe the flight of a giant airship over Wembley. Allison was prominent on the BBC now. He remained an Arsenal director, but sensitivity to bias in the media had yet, it appears, to reach paranoid levels.

Huddersfield were the favourites. They had beaten Aston Villa before knocking out Sheffield Wednesday and, in Alex Jackson, had the man of the Cup thus far. But Chapman got his tactics right and the players, especially the pivotal James, carried them out. There was an early assault in which young Bastin so troubled the great Roy Goodall that Arsenal had three chances, all missed, before James and Bastin worked a prearranged ploy. James had asked the winger to get ready for a quickly taken free-kick. In the seventeenth minute the opportunity came. James got the referee's nod, sent Bastin clear, and waited. Bastin drew Goodall and returned the ball to James, who drove it past the Huddersfield goalkeeper, Hugh Turner.

The *Graf Zeppelin* then appeared, drifting at such an audaciously modest altitude that the spectators on the upper rim of the great bowl might have been tempted to duck. It was not a popular sight only 12 years after the end of the war, this reminder of German bombing raids on London, and some players seemed understandably irked by the intrusion (although a few observers subsequently read Hitlerian mischief into the incident, the Nazis were still an opposition movement at the time and it was not until 1936 that Joseph Goebbels used airships for propaganda purposes).

In the game itself, Arsenal came under sustained pressure but absorbed it and eventually counter-attacked with lethal speed, all in a way that was to become familiar. James, lying deep, tamed the ball and swiftly sent it forward to Lambert, whom Huddersfield's defenders could not catch as he raced away and scored. There were only 10 minutes left. Arsenal's first trophy was won. Huddersfield had been the team of the Twenties. But that decade had gone. The team of the Thirties was about to emerge.

After the Arsenal players had bathed and changed, they were photographed with the Cup against the background of Wembley's soaring terraces, now empty and litter-strewn. Parker was holding the trophy. To his far left Allison, trilby at a jaunty angle, shook hands with chairman Hill-Wood. To his right Jack, in a three-piece tweed suit and plus-fours, looked more the country gent than serial Cup winner. And almost out of picture there was Chapman, his own plus-fours almost concealing the quirkiest of details: hooped socks, just like those of his team. But his face was almost impassive. His thoughts often seemed to be somewhere else. Ahead of the game, usually.

Arsenal had two League matches still to play and lost them both – to Sunderland and Aston Villa at Highbury – finishing fourteenth, their lowest position of Chapman's five seasons. The Sunderland match was the first Ron Jennings ever saw: the one that convinced his mother the players had overdone their Cup celebrations. But there was no concern. The people knew. They had voted with their feet, raising the average attendance to 36,000. Not that Chapman needed any more money for the moment (though, having lost out on £500 when Arsenal failed at Wembley in 1927, he would now be getting a fat-cat bonus). Not in team-building terms. He contented himself by awarding a professional contract to George Male, now 20 and awaiting conversion from wing-half to right-back, and taking on the 17-year-old-defender Leslie Compton, initially as an amateur. Between them they would make nearly 600 appearances for Arsenal. Chapman did, however, try to find an unusual solution to the goalkeeper problem by signing one from abroad.

Rudi Hiden was only 21 but already chosen by Hugo Meisl to figure in Austria's Wunderteam. In May he had been outstanding in a scoreless draw with England, captained by David Jack, in front of more than 60,000 in the Hohe Warte Stadium in Vienna. Several English clubs made offers but it was Chapman who agreed a fee of £2,500 with Hiden's club, Wiener AC. Hiden landed at Dover only to encounter a storm of opposition in which Charles Sutcliffe, chairman of Burnley and a long-time member of the League management committee, declared: 'I feel the idea of bringing foreign players to play in League football is repulsive to clubs, offensive to British players and a fundamental sign of weakness in the management of a club.' Given that Chapman's Arsenal had just won the Cup while Sutcliffe's Burnley were being relegated, it might have been thought an ill-timed observation, but the players' union and Ministry of Labour agreed to the extent that protectionist regulations were agreed and put in place by the FA. These lasted until 1978, when Tottenham signed the Argentine World Cup winners Osvaldo Ardiles and Ricardo Villa.

The regulations did not, however, cover those of amateur status and so Chapman was able to recruit Gerry Keizer for the 1930–31 season. Keizer had been a young understudy to the goalkeeper at Ajax in Amsterdam when he moved to Kent, supposedly in order to improve his English, and started playing for Margate in the Kent League. The club was being used by Arsenal as a nursery in which the development of young players could be monitored. But Chapman was to waste little time in calling the Dutchman into his first-team squad to compete with Bill Harper, the Scot having returned from his sojourn in America, and Charlie Preedy.

The first World Cup took place that summer. Without James or Jack, Goodall or Jackson. None of the four British nations (Northern Ireland had by now separated from the Republic) was involved, because they had left FIFA after a dispute about the Olympic Games, at which Uruguay had become football gold medallists two years earlier. Accordingly, and because 1930 marked a century of Uruguayan independence, the World Cup was held there. Because of the economic depression, only four European countries went to Montevideo and only Yugoslavia reached the semi-finals, in which they were beaten 6–1 by a host nation featuring the game's first black star, the dazzlingly creative José Leandro Andrade. Uruguay went on to win the final, a local derby against Argentina watched by 93,000 in the new Estado Centenario (the opening-day contest between France and Mexico had drawn a more typical 1,000 to a less capacious arena). Chapman could follow the tournament only through the newspapers. He was already a follower of the world game, though, enjoying his friendly debates with Hugo Meisl and Jimmy Hogan as the Austrian built what was to become his country's most renowned team.

In Germany unemployment was rising – and Hitler's stock with it. Britain, though jobs were increasingly scarce here too, had taken a different political direction. The previous year's 'flapper election' – the first enfranchising women over 21 – had produced a hung parliament in which Labour had the highest number of seats. With Liberal support Ramsay MacDonald had formed a government and included a woman, Margaret Bondfield, in his cabinet, as Minister of Labour. Sir Oswald Mosley, whose gifts MacDonald had acknowledged since his return to the House as Labour MP for Smethwick in 1926, was made Chancellor of the Duchy of Lancaster at the age of 29, also with special responsibility for solving the employment problem, but he wanted to go faster than the party and was certainly more radically leftward, calling for nationalisation of the major industries – the 'commanding heights' of the economy, as Labour, borrowing the phrase from Lenin, was to call them – a widespread programme of public works and high tariffs to protect Britain from international competition. That Mosley had been given a non-cabinet post was, however, significant. After his plan was rejected by the cabinet in May 1930, he quit and returned to the back benches.

Obscurity did not suit the handsome, charismatic and hopelessly arrogant baronet, however, and at length it was off to Rome to meet the man who really didn't mess about. On his return from the encounter with Mussolini, Mosley was to become the beguiling face of British fascism. If he ever had any thoughts about riding the crest of a sporting wave as Mussolini and Hitler were to do, he at least had the wisdom not to try these out at Chapman's Highbury. For Mosley was overtly anti-Semitic and Chapman counted many Jews – not least Hugo Meisl – among his friends.

REACH FOR THE SKY

It had been a memorable sporting season for more than one Chapman, because in January 1930, while Arsenal were beginning their successful Cup campaign, Herbert's son Kenneth had become the first of the boys to make his debut for Harlequins rugby club, of which he was to be captain before and briefly after the Second World War (and in the few matches played during the conflict). The duties of president and secretary were taken by Adrian Stoop, a former England player after whom the club's ground was to be named. Although Stoop was the dominant figure at the club, Chapman became a respected lieutenant – and a playing contemporary was Douglas Bader, a fly-half being tipped for England when his Bulldog aircraft crashed in December 1931.

Bader was a 21-year-old pilot officer in the Royal Air Force based at Kenley, Surrey. Nine days earlier he had played for the Combined Services against the South African tourists and done well enough, many thought, to earn a call-up for the Five Nations championship. The following Saturday he had turned out for Harlequins and on the Monday he had returned to his daredevil ways, blithely ignoring – not for the first time – orders not to try aerobatics at low altitude. The tip of a wing touched the ground and he was taken to hospital, both legs so badly mangled that they had to be amputated. He was nevertheless to return to flying in time for the Second World War, in which he was much decorated for bravery and imprisoned by the Germans. Bader made so many attempts to escape that he was sent to Colditz Castle, where he was eventually liberated by American forces in 1945. He then became an executive for Shell and was much in demand as a speaker. For one who fought so valiantly against Hitler, he had views that even then might have raised the odd eyebrow, once responding to criticism of Britain from black Commonwealth leaders by saying they 'could bloody well climb back up their trees'. He found it amusing that, in the film *Reach for the Sky*, the distinguished actor Kenneth More could portray him as quiet and restrained; little more than the pipe he smoked was accurate in this respect.

Shortly after the premature curtailment of Bader's rugby activities, Bruce Chapman joined his brother on the Harlequins' playing strength. Kenneth – known as Ken – was the more successful player, initially a centre three-quarter like the more naturally gifted Bruce but then, as he bulked out, a forward, and an especially useful place-kicker who scored a total of 662 points for the club, mainly through conversions (194) and penalty goals (72). He even had a trial for England. Ken also became a prominent administrator in the national game, serving as president of the Rugby Football Union in the mid-1960s, when his late father's voice could be detected in a message deploring 'an increase in the desire to win at any cost, and in particular the spread of rough, over-violent play'. Ken died in 1989 at the age of 81 and was remembered as a good chap with a sense of humour. Even when suffering from Parkinson's, he would make a post-match trip to the bar, murmuring: 'Let's go and spill some beer.'

That his father had been a family man, however stern at times, was incontrovertible. Herbert was once asked to define the greatest moment of his life and replied: 'Hearing that my first son had qualified as a solicitor.' Yet the difference between the family among which Herbert was brought up and the one he and Annie created said a lot about the intervening few decades. Herbert's father and mother could not read or write. Herbert's children all went to fee-paying schools and grew up socially above star footballers, let alone sweating miners. Instead of the grimy red-brick cottages of Kiveton Park, they had known lawned suburbs and cricket in the back garden during the holidays. They could listen to the radio and go to the cinema and, with their parents' permission, use the telephone to tell their friends about it. But their choice of sport was most socially interesting, because it identified them in class terms. Chapman wanted them to be middle-class. Just as his parents had been relieved when he stayed out of the dark shafts of the Kiveton pit, Herbert seemed anxious that Kenneth and Bruce remain aloof from professional football (unlike the sons of, say, Brian Clough and Sir Alex Ferguson in later, less class-defined times). Herbert, indeed, appeared to consider himself now middle-class, or employer as opposed to employee, unlike his late brother John, a union man to his grave.

There were, incidentally, no more Herberts to appear on the family tree as the Christian name went out of fashion. It seems always to have had something of a connotation, for Herbert Henry Asquith, who had been born at Morley, near Leeds, was known as Herbert to family and friends until he was married for the second time to Margot Tennant, the daughter of a baronet, who preferred to call him Henry.

CLOSE TO PERFECTION

To Chapman, as if in recognition of his success, the cricket season of 1930 delivered something special. The 21-year-old Donald Bradman came with the Australian tourists and introduced himself with an innings of 236 against Worcestershire. He became the youngest batsman to score a thousand runs in May and, in the Test series, began with 131 in the first, which England won, then a 254 that was instrumental in Australia's levelling victory. At Headingley, the Leeds headquarters of Chapman's Yorkshire, Bradman struck a century each before lunch, tea and the close of play. He was out for 334 the next day. Rain denied Australia another win but Bradman's 232 helped them to clinch the series at Old Trafford (where Fanny Walden, now an umpire, was to stand his first Ashes match four years later, Bradman scoring 30 in the one innings rain permitted him). Even the great Jack Hobbs had been overshadowed and, to Chapman and all other cricket-lovers, Bradman must have seemed like a creature from another planet.

Within a couple of weeks the wife of a US state auditor gave birth in Wapakoneta, Ohio. The boy was named Neil Alden Armstrong and he, rather than come from another planet, would go to one. He would be the first man to set foot on the Moon.

Chapman had goalkeepers on his mind and, as training in preparation for the 1930–31 season culminated, made the decision to start with Keizer. An impetuous performer with an off-the-field penchant for fast cars, the Dutchman lasted a dozen matches before giving way to Harper, who in turn was dropped in favour of Preedy, who then gave way to Harper for the rest of the season. It was to be another momentous one and yet, at the end of it, Arsenal still didn't have a satisfactory goalkeeper.

Leslie Compton had been engaged as a possible long-term replacement at right-back for Parker, who would be 33 next birthday, and the youthful element of a side featuring Bastin, 18, and Hapgood, 21, was enhanced by Keizer as initially Arsenal took the First Division by storm, starting with 4–1 wins at first Blackpool then Bolton and dropping only two points until, 10 matches in, came defeat at Derby. Aston Villa posed the toughest competition while Sheffield Wednesday were clearly reluctant to give up their title. But Arsenal had an irresistible combination of prolific attack, in which Lambert was to set a new goalscoring record of 38 in a season, and tight defence. They answered any questions raised at Derby with a 5–2 win over Villa and before November was out had also scored five against Middlesbrough and Chelsea.

Just after Christmas, they beat Blackpool 7–1. Then the friendly rivalry with Villa – respect flowed between the sets of players – was renewed in the Cup. It was the tie of the third round and let no one down. At Highbury, Lambert and Jack secured a replay and 74,000 at Villa Park saw Jack strike again, and Hulme twice, giving Arsenal a 3–1 victory. Their next assignment should have been easier on the face of it, but mid-table Chelsea beat them. The response was awesome: Grimsby Town were thrashed 9–1, Leicester City spanked 7–2 on their own ground during a nine-match spell in which 40 goals rattled in. From even the one match of the whole season in which they failed to score – at home to Huddersfield – came a point.

Only once were they humbled. It was away to Villa, whose superb centre-forward 'Pongo' Waring, outstanding with Billy Walker in a 5–1 rout, took the opportunity to tease Chapman about his habit of signing centre-forwards: 'I bet you'd like to sign me, Herbert!' He surely would have done. But at least he had lightened his load by selling Halliday to Manchester City for £5,700 (only £300 less than he had paid the previous year) and was to raise a further £2,500 by letting Jimmy Brain go to Tottenham early in the next season. Brain had been Arsenal's top scorer for four consecutive seasons. This was Lambert's second year of supremacy and he would manage one more; Chapman, meanwhile, would continue to hunt centre-forwards.

The memoirs of the journalist Donny Davies described his team's style thus: 'They deliberately and ever so artfully fell back on the defensive, and positively invited attack for fully 80 per cent of every match in which they played. Years went by before opponents rumbled that this falling back was . . . a vital part of an overall plan to lure opponents further and further away from the close protection of their own goal . . . until the time was ripe and the situation apt for the crucial counter-attack! Then would come the long ball driven to the remote right wing and with a capacious swerve on it to elude the opposing back. Followed by a flash of Hulme's heels, a swift low cross . . . and there would be the ice-cool Bastin leisurely picking his spot.'

It was the football of the future. Whether or not anyone noted that James 'played between the lines', he did. He was often to be found floating between the wing-halves and attack. Ivan Sharpe said he filled the gap where the old centre-half used to be but the system seems to have been a sort of 3–2–1(James)–1(Jack)–3. There were lots of crossfield passes to disconcert the opposing defence but other teams did that; the distinguishing feature of Arsenal was how quickly and directly they turned defence into three-pronged attack. In this sense, a search for a modern equivalent might lead to the Chelsea whose 4–3–3 became *de rigueur* in the Premier League after José Mourinho's arrival in 2004.

Not that Arjen Robben, in his era, could have been expected to match the 28 goals Bastin got in the League during the 1930–31 season, only 10 fewer than the rampant Didier Drogba equivalent Lambert (though the left-winger was an ever-present and the centre-forward missed eight matches). Throughout Arsenal set a near-relentless pace and the title was safe before a 3–1 win at Newcastle in late April. It had been brought south for the first time. Chapman had dreamed of building a Newcastle in the capital and now the reality dawned as his team completed their season by beating Bolton 5–0 in front of a large and exultant home crowd. Many were to look back on that 1930–31 side, with its one flaw – often of limited relevance, so diligently did the defenders protect whoever was between the posts – as the best Chapman ever produced. Bastin certainly thought so. His reminiscences made it clear. And there were statistics to buttress it, not least a points total of 66 that would not be equalled until the flowering of Tottenham's great Double team 30 years later.

The streets were thronged. The nimbies who had tried to send Sir Henry Norris back to Plumstead now partied, singing the praises of Chapman and his men. It was a fine time to be an Arsenal fan, even if you were just a boy and didn't have the price of admission on a match day – and sixpence (2½p) was a lot to young Ron Jennings.

He began by following the club's exploits from afar. The family lived in Hackney, closer to the home of Clapton Orient, where he would wait for the gates to open and scurry in to watch the final 10 or 15 minutes of their Third Division match. Or, if Arsenal were on the radio, he would listen to George Allison's commentary, he and his elder brother using the knobs and dials to tune in and each taking an earpiece. And less than an hour after the final whistle the Saturday sports papers would appear on the streets. 'The *Evening Standard*, *Evening News* and *Evening Star* all had their own editions,' Jennings recalled, 'with updated League tables and a different write-up of the afternoon's game – and we'd get one of each.' Any pocket money left would go on comics with football content.

He had to earn most of it; parents seldom had coppers to spare and so the local boys had to be resourceful. 'I used to have a few chalks in different colours. I'd use them to draw a picture outside our house. I'd make it more interesting with fragments of coloured glass and ask passers-by to give me a penny. Now and again I got a ha'penny. But life was tough in the early Thirties and, when my father got the sack, I started giving anything I got to my mother so she could buy a piece of meat or something. At the end of our street was Chatsworth Road Market and we used to go scrumping under the stalls and get bits of veg that had been chucked away. My mother would cut off the bad bits and cook the rest. But she'd often let me keep a penny so I could buy my football comics.' When he started going to Highbury, he found that turnstiles, like poverty, could be surmounted. 'If you were a kid and got into a crowd, you could just be dragged in along with the rest. That day when they paraded the Cup was particularly memorable – it made me so proud to look at that trophy. They wheeled it round in this old pushchair – with someone holding it so it didn't topple off!' Sometimes in midweek, during school holidays, he would walk several miles to Highbury in the hope of seeing the players run in the streets surrounding the ground. 'Also there was the Bank of Friendship pub on Blackstock Road and the bookmaker's next door. After they'd finished training, they'd be in one and then the other. I'd wait outside for their autographs – those all got lost during the war, I'm afraid.'

227

In fact they figured in a clear-out by his mother. 'I had every-body's! They were all so willing to sign. Including Mr Chapman.' Even as a boy, Ron had an awareness that Arsenal's manager was a special one, every bit as famous as Alex James or David Jack. 'He changed so much. And the papers were only too happy to exploit him. He didn't hesitate to buy – Arsenal were like Chelsea after Roman Abramovich came in or, later, Manchester City.' But there were no security guards or smoked-glass windows then. 'Mr Chapman was such a lovely man to encounter. Whether he was especially anxious not to disappoint a young boy I don't know, but he never hesitated to sign his autograph. And he's always have a cheerful greeting for us. "Hello, boys," he'd say. "Hello, Mr Chapman," we'd reply. Even when we talked among ourselves it was "Mr Chapman." He was idolised. We would have given anything to have a statue of him in the playground.'

HANDSOME HIGHBURY

The names, at least of the outfield players, had begun to roll off the tongue in 1930–31 – after Preedy or Harper there were Parker, Hapgood, Jones, Roberts, John, Hulme, Jack, Lambert, James and Bastin – and it was not entirely due to consistency of performance because Whittaker was producing an overall level of fitness to which football had never been accustomed; Chapman made no secret of his debt to the man for whom he had rudely demoted a club servant. Bastin had played in all 42 matches of the League campaign, Parker in 41, Roberts and James in 40, Hapgood in 38. That Lambert, along with Jack, managed only 34 made his goalscoring return all the more remarkable (including FA Cup, it was 39 goals in 36 matches). In all Arsenal found the net 127 times in the League, one fewer than Villa in a season of such net-bulging entertainment that even Leeds United, who were relegated, scored only one fewer than Chapman's Huddersfield had done when taking the title in the last season of the old offside law. Arsenal more than any side, however, gave flesh to

Chapman's notion about football's obligation to live with the pace of the times. 'Spectators want a fast-moving spectacle,' he wrote in his column, 'rapier-like attacks that have the spirit of adventure, and ever more goals. The heavier the scoring, the more appealing is the match.'

The FA Cup final of 1931 had been won by West Bromwich, who were also promoted from the Second Division. On 25 April they had beaten a Birmingham managed by Leslie Knighton and captained by Ned Barkas, who had played under Chapman at Huddersfield. Five days later there was a stormy by-election in Ashton-under-Lyne, where Chapman had worked and played in his youth, brought about by the death of a Labour MP, Albert Bellamy. There were candidates from Labour and the Conservatives and also the New Party, which Sir Oswald Mosley had formed a day after his resignation at the end of February with the help of a £50,000 donation from Sir William Morris – later Lord Nuffield – the industrialist responsible for, among other vehicles, the Morris Minor and MG Midget. It was to prove one of Nuffield's less noble causes, developing into the British Union of Fascists with Mosley playing the part of Mussolini and the 'Biff Boys', eagerly led by the England rugby-union captain Peter Howard, shouldering the burden of resistance to hecklers in an unceremonious manner of which Il Duce would have approved.

An advance party of Biff Boys, mainly rugger types in plus-fours, were in evidence at Ashton, to which Mosley journeyed as party leader, dominating the campaign in the unemployment ravaged town. His meetings attracted audiences of several thousand at whom he would jab a finger as he paced the platform, exercising oratorical skills of a class that had impressed even parliamentary connoisseurs. His candidate, Allan Young, polled 4,472 votes, a majority of which were assumed to be formerly Labour. The Conservatives gained the seat with a majority of 1,415 and an angry crowd on the market square called Mosley a traitor to his former party, perhaps forgetting that he had started out a Conservative before veering so far to the left that Aneurin Bevan supported him on industrial and employment policy. Mosley sneered at the scowling proletarians, more convinced than ever that his nation needed such a blast of fresh air as Mussolini had given Italy and Hitler was about to pump into a terribly deflated Germany.

Most of the world was suffering. France announced that it could not afford to send a team to the Los Angeles Olympics the following year and in Britain the government, while MacDonald remained at the head of the cabinet table, became one of national unity that promptly cut unemployment benefit along with state salaries. The jobless total was about to reach a nadir of 3.5 million – half the notional workforce – and the League attempted to limit the effect on attendances by banning radio broadcasts of matches (the FA kept the final on the air). And yet Highbury was a picture of prosperity, with the most handsome edifice in football about to rise opposite a main stand itself doomed to sacrifice on the altar of Arsenal's greater glory. While the North Bank terracing was built up to increase the ground's capacity from 60,000, Claude Ferrier, an acclaimed architect whose works had included the Army and Navy Club in Pall Mall, made plans to modernise its style and comfort with a new West Stand which, when it opened at the end of 1932, would make Archibald Leitch's enclosures seem a little out of date. It even had an electric lift.

Amid such splendour Alex James began to wonder if his contribution had been adequately recognised. An abrasive product of the heavily industrial region around Glasgow that was to produce so many outstanding managers as well as players, he often clashed with Chapman over pay. James was ahead of his time on this issue, believing that stars such as himself should be remunerated as such while the manager naturally aligned himself behind the argument that equality was more conducive to the team ethic. Unless Selfridges made a special arrangement with James, of course; that was a separate matter. Now James rebelled, refusing to sign for the 1931–2 season. Chapman rang to say the club had decided to send him on a cruise to think things over and, on the day of embarkation, he was duly accompanied to Tilbury docks by one of Chapman's assistants, John Peters. There he saw a cargo boat, one of the sort that took passengers unable or reluctant to pay the fares sought by more luxurious vessels. Upon protesting, James was told it was Chapman's orders that he should board. He complied and although, upon reaching Bordeaux, he accepted a relayed offer to return and report to Arsenal for pre-season training, he claimed to have enjoyed the experience. He signed a week before the opening fixture. And so James's large and boisterous Alsatian dog – 'Gunner' – never had to be renamed.

Even though Chapman had always afforded James special treatment, which included allowing him to get out of bed later than the other players on match days – there was an indulgence later mirrored by Matt Busby's towards George Best and, in a different way, the leeway given to Eric Cantona by Sir Alex Ferguson – further strains were to be exerted on the manager–player relationship. But Chapman's trick had broken the most serious impasse. James was back in the fold.

LAST PIECE OF THE JIGSAW

The 1931–2 campaign was preceded by not only the distractions over James but fevered speculation about the possibility of a Double which Chapman's players may have allowed to enter their heads. A blank was fired in the opening match, which West Bromwich won with a single goal at Highbury, and the new-year visit to The Hawthorns was to bring Arsenal's seventh defeat; in the whole of the previous League season, they had sustained four. But at least Chapman, with his only significant change of personnel, had found a goalkeeper of the required standard.

Keizer had gone to Charlton Athletic – he was also to have a spell at Queens Park Rangers before returning to Ajax in 1933 – and Preedy begun the campaign. Within three months, however, Preedy's Arsenal career was over as Chapman acquired, in Frank Moss, the last piece of his jigsaw. From then the concession of goals became even less frequent than in the previous season. Moss appeared just after Chapman's Arsenal had embraced air travel, flying to Paris for the annual Armistice Day match against

Racing Club (a 3–2 victory further distinguished by Chapman's acting as one of the linesmen), and within weeks four clean sheets were kept in five matches. Chapman had solved his problem – and by going to a familiar place, paying £3,000 to Oldham Athletic, from whom he had so craftily acquired Ted Taylor for Huddersfield in 1922. It proved another brilliant deal; Moss, like Taylor, went on to represent England.

The Cup coincided with Arsenal's revival. First it invited Darwen, heroes of the Victorian age, to Highbury for an 11–1 thrashing but there was consolation in the parting gift of a set of Arsenal strips; red and white promptly became the Lancashire club's colours. Plymouth Argyle were the next visitors to Chapman's domain and again there was romance because Bob Jack, father of David, was (still) the Devon club's long-serving manager – he had guided them from the Southern League to the upper half of the Second Division – and Bill Harper was his recently signed goalkeeper. Four goals went past Harper, two past Moss. Arsenal's League form was looking up again, with Moss and the defence especially impressive; only 14 goals were conceded in the 22 matches that led to Wembley. A 2–0 win at Portsmouth set up another Chapman derby, a rerun of the 1930 final against Huddersfield at Leeds Road.

Chapman had done his homework, as usual, and when Hulme won an early corner Roberts knew what to do. The defender had never scored in the Cup (and was never to do so after that day at Leeds Road). He had scored only one goal in the League (and was to add only three before his retirement five years later). Yet he trotted forward and, when Hulme placed the ball on his forehead, directed it into the net. The trusty rearguard did the rest. And it ended 1–0 to the Arsenal in the semi-final as well.

Manchester City were the opposition at Villa Park. They were building a fine side, with Matt Busby in midfield and the brilliant Eric Brook on the wing, but could not break Arsenal down and were confounded by the final kick of the match, Bastin scoring after a long, relieving ball from James had been hooked into the goalmouth by Lambert.

In the final Arsenal would face Newcastle and, given the disparity between the teams' defensive records, be favourites. Except that James's fitness was in doubt because of knee damage suffered at West Ham in late March. Even Whittaker struggled to repair this one and three days before the final Chapman took time out from the team's preparations at Brighton to announce a line-up in which James and Hulme did not figure; the replacements would be George Male and Pat Beasley, an 18-year-old winger signed from Stourbridge of the Birmingham and District League for £550 a year earlier who had only just made his first three League appearances as Hulme's deputy. Back at Highbury, James and Hulme were receiving treatment and the *Daily Sketch* had the idea of getting them to run around the pitch, taking a photograph and using it with the headline 'The Two Fittest Men In Football'. Chapman, though irate, ordered them to come to Brighton, to whose Goldstone Ground some 40 photographers flocked to see a double fitness test. Both James and Hulme appeared to pass and Chapman duly amended his team. And then another photographer arrived, claiming that his car had broken down and pleading with Whittaker to let him have just one shot. Whittaker kindly agreed and, once the camera had been mounted, challenged for the ball with James, who fell clutching his knee. Almost weeping, James was carried to the dressing room. 'He would not let the doctor touch him,' Whittaker recalled, 'and shouted at me to get everyone out of the room. Even Chapman had to go.' Male was back in the side. Poor Beasley stayed out. The outside-left position that had been his for a day went to Bob John, with Bastin moving into James's midfield role.

The King had enjoyed 'Abide With Me', which was beautifully sung as usual – this was an England both patriotic and still accustomed to making its own music – and was such a regular by now that he took a keen interest in the exchanges. He saw Arsenal go ahead in the fifteenth minute after Hulme, his fitness hard to question, crossed handsomely. As players of both sides converged, Newcastle's goalkeeper, Albert McInroy, seemed to be distracted by his colleague Jimmy Nelson and took his eye off the ball. John, who had cut in from the wing as all Chapman wingers were encouraged to do, unflinchingly headed into the net. Both Pathé and British Movietone had slow-motion replays now and McInroy might have regretted that. As might the referee, Percy Harper, and the linesmen who let the Newcastle inside-forward Jimmy Richardson scoop back what looked suspiciously like a dead ball for Jack Allen to equalise.

Had it crossed the line? The adjacent Hapgood certainly thought so and stopped, expecting the award of a goal-kick. But referee Harper swiftly turned away from the couple of Arsenal players unable to resist a pointless protest before Parker told them to get on with the game. *The Times* was to talk of 'the most controversial goal in English football history'. Arsenal still had 52 minutes to regain the lead but the expression of Chapman, wearing rimless spectacles as he sat next to Whittaker on the bench, did not suggest optimism. As he sportingly conceded afterwards, Newcastle were the better side after half-time and deserved the winner scored by Allen 18 minutes from the end. Nor did Chapman moan about the validity of the equaliser. Even though it might have lent weight to his idea of 'goal judges', who appeared, more or less, in the form of UEFA's 'additional assistant referees' some 77 years later (and 'goal-line technology' came four years after that).

In the remaining few League matches, Everton held on to deprive Arsenal of the title, which meant that Chapman had repeated his honourable but frustrating double of 1928: his players were the runners-up in both competitions. The margin was only two points but Everton had scored more, mainly due to Arsenal's patchy form in the first third of the season. It was also noticeable that Arsenal's results tended to suffer in the absence of James. But Lambert and Jack had still struck at a decent enough rate, Bastin and Hulme weighed in from the wings and Charlie Jones more than justified his conversion to right-half. By most clubs' standards it had not been a bad season at all. It had just taken a long time to get going.

ARSENAL: AMASSING THE LEGACY

FIT FOR A PRINCE

Chapman, as ever, had been looking ahead. Lambert was coming up to 30 and so in March, several weeks before the Cup final, the Grimsby centre-forward Ernie Coleman, six years his junior, had been purchased for £7,500. There had also been a £10,000 bid for Jimmy Dunne, who had scored 36 goals in 39 matches for a struggling Sheffield United in 1929–30, keeping them in the First Division, then 50 in all competitions the next season and was still going strong, but United had insisted on keeping their brilliant Irish attacker (they were eventually to relent, Chapman subsequently obtaining Dunne for £8,250). Other than this, a £3,000 investment in Frank 'Tiger' Hill, who came from Aberdeen under something of a cloud cast by betting allegations and was to be a tough tackling contributor to the next few seasons, would suffice. The club was well furnished with young players such as Male, who would take over from Parker at right-back, ready to fill the stalwarts' boots. Replacing David Jack, now 33, would be difficult but Chapman already had some candidates in mind. With the squad in good health, there was time to turn his attention to other developments at the club, above all – literally – the stadium, where the lower structures of the new West Stand had been in place even as James gave newsreel viewers an assurance of his fitness 10 days before the Cup final.

One of Chapman's bright ideas had perished when the League

warned Arsenal off a takeover of Clapton Orient. The plan was to use the Third Division club to develop players for Highbury and, to this end, he approached Jimmy Seed, the talismanic inside-forward of a successful Sheffield Wednesday whose career was ending due to a knee injury, and had him appointed Orient manager on £12 a week by a compliant board. At least this was to show that Chapman had an eye for a manager as well as a player, for Seed was soon to go to Charlton Athletic and swiftly have the club promoted twice, then keep them in the First Division's top four until the outbreak of war. But the 18 months to which Chapman had consigned him at Orient were something of a nightmare. Without the money Arsenal had been expected to pour in, the club struggled. The League – or later Leagues after the formation of the Premier – in England continued to set their face against nursery clubs of a different division, although they became accepted in other European countries.

Work on the new stand now began in earnest and Chapman, whose organisation of success on the field had made it feasible, supervised everything with the attention to detail that Arsène Wenger was to accord the London Colney training ground before its opening in 1999. His relish for innovation was also evident in the installation of floodlights, which, although he knew they would not be allowed for official matches, could be used for training. He had seen floodlit football while in Austria with Hugo Meisl and was excited about what it could bring to the game, not least the proportion of spectators who were always missing when matches kicked off on workday afternoons.

Another suggestion was for artificial pitches; Chapman, no doubt foreseeing the injury problems players were to encounter when the early plastic surfaces appeared half a century hence, wrote that manufacturers should be challenged to produce a rubber surface. But nothing came of it. At Arsenal, though, he had an all but free hand. Having ordered a radical refurbishment of the dressing rooms, he was offered undersoil heating, but rejected it because the plans entailed raising the pitch unduly. One notion he did accept was that of a 45-minute clock. The

FA, arguing that it would erode the referee's authority, ordered it to be removed and so a normal timepiece was erected at what became the Clock End. Not uniquely: there had been a clock at Villa Park for many years.

Meanwhile, Chapman was negotiating with the Underground Electric Railways Company of London to have the Gillespie Road station, improvements to which Arsenal were partially paying for, renamed after the club. Eventually Arsenal (Highbury Hill) was decided upon. Tickets and maps had to be reprinted before the official change in November. By then the stand was only weeks from completion and – coup of coups – the Prince of Wales came to Highbury in December for its grand opening. The Prince, later and only briefly to become Edward VIII, saw a 4–1 victory over Chelsea in which Bastin scored twice. If there had been a two-week delay, he might have enjoyed even more a 9–2 beating of Sheffield United featuring a quintet of goals from the apparently irrepressible Lambert, who featured in only 12 matches that season yet ended up with 14 goals. The machine was firing on all cylinders again. Even the new component, Coleman, scored 24 in 27.

BLACK DAY AT WALSALL

An early home defeat at the hands of West Bromwich, who were proving a bogey team since their return to the First Division, had been the only one in the opening 14 matches. Arsenal did succumb 5–3 away to Aston Villa but the slaughter of Sheffield United completed a sequence of five consecutive wins and only twice during the season was the machine to stall. Over Christmas and New Year five matches yielded only three points. Still, the Cup was starting and, because Arsenal had a far from daunting tie away to Walsall of the Third Division (North), Chapman thought it might be a sensible time to have a look at some of his reserves.

To an extent his hand might have been guided by injury to

Eddie Hapgood and the flu from which Bob John, Jack Lambert and Ernie Coleman had been recovering, but Hulme played for the second team the same day, as did Horace Cope, the obvious deputy for Hapgood at left-back, while John, Lambert and Coleman were among those on the train to the West Midlands, so there was definitely an element of unforced experimentation. The beneficiaries – or, as it turned out, victims – of this were Tommy Black, who replaced Hapgood, Charlie Walsh, who came in for Lambert or Coleman at centre-forward, Billy Warnes in Hulme's place on the right wing and Norman Sidey for John at wing-half. Black, Walsh and Warnes were making their debuts for the first team. Sidey had made one previous appearance.

The build-up had the usual David-against-Goliath charm. The Walsall team, a local leather manufacturer estimated, had been assembled for £18 less than the value of Arsenal's boots. Chapman liked that. It was his feel for a story, after all, that had conspired in Arsenal's becoming the most glamorous of clubs (the sort any Third Division outfit would dream of tripping up). His team went north in the railway carriage Chapman had ordered to be specially adapted and decorated in Arsenal colours for travel to away matches and on a cold and misty afternoon they ran out in front of the raucous 24,000 packed into Fellows Park.

It was a typical third-round scene, complete with muddy pitch and opponents who tackled as if bent on making 'Tiger' Hill look toothless by comparison. Chapman's wingers were regularly clattered and Warnes, intimidated by both this and the crowd's proximity, had little effect on proceedings. Walsh, so nervous beforehand that he put on his boots before his socks, rose too early to a cross and the ball bounced off his shoulder. Meanwhile, Bastin and James became irritable. On the hour Walsall took the lead through a header by Gilbert Allsóp and 10 minutes later, as Arsenal strove for an equaliser, a clearance was picked by the home attacker Bill Sheppard, who had been regularly troubling Black and now swept past him into the penalty area. Black, in his frustration, hacked down Sheppard, who got up and put the kick past Moss. The noise was deafening. The crowd was swollen beyond capacity when the gates were opened 15 minutes from the end, as was the custom, to let people out; thousands who had initially failed to gain admission flooded in and the terraces overflowed. There were even a few on the pitch. They thought it was all over – and it was now. The Walsall heroes were carried shoulder-high.

Back in London, young Ron Jennings and his brother were crouched by their radio and, as their disbelief unfroze, tears flowed. Elsewhere, cackles were heard as the news of Walsall's achievement spread throughout the land, for Arsenal, with their big spending and lofty stadium building, had come to represent metropolitan affluence in a decade when much of provincial England was suffering terribly. Chapman, with a foot on both sides of the divide, would have understood that.

Not that the immediate aftermath of Walsall involved much sociological contemplation. Chapman seethed. Black in particular was shown no mercy, being sold six days later. On the train back to London the 24-year-old Scot was told he would never appear for Arsenal again; he had let the club down with that ridiculous tackle and need not even come back to Highbury for his boots because they would be sent to his home along with some forms to sign. These turned out to be the documents of a transfer to Plymouth Argyle which went through on the Friday. Black did well in the Second Division, helping Argyle to finish fifth in 1936–7.

Neither Walsh nor Warnes was to make another appearance for Arsenal. Walsh went a week after Black and made 10 appearances for Brentford, contributing three goals to the latter stages of their Third Division (South) championship season. Warnes left at the end of the season, when he was signed for Norwich City by Tom Parker at the outset of the former Arsenal captain's managerial career, and featured in the winning of the Third (South) title. He continued to do well in the Second Division for a few years.

Chapman had been so angry, especially with Black, because it had looked as if Arsenal had paid for their manager's complacency. As his lieutenant Bob Wall said many year later: 'I have always held the opinion that Herbert could have played the others [those left out were surprised when the team was announced on the train], and he did not, because he took the view that this was an easy game and he would like to give some of our young players a taste of a Cup tie. Herbert had a great fetish for planning ahead and for once this philosophy failed him.'

Norman Sidey was retained as a trusted stand-in, making 43 further appearances over the next five years. He stayed in the team for the first match after Walsall, a 2–1 win over Manchester City at Highbury, and, although there was a brief wobble after an 8–0 home win over Blackburn that featured Coleman's second hat-trick in a month, Arsenal were restored to their former vibrancy. In a new look, too. Chapman had always believed in visual contrast as an aid to identification by team-mates, hence the yellow boots of his youth. He had put white hoops in Arsenal's red socks in 1931 and now, in a further endeavour to increase the speed at which his players could fix the positions of their colleagues while choosing a pass, he changed the socks to blue and white hoops. At the same time – March 1933 – he had the shirt sleeves altered from matching red to distinctive white, along with the collars and cuffs.

The idea had crystallised in his mind after a conversation with a friend, the sporting cartoonist Tom Webster, who had enjoyed a round of golf with the Chelsea chairman, Claude Kirby, while wearing a sleeveless blue jumper over a long-sleeved white cricket shirt. Kirby had gone to David Calderhead and suggested his players could be kitted out in something similar, but the Chelsea manager had been unimpressed. Not so his friend Chapman. He had asked for an artist's impression from Webster, who had duly got out his pen and red ink, and the result prompted Chapman to have the club apply to the League for permission to change to a white trim. On 20 February it was granted. Eleven days later, at 2.30 p.m. on the eve of a match against Liverpool at Highbury, Chapman rang the Nottingham factory of Hollins and Co., a textile manufacturer, and placed a rush order for 10 sleeveless jumpers in pillar-box red Viyella (a mixture of merino wool and cotton). By 6 p.m. they were on the way to Highbury and the following afternoon Chapman's players trotted out wearing them over the long-sleeved white shirts that were the club's change strip. They were of a brighter shade than the traditional shirts and quite a few whistles came from the crowd. The combination of three garments lasted just four matches and may have been uncomfortable for the players. Or maybe it was just jinxed. At any rate, Arsenal lost to Liverpool, Wolves and Newcastle, picking up a point only at Leicester during their worst spell of the First Division season. But then properly made shirts to the new design arrived and normal service was resumed. The look survived and, when Arsenal marked the final season at Highbury by reverting for 2005–6 to the redcurrant shirts abandoned after the First World War, there was never much doubt that it would be temporary. Chapman's change had become immortal.

In red sleeves or white, red socks or blue, his team were rampant in the League in that 1932–3 season. Bastin scored 33 from one wing, Hulme 20 from the other and Coleman and Lambert averaged around a goal a match; it didn't seem to matter which centre-forward played and yet Chapman, ever craving improvement, still searched. The team's totals for the season were 58 points, 118 goals scored and 61 conceded – all marginally less impressive than in the first successful title campaign but more than worthy of champions nonetheless. James missed only two matches – and it would have been one but for a refusal to travel to Belfast for a friendly against Cliftonville towards the end. He was dropped for the final League fixture against Sheffield United at Bramall Lane and replaced by Charlie Jones, who, as club vice-captain, instead had the honour of collecting the championship trophy from League president John McKenna. As in 1930–31, Villa were second and Wednesday third.

To revisit Donny Davies's lyrical caricature: 'The long ball . . . with the capacious swerve on it . . . a flash of Hulme's heels . . . and there would be the ice-cool Bastin.' The wingers contributed more than ever to the retrieval of the title from Everton and yet Davies and his contemporaries were not always wholly effusive about Arsenal's game, tending to praise mainly its cleverness and efficiency rather than its looks. But it must be borne in mind that their accounts, however fair and well written, were from a provincial perspective. Davies began writing for the *Guardian* only in 1932 and so, before the last full season of Chapman's career, would have seen Arsenal in away matches, in which many of their victories were narrow and therefore more likely to resemble smash-and-grab exercises than, say, the 8–0 win over Blackburn, an 8–2 trouncing of Leicester or a 9–2 triumph over Sheffield United (all at Highbury in 1932–3). And there may have been an element of bruised northern pride because the League championship had never been taken south of Birmingham before Chapman's Arsenal got going. The art of the counter-attack, furthermore – the art on which Chapman had always worked, the tactical principle that had led him to engage Lloyd Davies at Northampton, Clem Stephenson at Huddersfield and now employ Alex James – was bound to have been viewed as somewhat dark; it was, after all, to be so when Brian Clough and Peter Taylor practised it at Nottingham Forest in the late 1970s and early 1980s.

Donny Davies had been a sportsman in his own right. He had played football for the England amateurs before the First World War and, after nearly starving to death in a German prisoner-of-war camp, recovered so well that he had a couple of seasons batting occasionally – and none too successfully – for the Lancashire first team. His portrayal of Chapman's Arsenal was as most of the country saw them, but not quite as Highbury did. Highbury was ecstatic, from Anna Neagle and Herbert Wilcox in the second poshest seats – Miss Neagle was said to have spurned invitations to sit in the directors' box because she became too wildly partisan during matches to be bound by etiquette – to a teenage Ron Jennings on the terraces.

Ron stood with other schoolboys or fellow workers from a factory in Holloway which produced statuettes. 'They were made out of plaster, which was baked and, when they came out of the oven, they'd have pock-marks on them – I was trained to be a finisher. There were about 20 of us, all Arsenal fans.' The lads earned 10s. (50p) a week and, although the gap between their income and that of their heroes was a little narrower than today, there was no question of a post-match beer. 'We couldn't afford it. Not that we felt a need for it. Not to drown sorrows anyway. Ninety-nine times out of a hundred we'd have won and everybody was going home happy.'

TEA WITH MUSSOLINI

In the FA Cup, Walsall's reward for beating Arsenal had been a trip to Manchester to meet the City of Busby and Brook. They lost 2–0 and had Jack Reed sent off – quite an achievement when the game allowed plenty of vigour, especially from aspiring giant-killers – near the end. City proceeded to the final, one element of which deferred to a long-held Chapman view in that the players had numbers on the back of their shirts. For the FA – if not quite yet the League – were relenting on this. They favoured the system that had been used at Highbury several months earlier during the Arsenal match against Meisl's 'FC of Vienna', when Chapman's players wore 1 to 11 and the Austrians 12 (outside-left) to 22 (goalkeeper). Now Everton wore 1 to 11, making Dixie Dean the English game's original No. 9, and City 12 to 22.

Because the King was again unwell, his son the Duke of York attended with the Duchess, leaving their elder daughter 'Lilibet', aged seven (and the future Queen Elizabeth II), and toddler Margaret in the care of nannies. Although the Duke's stammer was well under control by now, the Cup was handed to Dean by the future Queen Mother, who charmed the Everton captain with her apparent interest in the match. Dean had scored one of three goals without reply, rounding off a remarkable spell for Everton, who had won the Second and First Division titles in consecutive years and now the game's most glittering prize. Unlike Arsenal, they did not have a dynamic, high-profile manager; the key to their success seemed to be Tom McIntosh's skill in linking the players and board. He was greatly liked, not least by Dean, who was thought to take part in the team-selection process and had shown admirable leadership during a pre-season tour, ordering his fellow players not to give the Nazi salute before a match played in Dresden with Hermann Goering present.

Before Chapman was afforded a close-up view of Italy's fascist leadership, there was time to lodge a protest with the League about the case of Walter McMillen, Cliftonville's centre-half. Chapman had made an offer to the young Northern Irishman after going through the proper procedures but then, he claimed, a journalist had tipped off another club – Manchester United were not named – who tendered more lucrative terms and got the player. McMillen went on to make only a couple of dozen appearances for United before completing his career with Chesterfield and Millwall. What happened to Chapman's complaint is not known. He had more than the usual post-season duties on his plate in that late spring of 1933, for this was his time to manage England. Sort of.

The initiative came from a senior FA member and a former referee, Arthur Kingscott, who was close to the octogenarian chairman and president Sir Charles Clegg. Kingscott quietly asked Chapman to look after the team in Rome. He thus became the first professional manager to have charge, however restricted, of an English national side. They began by drawing 1–1 with Italy in front of a full-house 50,000 in the Stadio Nazionale del Partito Nazionale Fascista (a title that left little to the imagination). The match took place in the presence of Mussolini, as the World Cup final was to do in the same arena a little over a year hence. Mussolini saw advantage in football. He sensed his luck in having the excellent Vittorio Pozzo in charge of the team and was to ride it hard during the long build-up to a tournament played in the unusually fine stadiums the regime had encouraged along with training facilities befitting the nation's new vigour.

This muscular fascism was embraced by Pozzo, decent and intelligent man though Brian Glanville deems him to have been. Pozzo was an Anglophile. After playing for Torino, he had gone to London to improve his English but soon moved to Manchester and got to know his favourite player, the United centre-half Charlie Roberts, and others with whom he keenly discussed the game. He had returned home to coach Torino and the national team, with whom he had begun a second spell in 1929. Two years later, a 2–1 win over Meisl's burgeoning Austrians had promised much and now here he was taking on Chapman in Rome, albeit on unequal terms, the Englishman being required to work with the FA committee's idea of a line-up.

Chapman would have approved of the decision to hand Eddie Hapgood his international debut, however, and there was hardly a shortage of individual quality with Cliff Bastin, especially, making his mark. Bastin was the man of the match, England's scorer and very much the centre of attention as the team bus inched its way through the crowds afterwards. The Italians chanted the winger's name and demanded his autograph. Meanwhile, he and other members of a side captained by Roy Goodall from Huddersfield sang marching songs from the First World War ('Tipperary', 'Keep the Home Fires Burning') to pass the time. The next day they were taken to meet Mussolini and a visit to the Vatican to see the Pope was also arranged before the party moved on to Berne, where Bastin scored twice in a 4–0 victory over Switzerland. And that was Chapman's career as part-time England manager. Played two, won one, drawn one, lost none, five goals scored and one conceded. Considering that both matches were away from home, it wasn't bad.

TOO BAD TO BE TRUE

No sooner had the 1933–4 season begun than Chapman took time out to pursue his belief in football coaching for children. Half a century before 'football in the community' became prevalent, he had a passion for the concept and Highbury became the setting for a series of sessions for boys that ran from 6 to 21 September. They had to be conducted after first-team training because Chapman got most of the squad and coaching staff involved. The boys, more than 80 at a time, would be divided into small groups and taught for three hours in one go, to a programme that had been prepared by Chapman in conjunction with representatives from the famous amateur club Corinthian (soon to amalgamate with the Casuals), who were co-operating with him in the initiative.

As it ended his team were getting over a patchy start in which they surprisingly lost to Everton, a club conducting occasional, and usually unsuccessful, experiments with the third-back game. Others did better with the system but Arsenal were its masters. Or, rather, Chapman was the master. In the 24 matches he supervised during the 1933–4 season – 23 in the League and a 3–0 Charity Shield victory over Everton – only 20 goals were conceded. When he took a team to Leeds Road for what was to prove the last time, the tactical battle between Chapman and his pupil Clem Stephenson was settled by the only goal, struck on the master's behalf by Jimmy Dunne, who had arrived from Sheffield as Jack Lambert moved across London to Fulham. Five weeks later Chapman picked the team to play Birmingham at St Andrew's. It was, characteristically, designed with an eye to the future. Only Jones had reached the age of 29 and seven players were 25 or under. Each of the wingers was 20: on the right the rapid Ralph Birkett, whom Chapman had just bought for £1,600 from Torquay United to compete with Hulme, and on the left Pat Beasley, progressing well and in the side now to let Bastin, still only 21 despite his rich experience, move inside as the creative deputy for James. At inside-right was Ray Bowden, who had come from Plymouth to replace the fading Jack as goalscoring inside-forward – on the recommendation of Jack's father – and was to prove outstanding value for £4,500, helping to win the second and third titles. Dunne was at centre-forward. He struck eight times in his first 12 matches. But he didn't score at St Andrew's on 30 December. No one did. For either side. Frank Moss kept his third consecutive clean sheet and Arsenal had lost one match of 14. They were heading steadily towards another title, leading the League despite the challenge of promoted Tottenham.

After seeing in the new year with his family in Hendon, Chapman travelled north to watch a match at Bury against Notts County, one of whose players interested him. He was already feeling the effects of a chill but the next day made a familiar journey across the khaki Pennines with their drystone walls to Sheffield to watch Wednesday, who were Arsenal's next opponents at Highbury, beat Birmingham 2–1. That was on the Tuesday and after the match he made the short trip to Kiveton Park, where he spent the night at the home of his younger brother Ernest. Upon returning to London he consulted the Arsenal doctor, Guy Pepper, who confirmed that his temperature was high and told him to rest. Instead, Chapman went to Guildford to watch Arsenal's third team play, explaining that he didn't often get the chance to see the 'lads'. On this occasion they included a 15-year-old Denis Compton, brother of Leslie and destined not only to win League and Cup honours with Arsenal after the war but to become one of English cricket's greatest batsmen. Only after seeing the lads beat Guildford City 4–0 did Chapman return home and, clearly suffering, go to bed.

He should have taken the doctor's advice earlier. Pneumonia had set in and the family gathered anxiously. Penicillin was not yet in use. Ten years later it would have been available, but now Annie and the children could only wait and hope. They heard him call out for his sister Martha, who had helped their mother to look after Herbert and the other boys in childhood. There were signs of a rally on the Friday but in the middle of the night – at 3 a.m. on Saturday, 6 January, the day of Arsenal's match with Sheffield Wednesday – Herbert Chapman passed away.

Many people connected with football remembered where they were when they heard of his death. Dick Parker, the Huddersfield director with whom Chapman had conspiratorially crossed the Pennines to sign Ted Taylor, had learned while Chapman was in Yorkshire that his friend was a bit off colour but knew no more until, arriving at Leeds Road for the day's match against Portsmouth, he saw the flag at half-mast: 'The meaning of it came like a flash.' Meanwhile, George Male, who lived near the West Ham ground, was walking to Upton Park station at the start of his journey to play at Highbury when the newspaper billboard confronted him: 'Herbert Chapman dead'. The last Male had seen of Chapman was on the way home from the Birmingham match; there had been no suggestion of ill health then. Cliff Bastin was nearly at the stadium when he heard the calls of the newspaper-sellers and was likewise stunned. 'It seemed too bad to be true.' In the dressing room, there was silence, broken only by the weeping of several players. 'Herbert Chapman,' said Bastin, 'had been loved by us all.' And the fans were as dumbfounded – Ron Jennings recalled seeing one of those billboards: 'I couldn't believe it. He'd gone, just like that.'

There was no postponement: life and the match went on. As the teams appeared, each player wearing a black armband, there was polite applause instead of the customary roar. Silence returned and, after the teams had stood to attention and the 50,000 spectators removed their hats and caps, four trumpeters sounded 'The Last Post'. The players then went through the motions. 'Despite the gloom due to Mr Chapman's death,' wrote the man from the *Islington Gazette* on the Monday, 'the match was a really good one, I am told. I am afraid that my thoughts were wandering and I do not remember a great deal of what happened.' Dunne scored for Arsenal in a 1–1 draw.

Chapman was survived by Annie and the four children – Ken was 25, Bruce 23, Molly 18 and Joyce 15 – by his brothers Tom, Matthew and Ernest and sister Martha and their families. The funeral, for which Martha bought a new coat, took place on the Wednesday. Crowds lined the Hendon streets as a Rolls-Royce hearse carried Chapman's flower-bedecked coffin from the family home in Haslemere Avenue to St Mary's. The shoulders of David Jack, Joe Hulme, Eddie Hapgood, Jack Lambert, Cliff Bastin and Alex James bore it into the church. The rest of the players formed a guard of honour as it entered to the strains of Mendelssohn's 'O, For the Wings of a Dove' from the church organ, after which the choir sang Chapman's favourite hymn: 'Nearer, My God, to Thee'. Several lorryloads of wreaths had been sent, many from overseas football associations or clubs, but only one was taken into the church. It was from Annie. Prominent among those outside was one from Kiveton Park Colliery Cricket Club. The church overflowed despite its 800 seats and, as one of Chapman's fellow parishioners was to recall, something of a scramble took place among photographers: 'There were people climbing all over the graves with cameras. Mr Chapman would not have approved.'

The card on the team's wreath read: 'To The Boss from the Players. Our hearts are sad and hopes well nigh shattered, but your inspiration, memory and affection remain ours for ever.' Upon which they journeyed to Brighton to prepare, with the professionalism Chapman would have demanded, for the FA Cup tie at Luton on the Saturday. The *Islington Gazette* also did its duty, reporting on the Friday: 'Remembering Walsall, Arsenal are taking their game at Luton more seriously than if the latter were a First Division instead of a Third Division side . . . Under Tom Whittaker, they have been getting ready . . . and it is hoped that John will have recovered from a strain in his groin in time. In that event, the team will probably be: Moss; Male, Hapgood; Jones, Roberts, John; Coleman, Bowden, Dunne, Bastin, Beasley.' John did pass his fitness test and, at Kenilworth Road, Dunne scored the only goal. It was not until Crystal Palace, also of the Third Division, came to Highbury at the end of the month that Arsenal won again.

Among the matches they lost while coming to terms with Chapman's death was the home derby with Tottenham. Their rise from the Second Division had allowed Chapman one more derby, a thrilling 1–1 draw at White Hart Lane in September when the gates had closed on a record crowd of 57,000 an hour before the start only to be pushed open again by the disappointed thousands, requiring police to restore order. The rivalry between the clubs, according to Ron Jennings, was as acute as now. But perhaps not so bitter: 'You could mix with Tottenham supporters, even at a match. There were disagreements, but I never saw a punch thrown.' Spurs finished third that season, behind a Huddersfield still thriving under Stephenson. Arsenal took their second successive title in a manner of which Chapman would have been proud.

So splendid had been their defending in the first half of the season that, despite the understandable dip in standards that followed the shock of his loss, the final goals-against total was the lowest recorded by champions since Chapman's Huddersfield in 1925. Although the goals-scored figure fell by 43 to 75, reflecting the many absences of James since he had been injured on the first day of the season, a team guided largely by Joe Shaw from the Sheffield Wednesday match afterwards (though the estimable Tom Whittaker also remained on hand to help George Allison, who initially acted as caretaker while retaining his seat on the board) remained champions by a margin of three points.

The concluding match was a 2–0 victory over Sheffield United, the club of Chapman's boyhood heart, and for the Arsenal fans gathered at Highbury there was a symbol of his enduring – some would say eternal – influence from the grave. Ted Drake was one of several players he had earmarked for Arsenal's future. He had tried to pluck the 21-year-old centre-forward from the Second Division towards the end of the previous season but Southampton would not part at that stage. Allison had, however, gone back to the Dell when the South Coast club looked assured of promotion and succeeded with a £6,500 bid just after Arsenal had been knocked out of the Cup by Aston Villa in March. Now Drake claimed both goals for Arsenal in their farewell to Highbury for the summer, taking his total to seven in ten matches since the move. He would score riotously the next season as Arsenal equalled Huddersfield's hat-trick of titles, staying tight at the back yet striking lethally once more, finishing with 115 goals.

The team benefited from two further additions secured in the summer by Allison, who had been confirmed as Chapman's successor with the increasingly influential Whittaker at his side and Shaw returning to his former duties with the reserves. Both of the new players were wing-halves and they became firm friends, if an odd couple in that Jack Crayston, a £5,250 signing from Bradford Park Avenue, exuded such grace that he was known as 'Gentleman Jack' while Wilf Copping, who cost £8,000 from Leeds United, bristled with craggy aggression; Chapman had resolved to buy Copping after noting his strength in adversity during the England match in Rome. As envisaged by Chapman, Crayston took over from Tiger Hill in Charlie Jones's old position while Copping replaced the 35-year-old Bob John, the last survivor of the pre-Chapman era. Despite the almost theatrical resonance of Allison's tones, he was accurately representing the master's voice.

HUMILITY OF THE BOSS

In a Pathé broadcast spliced with scenes from the funeral, Allison had paid particularly eloquent tribute to Chapman in declaring: 'At Highbury the whole playing staff, and the whole ground staff, called him "The Boss" and it was a term of affection, a sincere expression of admiration, not a mere title for a master.'

In no sense had Chapman been a boss before God. While football had mourned a dominant personality, the tranquil community to which Chapman always returned had lost a humble servant. When at church Chapman had acted as a sidesman, or usher, waiting at the end of each row of pews for the congregation to slip their pennies into the collection plates and performing other simple duties. It took a lot to make him miss a service and his friend the Revd Norman Boyd had told the hundreds of unfamiliar faces at the funeral: 'There have been Bank Holiday mornings at the height of the Cup and League competition when the busiest man in football was to be found at the altar of this church.'

The vicar had done Chapman's stated footballing principles proud with this tribute: 'Football is a game. And in a game nothing matters as much as the spirit in which it is played. The dangers of professionalism are obvious and against them Herbert Chapman steadfastly set his face.' Later the parish magazine, while acknowledging his success in the world of sport – 'his team played splendid football, as clean as it was clever' – added: 'At St Mary's he will long be remembered for his quiet, firm and kindly but unassuming manner.'

The newspaper obituaries had naturally concentrated on his contribution to football. James Catton, confessing to have 'induced him to attach himself to Arsenal', wrote in the *Observer*: 'His achievements as a team-builder, and his strategical addresses to the players prior to their matches, have made this club one of the most famous not only in England but abroad.' Catton also alluded to his human qualities: 'For the welfare of players he was deeply concerned, as his discipline was tempered by thought for the future of the young men in his care.' There was no mention of his difficulties in Leeds. Nor, the following day, in *The Times*, which lamented the untimeliness of his death, saying: 'He was only 55 years of age and, much as he had accomplished, he had such vitality and determination that there seemed even more for him to do in the future.

'His main interest was in making the game pay and giving the public what it wanted. His enormous transfer deals when he came to Arsenal – roughly £20,000 was paid out for Jack and James – his schemes of playing football by floodlight, of numbering the players, of building new and comfortable stands, all were shaped to the same end – that of getting people through the turnstiles and giving it the football and the amenities which would make them come again. Even Chapman could not always get his own way and the game is still played by daylight and players still go unnumbered, but his spectacular career has been amazingly successful, so successful indeed that a novelist would reject it as too far-fetched.'

Perhaps most poignantly, the *Jewish Chronicle* praised Chapman for his charitable efforts while calling him a 'great friend of the Jewish people'. During his time at Highbury many Jews had become supporters and the *Chronicle*'s kind words prompted George Allison to write to the editor: 'I am happy to think we have a large number of Jews who derive healthy entertainment and get enjoyment from the demonstrations of sportsmanship which they see at the Arsenal ground. For many years it has been our great pleasure to contribute to Jewish charities and to help those deserving causes which Jewish organisations have "fathered" and I am conscious that we are only able to do this to the fullest degree because of the support which we receive from the Jewish community.'

Before Chapman's time, Jewish football enthusiasts in London had been working-class people from the East End who tended to gravitate to Tottenham. But Arsenal attracted a more mixed crowd including middle-class fugitives from persecution in Europe and Chapman, with his Jewish friends including Hugo Meisl, would have found it easy to get on with those attracted by Arsenal's aura. The film producer and director Emeric Pressburger arrived just too late for him. Pressburger was born in Hungary and became a screenwriter in Berlin. After the Nazi grip tightened in 1933, he fled his apartment – he said he left his key in the door so the storm troopers didn't have to break it down – and worked in Paris before moving on to London in 1935. He was already an Arsenal supporter when Alexander Korda introduced him to Michael Powell, with whom he was to make 20 films in as many years, including *Black Narcissus*, *The Red Shoes* and *The Tales of Hoffmann*. Pressburger carried his footballing passion through the rest of his life.

HURRAH FOR THE BLACKSHIRTS!

If Chapman had been a great friend of the Jewish people, he had been a friend in need. Anti-Semitism had been sweeping through Europe and not always stopping short of Dover. In London's East End, where many Jews had settled, the British Union of Fascists had been recruiting well, and marching energetically. Harrumphing in some more elegant quarters, earnestly theorising in others, the BUF was a strange coalition of the fearful working class, crusty generals and agile intelligentsia. But, then, its leader was an odd mix himself.

Mosley had spent the summer prior to the party's launch in 1932 on the Venice Lido, writing a book – apparently without a trace of irony – on the need for British youth to abandon decadence and join a classless movement. His private life hardly exuded the wholesome discipline he prescribed for the nation. After beginning an affair with Diana Guinness (née Mitford), he had encountered understandable domestic turbulence and at one stage decided to be honest with his wife Cynthia, known as Cimmie: he would own up to this case of adultery and at least a goodly proportion of his past ones. Cimmie listened and, when he had finished, exclaimed: 'But they are all my friends!'

Cimmie had become ill and died in 1933, just after Mosley had gone to Rome and been photographed with Mussolini on his balcony. Mosley adopted a stiff-arm salute and unambiguous title: 'The Leader'. Next for the trip to Rome was Lord Rothermere, who promptly aligned the *Daily Mail* with the BUF. No sooner had the Chapman obituaries been absorbed than the *Mail* printed a paean under the infamous headline: 'Hurrah For The Blackshirts!' A week later the paper called the BUF 'a well organised party of the right ready to take responsibility for national affairs with the same directness of purpose and energy of method as Hitler and Mussolini'. With such support, membership of Mosley's party reached 50,000 by the middle of 1934. Mosley spoke in various cities. A rally at the Albert Hall in London attracted 10,000, then 12,000 packed into Olympia. The latter was to prove a significant event. Outside, a horde of Blackshirts faced just as many anti-fascists of generally leftwards persuasion. Inside, hecklers were roughly, even brutally, treated and the BUF acquired such a thuggish image that Rothermere withdrew his support and membership plummeted.

AFTER CHAPMAN: THE ALLISON YEARS

There was still plenty to celebrate at Highbury after Chapman, not least the rise of the new stand he had envisaged. When it was opened in 1936, Arsenal proudly announced the culmination of a 10-year programme that had begun almost as soon as Chapman got his feet under the managerial desk. In 1935 the North Bank terrace had been covered and so only the new Clock End, to which Chapman's beloved timepiece had been moved, was open to the elements. Highbury became a uniquely handsome and comfortable football ground with the new East Stand, which had three tiers, the upper two all-seated, and a façade that greeted visitors emerging from the Tube station with the unwritten message that they had arrived at a place of substance. Style, too: Art Deco had come from Paris only in 1925 and now, with the matching West and East Stands, Arsenal had brought it to football. Chapman had even commissioned a new club badge in the Art Deco style which was placed over the main entrance to Highbury and inlaid into floors as part of what amounted to a rebranding.

Even the club's pre-match entertainment – the Highgate Silver Band had changed its name to incorporate Arsenal's – had star quality now. Its repertoire would include medleys from Chopin or Liszt as well as popular favourites and its 78rpm gramophone recording of the march 'Blaze Away' was said to have sold a million in the year of Chapman's death. The Arsenal band had two further hits in 1935.

The architect Claude Ferrier had died in a road accident in 1935, but his partner William Binnie had completed the East Stand, in whose stately foyer the bust of Chapman was unveiled in October 1936. The ceremony was conducted by the Revd Norman Boyd in the presence of Annie, the four children, two of Chapman's surviving brothers and the directors, players and staff. The East Stand had cost £130,000 – nearly three times as much as the West, but the Chapman years had paid for it. Rough calculation produced figures of £100,000 spent on inward transfers during his time in charge with £40,000 recouped, or a net cost of around £7,000 a season for all that glory and the increased gate income it generated. Meanwhile, the players' wages were at least notion-ally pegged. Chapman the entrepreneur had been lucky in that sense for, although the concept of a maximum wage seems quaint today, it is worth reflecting that he would hardly have been able to build the grandeur he did if the players of his time had taken the same share of the game's revenue as in the boom years of the Premier League. Chapman was able to leave Arsenal with the most up-to-date stadium in the country and the beginnings of a tradition for spectator comfort that was duly observed in the design and construction, when Highbury became obsolete at the turn of the more moneyed third millennium, of the new Emir-ates Stadium with its generous legroom and fine facilities. To the ghost of Sir Henry Norris, it must all have seemed such a gratify-ingly long way from Woolwich.

In 2003, three years before the Emirates Stadium opened, Pete Winkleman had moved Wimbledon FC to the new town of Milton Keynes and there had been much criticism of this example of 'franchise football' – and of the FA for allowing it. Winkleman, a property developer, might have pointed to the precedent created by Norris, without whose initiative it is doubtful that Chapman would have chosen to build his Jerusalem – or his Newcastle of the south – in north London's relatively fertile land. There was, it had soon transpired, room for both Arsenal and Tottenham Hot-spur, who opened their own atmospheric East Stand (to Leitch's more orthodox design) for the 1934–5 season. Although it ended with their relegation, the rivalry had already done much to spice the supporters' lives, as the huge crowd for Chapman's final derby had emphasised.

Ron Jennings had left school and was 14 when he went to work in the statuette factory of the Art Figure Company. From then it was Highbury every weekend, first team or reserves. He could pay to get in and have his chocolate. 'My life was wonderful,' he said. 'I loved sport and when I started to earn a bit more I went to speedway as well. After the war my brother and I became season-ticket holders in the West Stand. I used to think I was a cut above then!' In March 1935 he had been in the crowd of 73,295 that set the Highbury record for all time; they saw Arsenal fail to score at home for the first time in two years but take a point, against Sunderland, towards yet another successful title campaign.

By now Drake was firmly established as Jennings's favourite: 'For me, Ted could do no wrong.' In 41 League matches he got 42 goals out of Arsenal's 115. It seemed a case of business as usual under Allison the figurehead and Tom Whittaker the trainer and tactician, both ably assisted by Joe Shaw. The struggle to replace Chapman was not yet evident. But in the next season James, now in his mid-thirties, became an irregular presence. Drake's strike rate appeared to fall in consequence. He had still struck a creditable 11 goals in 17 matches when Arsenal went to Villa Park – and there Drake restored his goal-a-match ratio in the most dramatic manner. He scored with his first attempt and six of the remaining seven – the other came back off the crossbar – to set a record for an individual in a top-division match.

Drake suffered from injury in the latter half of that 1935–6 season and Arsenal slipped to sixth. But they won the FA Cup, Drake's goal overcoming Sheffield United. By now Jennings could make the short trip to Wembley to support the team, although he remembered uncomfortable aspects of the occasion. 'Highbury was said to have the best toilet facilities in the country,' he said, 'but even there you sometimes had to cross your legs. At Wembley you had to get in place by half past one for a three o'clock kick-off and, if you wanted a pee, you might have to go all the way to the top of the terracing, then down to the toilet and back again. It was terrible. So you can guess what happened in lots of cases.' Letting off steam at Highbury was a pleasure. 'One thing that was always good fun was everyone putting a few pence in and drawing a number from one to eleven. If your player got the first goal, you took the prize. One bloke was always complaining that he got the goalkeeper. He was a very tall chap with long arms – so long his mac finished halfway up them. Every time we didn't score he'd want a corner. We used to call him "Pointer" because he'd be pointing at the corner flag and shouting. What you didn't get was swearing. Well, maybe the odd word when someone got excited. But nothing like the blatant bad language you hear today.'

Arsenal rose to third in 1936–7 and won another title – Drake's second – under Allison the following year. Early in the campaign Allison helped Chapman's friend Gerald Cock to arrange the first television broadcast of live football. It featured a phase of a match between Arsenal's first team and reserves at Highbury and towards the end of the season, although the League remained wary of the new medium, the FA allowed the Cup final (Preston 1 Huddersfield 0) and the oldest international (England 0 Scotland 1) to be shown. Because there were only 10,000 television sets in Britain at the time, more people would have watched the events at Wembley than in the homes of the avant-garde. The most memorable television event that year, however, was to be Neville Chamberlain's optimistic declaration on his return from Munich with a piece of paper. Rearmament was nevertheless a major factor in the fall of the unemployment total, now 1.5 million.

Despite the title triumph, the great Arsenal team was breaking up. Of Chapman's original champions, Bastin and Hapgood remained key men but Roberts had broken a leg, Hulme had faded and been transferred and James retired. The brave and agile Frank Moss had been obliged to quit aged only 27 after dislocating a shoulder in a match away to Everton. With no substitutes, the goalkeeper swapped jerseys with an outfield player; he even scored one of Arsenal's goals in a 2–0 win. But Moss made only a handful of first-team appearances in the ensuing two years before moving to Scotland to manage Hearts. There, a promising start to his new career was curtailed by the war.

Hulme had moved to Huddersfield during the 1937–8 season and, after winning a Cup runner's-up medal, also decommissioned his boots. He was to manage Tottenham for four post-war years and then choose journalism as the next venture of a life that lasted 87 years. Roberts contributed 13 appearances to the championship campaign – he was one short of qualification for a medal when injury struck – and then became reserve trainer for just one season before his life was brought to a cruelly premature end.

In 1938–9 Arsenal broke the world record once more in their efforts to replace James, Allison handing £14,000 to Wolves for Bryn Jones, who had not settled to his new surroundings when the war began and was 34 when football resumed; he ended up running a newsagent's near Highbury. Jones missed the concluding match of his first season, Brentford being the visitors and the occasion enabling Highbury to continue its ground-breaking habit when it became the setting for *The Arsenal Stadium Mystery*, a film in which Allison appeared along with some of his players and uttered the immortal line: 'It's one-nil to the Arsenal.' He added: 'And that's the way we like it.' In one scene Allison is shown giving the players tactical instructions, but this was hardly his strength. With his booming voice – plummy enough for the BBC, despite the northern origins he had shared with Chapman – he was more of a showman than a coach. Arsenal beat Brentford 2–0 but finished in fifth place, having won fewer than half of their matches and scored a mere 55 goals. For many clubs it would have been satisfactory, but Allison's management was failing. He was to be granted an unwelcome sabbatical, for the third League match of the next season – a 5–2 win at home to Sunderland in which Drake scored four times – was to prove Arsenal's last official fixture before the Second World War.

A SMALL AND COMFORTABLE WORLD

Sir Oswald Mosley and Diana Mitford had been married in 1936, at the home of Joseph Goebbels. Hitler was a guest. After the outbreak of war, Mosley was ordered to be detained along with other officials of his BUF, but Winston Churchill, newly installed at 10 Downing Street, made his three-year imprisonment as pleasant as possible, allowing him to be joined by Diana and accommodated with their baby son Max in a cottage in the grounds of Holloway Prison, where the couple employed other prisoners as servants. After the war Mosley started the Union Movement, which called for Britain's integration with Europe and an end to immigration from the Commonwealth (India and most other former Empire territories had achieved independence in the immediate post-war years). He and his wife ended their days in Paris, living near the Bois de Boulogne mansion of their friends and fellow travellers the Duke of Windsor (whose abdication had led to the Duke of York's coronation as King George VI) and Wallis Simpson. What a small world it had proved.

What a comfortable world, too – and how different from the existence Mosley had envisaged for those he perceived as enemies of the state. When in their Holloway cottage, a mile from Highbury, he and Diana would have heard the bombs that fell on Arsenal's stadium during the Blitz, destroying the North Bank. The enemy may have considered the stadium a legitimate target because it was a headquarters for air-raid patrols. Bombs fell on Hendon, which was near munitions factories, and one attack close to the Chapman family home in Haslemere Avenue killed 85 people while destroying hundreds of homes. In all, the Blitz claimed 20,000 lives in London and as many in the rest of the country. Meanwhile, the Duke of Windsor had been installed as a somewhat reluctant Governor of the Bahamas in order to keep him and the Duchess out of the way, lest the war effort of Churchill's government be complicated by their appreciation of the other side's point of view. Mussolini was in Rome, preening

himself more pensively than usual, facing up to the biggest decision of his life – whether or not to enter the war on Hitler's side
– and about to get it wrong.

THE WORTHY WHITTAKER

Arsenal took part in regional football during the war but resumed
participation in the FA Cup in January 1946 without Drake, who
had been forced to retire with a slipped disc. The tie with West
Ham took place over two legs and a 6–0 defeat in east London
left Allison's team with little more than pride to play for a home,
where they won 1–0. The club's debt had risen and at the end of
the first League season since the war, 1946–7, in which a new
Arsenal finished thirteenth, Allison stepped down as manager.
He had come off the board to take over from Chapman on an
annual £3,000 – more than the basic salary the great man had accepted in his last contract, signed a few months before his death
– but was never up to the near-impossible job it became.

Whittaker, who had flown for the RAF during the war, took
charge in the summer of 1947. Arsenal won the League in his first
season, with the likes of Joe Mercer and Jimmy Logie bedding
in, and the Cup two years later. They were champions again in
1953, but gone were the days of dominance. Whittaker tried to
recreate the star quality of James's pomp with a covert bid for
Stanley Matthews, but the maximum wage kept the great winger
at Blackpool and Arsenal were three years into a trophy famine
– it was to last 17 years – when Chapman's protégé died of a
heart attack at the age of 58. Whittaker had said of Chapman
that he was 'the 25-hour type of man', often working through his
lunch hour and into the night, and ventured: 'It was this devotion
to duty that killed him.' Now Whittaker, on whom the cares of
managing Arsenal had weighed heavy, was gone at hardly a great
age. It was 1956. The following year Allison, having reached 73,
succumbed to recurrent illness.

By now James, like Roberts, had gone. Herbie Roberts had

THE LIFE AND TIMES OF HERBERT CHAPMAN

left for the war, fallen ill and died at 39. It was a fate unbefitting one of Chapman's most likeable, modest and restrained characters: a polite man who, for so diligently carrying out the role of destroyer allotted by Chapman, had been booed and jeered on every away ground and not seemed to mind a bit. He was the most prominent of nine players registered with Arsenal who perished amid the conflict.

Although James was also to die relatively young, he at least survived the war and returned to Highbury to coach youth teams before falling to cancer in 1953, when he was 51. James had joined Hulme in trying the creative side of journalism. Just as many of today's retired footballers maintain a connection with the game through television and radio, those of the Chapman era gravitated to newspapers. Ivan Sharpe, who had trained properly and remained a journalist while playing for Chapman at Leeds City, was among the most distinguished sports writers of the inter-war period and beyond. Charlie Buchan even took part in the formation of the Football Writers' Association in 1947; he was one of a group of chroniclers returning by ferry from an England victory over Belgium in Brussels when the idea arose. Thus began the annual Footballer of the Year election by journalists, with its distinguishing feature that, as well as outstanding play, a candidate's moral example should be taken into account; Buchan suggested that and his old boss Chapman would certainly have approved. It was first won in 1948 by Stanley Matthews and annually presented at a dinner on the eve of the FA Cup final until 1954, when Tom Finney's subdued performance at Wembley was partially ascribed to several hours nervously waiting to collect his trophy on the Friday night instead of resting in readiness for the big event. His Preston lost to West Bromwich, disappointing many who had hoped Finney would win the Cup as Matthews had done the year before, and thereafter the dinner was brought forward to the Thursday.

Buchan went on to commentate for the BBC and co-found a much loved magazine. Between 1951 and its demise in 1974, *Charles Buchan's Football Monthly* brought the game and its players to life for enthusiasts of all ages with its earnest interviews and portraits, often in colour. It could be purchased, no doubt, from Bryn Jones's shop. The likes of Ron Jennings would swell the custom there on match days. Except when serving in the RAF during the war, Jennings remained a constant supporter until Highbury closed and then moved to the Emirates until after his ninetieth birthday in 2010, when he returned to his technological roots and, instead of listening to the club's matches through an earphone, began watching them on television. He remained lean, fit and active. Smartly turned out, too. When complimented on his appearance towards the end of the 2012–13 season, he smiled and said: 'I think I got that from Mr Chapman. When the Arsenal team ran out, they were always immaculate. Clean-shaven – not like today – with their hair in place. There were rumours that he inspected them before they went out.'

BUSBY AND THE EUROPEAN DREAM

On the day that Herbert Chapman had died, Manchester United had lost 5–1 at Lincoln in the Second Division. It could have been worse because, also on that afternoon, Stanley Milton made his first appearance in goal for Halifax Town in the Third (North) away to Stockport County, whose 13–0 victory was the heaviest inflicted in the League's history. But Manchester United's troubles continued and they were almost relegated to the Third (North) that season. They were promoted to the First in 1935–6, then relegated, then promoted again and entered the war as what might have been known – for the yo-yo had become popular in the 1920s – as a yo-yo club. The war, moreover, left Old Trafford a bombed wreck. United were not alone in being disrupted by both the Luftwaffe and the lost years; Arsenal were among the competitors who suffered and Tom Whittaker deserved much credit for the revival there. But United's rise from the rubble was spectacular. Within a year of the League's resumption they had finished runners-up. Within another year they had done the same while winning the FA Cup. Then they finished second, fourth, then second again while building the side that would become champions in 1951–2. And Matt Busby was only starting. He was doing for Manchester United what Chapman had done for Arsenal and, although tragedy was to intervene, his legacy must be deemed comparable.

After assembling, with his immensely regarded assistant Jimmy Murphy, a young team that had won consecutive English championships and was tipped by many to succeed Real Madrid as the leading force in Europe, Busby saw many of them perish – as Busby himself nearly did – in the Munich crash of February 1958. He then built again and won two further titles and one more FA Cup before fulfilling a dream by lifting the European Champions' Cup in 1968. Just as it might be rhetorically asked if Bertie Mee, George Graham and Arsène Wenger derived inspiration from the scale of the institution Chapman had developed at Arsenal, an analyst of Sir Alex Ferguson's extraordinary achievements would have to acknowledge the creation during the Busby era of the intangible factor to which Ferguson once referred as 'our club's DNA'. Busby had his own style but, with one possible exception, no manager since Chapman has made so much that was to prove so durable. Bill Shankly gave Liverpool the foundation for success that Busby had provided for United. Shankly was assisted, and later followed, by Bob Paisley, under whom the flow of trophies into Anfield increased. Busby and Paisley had been close friends since their time as team-mates at Liverpool and it is impossible to believe that Busby's studies of the game, at least, had not been based on the Chapman syllabus. He approached management in a remarkably similar way and later said of Chapman: 'In transforming Arsenal he transformed the game of football.'

Busby, like Paisley, Shankly and Chapman, had been born into a coal-mining community. He lost his father to a sniper at Arras but was invited south at 18 from Lanarkshire, where his heroes had included Alex James and that other celebrated Scottish émigré Hughie Gallacher, to join Manchester City. This was in 1928, between the twin peaks of Chapman's powers: after Huddersfield had won three titles and before Arsenal got off the mark. The City manager was Peter Hodge, who astutely converted Busby from an inside-forward into a wing-half. City became the leading club in Manchester and, after losing the FA Cup final in 1933, won it the following year.

Liverpool had to pay £8,000 for Busby, who became captain and looked after a young Paisley when he arrived from Bishop

Auckland in County Durham just before the war. The conflict was to signal the end of Busby's playing days. He and other members of the team signed up. Paisley became one of Montgomery's Desert Rats, serving at Tobruk and El Alamein, and ended up on one of the tanks that liberated Rome a few months before Mussolini, by now a fugitive in the northern lakes, was captured by partisans, shot dead and dangled from the canopy of a petrol station in Milan. Paisley returned from the war to make a belated debut for Liverpool and won a championship medal in 1946–7. When his one-club career ended, he stayed on at Anfield as physiotherapist (self-taught) before joining Shankly's famous Boot Room and eventually graduating, with apparent reluctance, to manager.

Busby became an army football coach, after which Liverpool wanted him to assist their manager, George Kay. But Busby had developed a vision of his own and, though only 36, was anxious to enact it as soon as possible. Manchester United offered the opportunity. From their chairman, James Gibson, he demanded, in essence, the power Chapman had assumed at Arsenal: control over recruitment, team selection and training. Despite Chapman's success, this was still regarded as revolutionary. The similarities with Chapman's approach were uncanny; Busby even told Gibson he had a five-year plan. And Gibson, who had offered three years, agreed to put two more on his contract. Busby returned to the army and, while coaching a regimental team in Italy, met Jimmy Murphy and offered him a job. At his first press conference, Busby promised to restore United's glories of 1907–11, a period in which they won the League twice and FA Cup, through developing their own young players – a policy that had already been put in place by Gibson and his secretary, Walter Crickmer – and the rest is an increasingly bulky volume of history.

The most famous club in Europe when Chapman died had been Arsenal and that remained the case almost until the outset of the Champions' Cup. The Hungarian national team's victory at Wembley in 1953 ridiculed English notions of superiority but they were to die hard and when, the following year, Honved brought Ferenc Puskás and other Magical Magyars to Wolverhampton for the most famous floodlit friendly, the narrow victory of Stan Cullis's side on a pitch made boggy by liberal pre-match hosing prompted the *Daily Mail* to hail Wolves as the true champions of the world. Even Charlie Buchan pronounced it a vindication of the British approach. All of this was too much for Gabriel Hanot. A full-back who had played for France, he now edited the sports daily *L'Equipe* and wrote: 'Before we declare that Wolverhampton Wanderers are invincible, let them go to Moscow and Budapest. And there are other internationally renowned clubs, AC Milan and Real Madrid to name but two. A club world championship, or at least a European one . . . should be launched.' And so it was, after Hanot had called a meeting of clubs in Paris – 15 attended – and FIFA given approval for its running by the newly formed Union of European Football Associations (UEFA), to start in 1955–6.

Scotland provided Hibernian, who were beaten in the semi-finals by Stade de Reims, but the Football League was not represented until Busby took Manchester United in the following season. It proved a spectacular introduction as, having beaten Anderlecht 2–0 in Brussels, they won 10–0 at Old Trafford. Borussia Dortmund and Athletic Bilbao were also overcome before the great Real Madrid knocked them out. Real proceeded to the second of five consecutive triumphs in the competition. The status that had once been vaguely accorded Arsenal was now the Spaniards' by demonstrable right. They had made Hanot's point with emphasis. Meanwhile, Cullis's Wolves, after they had temporarily replaced the stricken United at the forefront of the English game, suffered a first-round knockout by Schalke in 1958–9 but put up a slightly better show the next year, removing Vorwaerts of Berlin and Red Star Belgrade before being thrashed 9–2 on aggregate by Barcelona in the quarter-finals: plenty there for the Buchan school to chew on.

Cullis had nonetheless proved himself an outstanding manager, along with Jimmy Seed, of the post-Chapman era. Cullis had built on the principles of Major Frank Buckley. He had, indeed, been a product of Buckley's youth policy as Wolves had moved from the Second Division to the upper reaches of the First before the Second World War broke out. It is fair to say that even Chapman, who liked the ball to be transferred forward without undue ceremony, did not so zealously make a principle of directness as Buckley, who, according to his erstwhile captain, had a military approach to management. 'If you didn't like his style,' said Cullis, 'you'd be on your bicycle.' And that style, as interpreted by Cullis, was to bring Wolves three titles after the war.

But it was only Busby who could create the equivalent of Chapman's Arsenal. As soon as he had taken over at Old Trafford – or Maine Road as it often became because of the damage done to United's ground during the war – there was a sense among Sharpe, Donny Davies and the other notables of the northern press that a version of the metropolitan citadel Chapman had built would be created on their territory. One that accommodated a more expansive and flowing style of football. Because of the technical attractions Busby had first noted while on tour with City in Czechoslovakia in 1936, he had always embraced the notion of an organised European game, and now it gave him, both before and after the agony of Munich, a chance to connect United romantically with the outside world. The culmination of Busby's European quest, a decade after the crash, sealed that relationship.

It was an opportunity Chapman never had. His Arsenal had been the toast of all Europe at a time when only reputation counted, there being no organised competition. But how would they have fared against the Bilbao who won four Spanish championships under Pentland or Garbutt in the seven seasons leading to the Spanish war? Or against the great Juventus who took five Italian titles in a row during the period, supplying the core of Pozzo's conquering side? It must have been frustrating for Chapman and his admirers not to know, for European competition had been just one of the innovations he had foreseen, wanted and seemed to be wishing into existence in that *Sunday Express* column of the early 1930s. When Brian Glanville later wrote of a 'triumvirate of Titans', he meant Pozzo, Meisl and Chapman. But

Pozzo and Meisl had jobs to which the crossing of borders was intrinsic. Although Chapman's land retained its status as football's capital, it was they who had that European feeling. Of the triumvirate, Chapman was the only Titan denied it.

THE BEST MANAGER
ENGLAND NEVER HAD

Even without European competition, Chapman might have commanded the international stage as well as the domestic, but for the FA's twin shortcomings of conservatism and isolationism. An extra five years on his life would have been useful, too. Whether the World Cups of 1930, 1934 and 1938 should be retrospectively wished upon him is another matter – especially 1934 and 1938, although he would surely have relished an opportunity to confound Europe's dictatorships. Not to mention Vittorio Pozzo and Hugo Meisl. What fascinating conflicts would have taken place among the members of this little gang. Pozzo, an amiable foe of the stopper centre-back on the Herbie Roberts model, emerged triumphant from each of the tournaments – albeit with some dubious assistance in the first. But the Germans used a stopper in 1934 and finished a creditable third. When Chapman's tactics had so much to offer, his restriction to two full international friendly matches in the early summer of 1933 should be viewed as a greatly regrettable anomaly.

He did, however, have one other match against an international team in the December of that year, just four weeks before he died. A very good team it was, too: Meisl's Wunderteam. For the friendly against Arsenal at Highbury, the Austrians came under the guise of 'the Football Club of Vienna' in order to circumvent an FA rule forbidding competition between clubs and countries. But it gave Chapman a chance to manage properly against a world-class side and his Arsenal proved more than their equals, winning 4–2. This was a year after Chapman had declared the Austrians unlucky to lose 4–3 to England at Stamford Bridge, saying they had carved the better chances with 'most clever scheming and expert footwork'. After the Highbury match Meisl took up Chapman's suggestion that he go to watch Sheffield Wednesday play Aston Villa. On his return he accepted an invitation to be entertained at Chapman's house in Hendon and, according to Chapman, confessed to doubts, saying: 'We have copied the old Scottish style, which pleases our spectators, but after seeing Sheffield Wednesday with their quick diagonal passes and their wonderful positional play it seems there are other possibilities about the game which we have not yet exploited.' They nevertheless proceeded to embark on a run of seven consecutive victories, including one in Turin, before falling 1–0 to Italy in that suspect World Cup semi-final in Milan. So clearly Chapman had built a world-class side, too, and Meisl wasn't just being polite when he said while presenting a gift to his friend at the Café Royal: 'Mr Chapman is undoubtedly the leading man in association football throughout the world.'

Tom Whittaker followed in Chapman's footsteps by working with the national team on a few occasions immediately after the Second World War, before Walter Winterbottom became the first England manager by title. But so deep and persistent was the failure of understanding between the FA and the professional game that even in 1950, when England finally arrived at a World Cup, the team was selected by a committee. It had streamlined itself, admittedly, into a committee of one: the Grimsby Town director and local fish merchant Arthur Drewry, who would become both chairman of the FA and president of FIFA. He presented the line-up to Winterbottom and on 29 June a bit of a shambles ensued. All that is widely remembered is the 1–0 defeat by the United States in the Brazilian city of Belo Horizonte. The campaign had begun with a routine 2–0 victory over Chile in the new Maracanã in Rio de Janeiro and ended with a respectable 1–0 defeat by Spain in the same stadium. But the notion of the English as all-powerful in the game, enhanced by the absence of a competitive measure while they stayed out of FIFA, was exposed to much ridicule.

That the order of the 1930s had also changed was evident from the early exit of Italy, who had parted company with Pozzo and lost several players in the Turin air crash, and the non-participation of the Germans and Austrians. Germany was in post-war disgrace, split between West and East, while Hugo Meisl's death in 1937 had signalled the beginning of Austria's demise as a major force in the game. A year later, the country had been annexed by the Nazis and its best players lent to the strength of a greater Germany; there would have been no room for a Jew in that set-up anyway.

The Latin Americans dominated the 1950 tournament and the best European performance came from Sweden under George Raynor, who hailed, like Chapman, from industrial Yorkshire and whose formative football years had been those of Chapman's predominance. Raynor's playing career had begun with Sheffield United and ended at Aldershot. After the war he had been recommended by the FA to their Swedish counterparts, who were looking for a national coach. An Olympic gold medal won at Wembley in 1948 was followed, in Brazil, by the elimination of Italy. A 7–1 thrashing by the hosts and further defeat by Uruguay, who would shock the Maracanã by winning the final, left the Swedes to contest third place with Spain, whom they soundly beat. Raynor then tried club management in Sweden and Italy but returned to his old job for the World Cup held in Sweden in 1958, guiding the hosts to the final, in which Brazil and a teenage Pelé proved too much for them, winning 5–2.

The quality of some of the players Raynor managed should not be underrated – Sweden had impressed Highbury in losing 4–2 in 1947, beaten England 3–1 in Stockholm in 1949 and, perhaps most impressively, drawn 2–2 in Budapest in 1953, shortly before the Hungarians came to Wembley and won 6–3 – but his achievements still raise the intriguing question of how Chapman would have fared with England in the 1930s. Even under the FA's amateurish management structure they achieved some excellent results, including the 1–1 draw with Pozzo's Italy that Chapman supervised. Six months earlier, Chapman had watched the 4–3 victory over Meisl's Wunderteam at Stamford Bridge. The Austrians had trained at Highbury at Chapman's invitation..

Chapman missed, by 11 months, a match that emphasised the contribution his Arsenal had made to the English game: an unprecedented seven of the club's players were picked for the national side in what became known as the Battle of Highbury. Pozzo brought Italy to his late friend's domain to face a relatively inexperienced England featuring Frank Moss in goal, George Male and Eddie Hapgood at full-back, Jack Barker (Derby County) at centre-half, Wilf Copping and Cliff Britton (Everton) the winghalves, Ray Bowden and Cliff Bastin the inside forwards and Ted Drake at centre-forward, with the 19-year-old Stanley Matthews from Stoke City on the right wing and Eric Brook (Manchester City) on the left. As if the bulk of the team were not enough, Arsenal supplied Tom Whittaker as trainer and even George Allison as radio commentator.

The trouble started after only two minutes. How it began depends on which account you trust. One mentions a foot-cracking tackle by Copping on Luiz Felipe Monti (note the Christian names: Mussolini didn't regard the Argentine-born as impure Italians, indeed at that stage differed sharply from Hitler on ethnic notions). Other versions imply that Monti stubbed his toe, which, given the seriousness of the bone damage, would have made him very unlucky indeed. A suspicion of home-town journalism lingers.

Whatever the truth of the matter, Monti's departure reduced the world champions to 10 men and, while they sought furiously to retaliate, England took advantage of their distraction with two goals from Brook and one from Drake – and still only 12 minutes had gone. The injuries sustained by England before the end included fractures of the nose and arm (Hapgood and Brook respectively) and damage to one of Bowden's ankles, while Drake was said to have been punched. Only Bowden of the Arsenal contingent missed the League match against Aston Villa three days later, however, and he was soon back in action. How many Italians went home with inflamed souvenirs of Copping's tackling is not chronicled by the English press, but at least Pozzo's side had offered some testimony to their status with a stirring second-half display in which Giuseppe Meazza scored twice and Moss was required to keep goal defiantly to maintain England's advantage.

Given the potential of the Arsenal nucleus, the class of Goodall and the likes of Britton, Brook and Sunderland's Raich Carter, and the rich promise of Matthews, Chapman would surely have been able to fashion an England side capable of proclaiming the case for WM and the swift counter-attack. But he died unable to envisage the FA providing conditions comparable with those of Pozzo or Meisl, or indeed those Chapman had enjoyed while building his champion clubs. He had written as much between the lines of his *Sunday Express* column, declaring that a team should never be picked by committee and continuing: 'When you have a dozen officials expressing their views as to merits of the players, without proper regard to blend and balance, the result cannot be satisfactory. Team picking is a complicated and scientific matter requiring expert knowledge and, in my experience, comparatively few directors are qualified to undertake it. I do not say this in a disparaging way. A director cannot have the same intimate knowledge of the men as those who live with them and come to know and understand those peculiarities of temperament to which all of us are heir.' But then he concluded: 'My ideal selection committee is composed of three. This is how I would have the England team chosen, or, at any rate, I would have three members of the committee specially charged to nominate the players.' This was almost certainly an instance of Chapman's famous tact.

When in Rome, he had done as the FA did. In 1933 he had given the team a pre-match talk – then disrupted his own half-time plans, most uncharacteristically, by misplacing the key to the dressing room. But it was a team nominated by the 14-member 'international selection committee'. It would therefore have been listed in 2–3–5 formation, for WM was long to remain the shape that dare not speak its name, at least in the land of its birth.

Even at Highbury later in 1933, when Chapman's Arsenal took on Meisl's 'FC of Vienna', the programme listed both teams in the already near-obsolete 2–3–5 formation. Arsenal were numbered 1 to 11 and Vienna 12 to 22; it was the method, let it be remembered, that had been used in the Cup final earlier that year. The principle of numbering was rejected by the League in 1934 but in those days radical matters were decided by the FA, who not only made it compulsory in League matches from 1939 but established – no doubt due to the influence of Stanley Rous – that each side should wear numbers 1 to 11. This had been introduced in the Scotland v England match in 1937 and it, rather than Chapman's 1 to 22, became the norm.

But the FA also ordered that players should be numbered by position – and seemed to ignore the invention of the centre-back. The right-back had to wear 2 and the left-back 3. Then came the right-half. The centre-half, though largely non-existent, wore 5. In other words, defences lined up with, from right to left, the numbers 2, 5 and 3. Had the reality of WM been acknowledged, the full-backs would have been 2, 3 and 4 with the centre-back, the Herbie Roberts, wearing 3. Not only that; the truth was to be ignored verbally by the perpetuation among the wider populace of the term 'centre-half' even after 1966, when England won the World Cup with a back four (this had begun to replace WM as the default formation after Brazil's World Cup triumph eight years earlier). Although it had been a misnomer since Chapman's day, 'centre-half' survived for more than 80 years after his death and survives now, at least in the argot of those who eschew the dull accuracy of 'central defender'.

Before the international against Austria at Stamford Bridge in 1932, Chapman had bemoaned the FA's unwillingness to fall in with the widespread club practice and employ three at the back. And in Rome he was heavily outnumbered by the selection committee; the 14 good men and true had overlooked Herbie Roberts and other stoppers, as they almost invariably did, choosing the more creative and traditional Alf Strange, of Sheffield Wednesday.

But Chapman continued to display an acute interest in the national team. He suggested in another of his newspaper columns that the England selectors should choose 20 of the most promising players and have them assemble once a week under the guidance of 'a selector, a coach and a trainer'. They would practise and exchange views and he thought the outcome would be 'astonishing'. Chapman added that he had no hope of such an international building plan being realised; it would be considered 'too revolutionary'. Yet he said other countries had been working along such lines, and improving. He was right that the English establishment would retain an island mentality. It was left to individuals to explore the game, and while Chapman was destined to become the best manager England never had – a title later bestowed on the less predictable Brian Clough – others did their best work abroad.

Jimmy Hogan's in Austria and Hungary is acknowledged, as are Raynor's later efforts with Sweden. Willie Garbutt, having made his lasting mark in Italy, chose 1935 as an opportune moment to head for the Basque Country of Spain and take over at Bilbao, where the latter of Fred Pentland's league and cup double seasons had featured a 12–1 defeat of Barcelona that remains the Calatan club's heaviest ever. Pentland had gone to Atlético de Madrid. Garbutt maintained Bilbao's supremacy with another title triumph in 1936 but conflict was to consume Spain before Germany or Italy and that summer Francisco Franco, with the support of Hitler and Mussolini, led the rebellion that started the civil war. Pentland went home to England and ended his career with short spells as assistant to the brilliant Harry Curtis, who had taken Brentford into the top half of the First Division, and then as manager of Barrow in the Third (North). Garbutt returned to Italy, only to discover that he had left a fire for a frying pan; in 1939, while with Genoa once more, he was directed to go back to his native land upon the outbreak of war.

As the footballing decade closed, Italy retained their world title. Pozzo had done it again. And it had been done more wholesomely than in 1934, when Mussolini had hijacked the tournament on his home soil; even the referees seemed to be under the influence of the dictator. 'FIFA are not organising this tournament,' declared Jules Rimet, 'he is.' Mussolini was said to have insisted on the choice of Ivan Eklind to referee Italy's semi-final against

Austria and, after the 28-year-old Swede had presided over a home victory, the final against Czechoslovakia, which was also duly won. Mussolini milked the chants of homage – 'Duce, Duce, Duce' – from the crowds. By now his hold on the nation was so firm that school teachers had to swear allegiance to fascism and children were taught to worship God and Il Duce equally. And look how well it was working! Those 11 manly specimens of the new Italy were champions of the world.

The 1938 World Cup took place against an even more troubling background. The Spanish war raged, Mussolini's forces had entered Abyssinia and Hitler's had swallowed Austria. Hitler had enjoyed his sporting triumph during the 1936 Olympics when, although Germany's football team had been knocked out early by Norway and Italy triumphed again, the host country dominated the medal table. If the four golds sensationally won by the black American athlete Jesse Owens had added up to a major embarrassment, Hitler had concealed it. Although he had priorities other than football in 1938, that really should have been an embarrassment, for three months before the World Cup had come the Anschluss and ordering of Austria players to join the German squad, which understandably failed to knit and went out after the first round of the tournament in France. Pozzo, meanwhile, proved himself one of the great international managers with victories over the hosts, then Brazil and finally the neutrals' favourites, the Hungarians, whose old-fashioned charm emphasised the robust modernity of the Italians. Chapman would have seen both sides of the argument. He was a pragmatist who could discern the beauty in the game. Goodness knows what, given the chance, he could have done for his country in the formative years of the World Cup.

After Chapman, Meisl became the next of football's international brigade to go. He died, like Chapman, in harness. He was 55 when a heart attack claimed him shortly before the Anschluss. The others outlived Chapman by at least a quarter of a century. Fred Pentland stayed in England after the Spanish Civil War and was 78 when he died in 1961. Willie Garbutt went three years later, at 81. He had left management after a final post-war spell at Genoa. Pozzo's last match in charge of Italy was at Highbury, where they were knocked out of the 1948 Olympic tournament by Denmark. He became a football writer with *La Stampa* and as late as 1968 covered the European Championship, won by Italy after a replay with Yugoslavia in Rome. He died that December at the age of 82. Hogan reached 91. He had enjoyed success in his native land before the Second World War, getting Aston Villa back into the First Division as champions, and later had a short spell coaching Celtic in Glasgow. Hogan watched the fruits of his Hungarian labour at Wembley in 1953 surrounded, appropriately, by junior players from Villa.

By then football had its second knight. The first, in 1927, had been Charles Clegg of the FA, and 22 years later Stanley Rous had become Sir Stanley. Rous had refereed the first Cup final after Chapman's death and then been appointed FA secretary. He was to become president of FIFA, overseeing the World Cup in England in 1966, and, although it was after his relinquishing of the FA post in 1962 that England let the manager pick the team, Chapman would have appreciated much of the work he did in tandem with Walter Winterbottom. Chapman, as an early advocate of a national coaching scheme, wanted one more ambitious than was to be founded in 1946 by the FA, but he accepted that in football politics was the art of the possible.

Rous, appointed in 1934, had immediately set about working from within to persuade the arch-conservatives. Meanwhile, Winterbottom had graduated from teacher training college and obtained a school post in his native Oldham. He had lent his skills as a centre-half to Mossley – a neighbour of the Ashton-under-Lyne and Stalybridge clubs for which Chapman had played in his youth – and in 1936 caught the eye of Manchester United, with whom he had a First Division season before his promise faded due to a spinal condition. At Carnegie College of Physical Training in Leeds he met Rous and after the war, during which he rose to the RAF rank of wing commander, he was called to the FA to be offered the new posts of director of coaching and

England team manager (they had to be combined to give him a sufficient salary). Among the coaches who proceeded to thrive were Ron Greenwood – founder of the West Ham 'academy' from which Bobby Moore, Hurst and Martin Peters graduated, becoming members of the 1966 World Cup-winning team – Bill Nicholson, Don Howe, Dave Sexton and Bobby Robson, who took England to the semi-finals in 1990.

As England manager Winterbottom had a 16-year-tenure of highs and lows. Early on there was a 10–0 victory in Portugal in which Tom Finney starred and towards the end a sequence of six consecutive wins in which 40 goals flew from the boots of such great players as Bobby Charlton, Jimmy Greaves and Johnny Haynes. But there were also the defeat by the United States in 1950 and twin spankings at the hands of Meisl and Hogan's Hungarians, who, after triumphing 6–3 at Wembley in November 1953, won 7–1 in Budapest six months later, prompting Meisl's brother Willy to write his much-quoted book in which he lamented the effects of Chapman's teachings. As if they had been more influential than Winterbottom's or anyone else's. Which, of course, they had been, given their demonstrable success on English fields (and the acknowledgements that were to follow from Busby and many others). But maybe they were not influential enough. Maybe the administrators of English football were just too insular, too sure of themselves, to make the most of him.

On at least one occasion Rous toyed with the idea of having Winterbottom concentrate on the coaching system while an England manager in the modern sense took charge of the senior team. A year after the latter of the Hungarian humblings, the FA secretary informally approached Jesse Carver – a prominent member of England's foreign legion, a peripatetic who had nevertheless stayed long enough with Juventus to guide them to the Italian championship in 1950 – but nothing came of it and only when Alf Ramsey arrived on the scene did England acquire a manager in the sense that Chapman might have been. Three years later, they won the World Cup.

NEARER TO GOD

There were to be seven grandchildren and Annie Chapman saw them all born and at school. Indeed the first to arrive – Richard Kenneth Herbert Chapman, the only child of her elder son Ken and his wife Jean – had left school by the time Annie was laid to rest next to her husband in the churchyard of St Mary's, Hendon, in 1958.

She had remained a familiar figure at Highbury on match days, when she continued to receive and attend to official guests in the ladies' tearoom; the men of the respective clubs commanded the main directors' area. She had two season tickets as well as a pension of £500 a year and the use of 6 Haslemere Avenue – which Arsenal owned – for as long as she wished. By 1942, however, she had left to live in Ealing. The club house would have been too big for just Annie, whose daughter Joyce was about to become the last of the children to marry and fly the nest; no doubt the German bombardment of factories near Hendon had also influenced her decision to move a few miles to the west.

Joyce had a gift for making cakes which she sold from a tea shop in Ealing. After her wedding in 1943 to Freddie Barwick, the manager of a wine merchant's, her mother moved into Hill Court, near the Hanger Lane roundabout. Later Annie changed to a ground-floor flat in the same development before spending the final two years of her life with Joyce and Freddie and their sons Roger and Peter in Weybridge, Surrey. She had been succeeded in the Highbury tearoom by her elder daughter Molly.

Since Herbert's death the family sporting tradition had been gloriously maintained by her boys in cricket as well as rugby, for in 1953 a history of Stanmore Cricket Club had said of Ken, its captain since the end of the Second World War: 'His brother Bruce is his only equal. These two magnificent cricketers have a style of their own making, unspoiled by stereotyped coaching. It is based on native ball-game-sense, good health and the tremendous enjoyment they find in all their doings. They bowl with every ounce of vigour they can muster. They bat for the sheer delight of seeing the ball, perhaps not the most suitable delivery, sail over the pavilion roof. Their fine example . . . raised the quality of cricket at Stanmore so that we were able to play and defeat the best clubs in the district . . . not because of individual superiority but because we were infected by the Chapmans' enthusiasm.'

Bruce had been forced to stop playing rugby because of a head injury in 1940 but Ken, who worked during the Second World War for the Ministries of Aircraft Production and Supply, returned to captain Harlequins for one more season before concentrating on his organisational skills. He became a director of many companies and in 1974, the year of his Rugby Football Union presidency, he also served as High Sheriff of Greater London. The brothers played the occasional game of football for the Harlequins team and, along with Molly, maintained the Arsenal connection.

There was one other child of the family. Harry Chapman Jr, who had been taken in by Herbert and Annie when his father died, was found a job at the Rolls-Royce factory in Derby but later gravitated to football and became manager of Shrewsbury Town in 1949. At the end of his first season, election to the Third Division (North) persuaded the club to place their fortunes in the hands of the former England winger Sammy Crooks and Harry had to settle for scouting for various clubs thereafter.

In Kiveton Park, life went on: more comfortably by and large, not least for a contemporary of Herbert Chapman's, one Lizzie Eddershaw. Herbert would have been seven or eight when Lizzie first attended the local school. Her father, like Herbert's – and almost inevitably – worked at the colliery. When she was married, it was to Will Hart, staunchly Methodist and excellent at football and especially well known to Herbert Chapman in that his sister Thirza was Chapman's girlfriend (this was before Annie moved into the village). The status of a housewife meant that Lizzie Eddershaw no longer had to take in other people's washing, an occupation that entailed lighting a fire under a copper tub and boiling, wringing and perhaps ironing the clothes and sheets in exchange for a few shillings a week. But, becoming a mother of two, Lizzie still observed the Monday routine in the washhouse. She kept a spotless home.

And then, in the early 1930s, around the time of her fiftieth birthday, science had eased her burden. She and Will had resolved to become the first people in Kiveton to own one of the new-fangled washing machines. Fortunately, there was a local supplier. This was Herbert Chapman: not the football manager now causing such a sensation in London but his nephew, the son of his brother John. He shared something of the elder Herbert's foresight and, after training as an electrician, had decided to sell the increasingly popular appliances, setting up shop in the ground floor of his home in Station Road, near the cricket ground. Where else for Lizzie to go? She took delivery of a large, enamelled Goblin machine with a hand-operated wringer on top.

The younger Herbert did well out of technological advance, selling radios and, some years after his uncle's death, the first television sets to enter Kiveton. But during the Second World War his wife died and he married his housekeeper. It was not a success. He developed a drink problem and died in 1955 at the age of 50.

Of the elder Herbert's sibling survivors, the middle brother was the first to go. Matt lived just long enough to follow the progress of his beloved Grimsby Town to the FA Cup semi-finals of 1936 only to lose to Arsenal at, of all places, Huddersfield, and was 61 when he died the next year. Martha, for whom Herbert had cried out in his last hours, went in 1940, at the age of 73 and in a Sheffield hospital, suffering from dementia and depression. Tom was 92 when he passed away peacefully in a nursing home near Grimsby in 1956 and six years later Ernest, aged 77, was cremated in Sheffield. In the family section of the graveyard at Wales lay 'The Best of Parents', John and Emma Chapman, whose journey from Derbyshire had led to so much. The tribute paid to Herbert by the Revd Norman Boyd of Hendon might have been written for their satisfaction as much as Annie's consolation.

It culminated thus: 'Those of us who have been privileged to enter his home at any time have recognised it to be what every Englishman means by the phrase "a true home". And there are many of us here who know perfectly well that apart from that happiness of his home, and the unfailing devotion of her to whom above all others our hearts go out today, success would have meant nothing to Herbert Chapman, if indeed it had been possible.

'Nor was Mr Chapman any less mindful of his duty to God. No doubt his interest in and connection with Hendon Parish Church were well known to his more intimate acquaintances . . . But of the tens of thousands who have thought of him as a man wholly absorbed in football there will be many who will learn with surprise that for many years Mr Chapman has held office here as a sidesman and Sunday by Sunday, if duty did not call him away from Hendon, he was to be found either at the morning or evening service. He carried his success with characteristic modesty and many members of the congregation here were quite unaware on Saturday morning that the man whom all England seemed to be mourning was none other than the figure so familiar to them as a fellow worshipper in Hendon Parish Church.

'The general public mourns a great sportsman. Football mourns a genius. The Church mourns a faithful and devoted son, and commends his soul to God.'

It is a journey of only a few miles from the graveyard at Hendon to the Emirates Stadium, where it is possible to look at Chapman's statue and the edifice it faces and – while this can only be educated guesswork – sense his approval of what has been built. He would not have approved of football's economics and the rampant, mindlessly destructive inflation that renders players and their agents unfeasibly rich while – to paraphrase

Denis Hill-Wood, heir to the noblesse oblige of the Chapman era – appearing to care little for the consequences on Doncaster. But Chapman would have greatly liked both the scale and state-of-the-art facilities of the Emirates Stadium, served now by plain 'Arsenal' station (Highbury Hill had been dropped in 1960) and others. Chapman would have liked the care for the balancing of the books for which Arsenal had become noted in the Arsène Wenger era and the way the club had defrayed the expense of their stadium's construction with the architecturally sensitive development of Highbury Square, which opened in 2010, the club's old home thus becoming the father of the new; he and Sir Henry Norris, who brought him to Highbury in 1925, would have heartily concurred on that, if little else. And for this legacy of footballing grandeur Herbert Chapman, after first counting the blessings, who had lived at 6 Haslemere Avenue, would have thanked God. He had made a life in Hendon for the sake of family and career entwined. Maybe the altar chair ended up in the right place after all.

BIBLIOGRAPHY

Bryon Butler, *The Official History of the Football Association* (Macdonald Queen Anne Press, 1991)

J. A. H. Catton, *The Story of Association Football* (Soccer Books, 2005)

Anthony Clavane, *Does Your Rabbi Know You're Here?* (Quercus, 2012)

Kevin Connolly and Rab MacWilliam, *Fields of Glory, Paths of Gold* (Mainstream, 2005)

Jack Cox, *Don Davies: An Old International* (Stanley Paul, 1962)

Keith Dewhurst, *Underdogs* (Yellow Jersey, 2013)

Jessica Fellowes, *The World of Downton Abbey* (Collins, 2011)

Brian Glanville, *Football Memories* (Robson Books, 2004)

John Harding, *For the Good of The Game* (Robson Books, 1998)

Simon Inglis, *League Football and The Men Who Made It* (Collins Willow, 1988)

Martin Kelner, *Sit Down And Cheer* (Wisden, 2012)

Conrad Lodziak, *Understanding Soccer Tactics* (Faber & Faber, 1966)

Graham Morse, *Sir Walter Winterbottom* (John Blake, 2013)

Simon Page, *Herbert Chapman: The First Great Manager* (Heroes, 2006)

Phil Soar and Martin Tyler, *Arsenal: The Official Centenary History* (Hamlyn, 1986)

Stephen Studd, *Herbert Chapman: Football Emperor* (Souvenir, 1998)

Phil Vasili, *Colouring Over The White Line* (Mainstream, 2000)

Andrew Ward, *Football's Strangest Matches* (Robson Books, 1999)

Julie Welch, *The Biography of Tottenham Hotspur* (Vision Sports Publishing, 2012)

Jonathan Wilson, *Inverting The Pyramid* (Orion, 2013)

Index